I0106978

Beyond Religion

Craig R. Vander Maas

Beyond Religion

Finding Meaning in Evolution

Integral Growth Publishing, LLC
Grand Rapids, MI

Copyright © 2023 Craig R. Vander Maas

All rights reserved. No part of this book may be reproduced
or transmitted in any form or by any means whatsoever
without express written permission from the author, except in
the case of brief quotations embodied in critical articles and
reviews.

For information about the author please visit:
www.craigvandermaas.com

ISBN 978-0-9972388-6-0 (soft cover)
ISBN 978-0-9972388-7-7 (hard cover)

Dedicated to

People everywhere that courageously seek truth,
that live principled lives,
that pursue ongoing personal growth,
that value compassion and understanding,
and who promote justice and fairness

Contents

Introduction

Does "Religion" Have a Future?

Religion is on the decline, particularly Christianity in Europe and North America. Attendance of church services in Europe has been on the wane for many years. The Pew Research Center reports in a May 29, 2018 article that while 46% of their European sample reports being "Christian", only 18% report regular attendance of church (i.e., attending church at least monthly). These Nonpracticing Christians primarily report a belief in a higher power or spiritual force but not a belief in God "as described in the Bible."

Not only are Europeans attending church less, fewer people are also describing themselves as Christian. Pew uses the term "nones" to denote those who identify as atheist, agnostic, or "nothing in particular." "The unaffiliated portion of the adult population ranges from as high as 48% in the Netherlands to 15% in Ireland, Italy and Portugal." "'Nones' in Western Europe are relatively young and highly educated, as well as disproportionately male." The four biggest reasons respondents gave for leaving religion were:

- gradually drifting away from religion   68%
- disagreeing with their religion's positions on social issues   58%
- no longer believing in their religion's teachings   54%
- being unhappy about scandals involving religious
      institutions and leaders   53%

Although Christianity is in decline in the United States as well, Pew reports that Americans are both more religious and more spiritual than those in Western Europe.

	Both religious and spiritual	Religious but not spiritual	Spiritual but not religious	Neither religious nor spiritual
U.S.	48%	6%	27%	18%
W. Europe	24%	15%	11%	53%

The Pew Research Center also published a report on October 17, 2019 with the headline "In U.S., Decline of Christianity Continues at Rapid Pace". "65% American adults describe themselves as Christians when asked about their religion, down 12 percentage points over the past decade. Meanwhile, the religiously unaffiliated share of the population, consisting of people who describe their religious identity as atheist, agnostic or 'nothing in particular', now stands at 26%, up from 17% in 2009." "The U.S. is steadily becoming less Christian and less religiously observant as the share of adults who are not religious grows. This is particularly true of Millennials."

David Kinnaman is president of the Barna Group, an evangelical Christian polling firm. He wrote a book in 2007 titled *UnChristian: What a New Generation Really Thinks About Christianity... and Why It Matters.* Through surveys and interviews Kinnaman describes perceptions of Christianity by young adults who are outside of the religion. "These days nearly 2 out of every 5 young outsiders (38%) claim to have a 'bad impression of present-day Christianity." "Among those aware of the term "evangelical," reviews are extraordinarily negative. Disdain for evangelicals among the younger set is overwhelming and definitive." Among "outsiders" ages 16 to 29 are the following negative perceptions of Christians:

Antihomosexual	91%
Judgmental	87%
Hypocritical	85%
Too involved in politics	75%
Out of touch with reality	72%
Old-fashioned	78%
Insensitive to others	70%
Boring	68%
Not accepting of other faiths	64%
Confusion	61%

Kinnaman wrote a follow-up book in 2011 titled *You Lost Me: Why Young Christians Are Leaving Church...and Rethinking Faith.* In this book he is looking at the perceptions of "insiders," i.e., young people who grew up within Christianity. "Millions of young Christians were also describing Christianity as hypocritical, judgmental, too political, and out of touch with reality." Kinnaman's research suggested 6 broad reasons for young Christians to drop out of the faith:

1. Overprotective
2. Shallow
3. Antiscience
4. Repressive
5. Exclusive
6. Doubtless, i.e., not a safe place to express doubts

Matt is a 30-year-old, married man who was raised Methodist but considers himself now atheist:

"I'm of the opinion that society functions better for more people when facts and logic are the foundation. When we lacked scientific knowledge, religion gave compelling explanations, or excuses for lack of understanding. That may have been necessary at the time. Now I think it holds us back and divides us unnecessarily."

Tom, a 34-year-old, married, behavioral therapist with a Catholic background says:

"I appreciate many aspects of many religious traditions. I like the notion that happiness is not derived from the acquisition of material possessions. I like the practice of meditation. I even like the idea that we are connected to our ancestors by practicing the same rituals and traditions that they did. What I completely reject is mysticism and unquestioned authority. Scientific progress has had a history of being stifled by established religions. A sense of communal belonging is sadly missing from today's culture, and for many, church is a good solution, but I find ethics and morality rooted in secular philosophy or a combination of multiple faith traditions to be more compelling than those that are preached at me from a single 2,000-year-old book."

"Frank" a 68-year-old gay man with a Catholic upbringing states

"There are many reasons for my dislike of organized religion. I feel it fosters oppression. They ask you to believe in something illogical and then represses your asking of questions. Also, it seems in this decade of the current political climate in the U.S., religion is a major cause of racism and bigotry. I feel religion is nothing more than a giant business trying to reinvent itself."

Given that there is strong interest in spirituality and the search for meaning in life, and given that people continue to have a strong need for community, it seems there is a need for something like "church," although an organization that is rational, that eschews magical thinking, and follows moral principles- that truly demonstrates love and advocates justice for all people.

What I suggest in the title of this book is that we go "beyond" religion. With that in mind, let me give you a brief summary of religion's history.

The History of Religion

Very early religion primarily entailed making sacrifices to gods to elicit favors (such as the conception of a child or rain for one's crops) and to avoid calamities. The better the sacrifice, the more likely it was believed to please gods. We can see this in the Hebrew scriptures in the myths about Adam and Eve, Noah, and Abraham and his descendants. The book of Leviticus gives detailed instructions about appropriate offerings. The greatest sacrifice one could make was of one's firstborn son, and there is significant evidence that human sacrifices were made in the ancient near east including in Israel, and that sacrifices were made to Yawheh as well as to other gods.

As societies grew from bands of families to clans, tribes, and chiefdoms there was need to establish laws and rules to keep order. Family members tend to care for and be altruistic to each other; large groups of strangers not so much. The birthplace of civilization is Mesopotamia, and one of the earliest legal codes came from there, the Code of Hammurabi. Several centuries later a similar code appeared among the Hebrew people, the law codes attributed to Moses. The twelve tribes in the Torah (the descendants of Abraham) combined into a larger group, a chiefdom, in which a leader was now is required. For the Hebrews that leader was Moses. Rules and laws were required to keep the people in line. The rules included the famous "Ten Commandments." To maintain a workable society, people cannot kill each other or steal from each other.

A religious revolution took place between 800 and 200 BCE in which religions in several places in the world began for the first time to concern itself with morality and to concern itself with issues of life and death. This period has been called *The Axial Age*; a term coined by Karl Jaspers. In *The Origin and Goal of History* (2010), which deals with the philosophy of the history of mankind, Jaspers said that in the Axial Age "man, as we know him today, came into being". Religious historian Karen Armstrong (2006) termed this "the great transformation".

> *Before the axial age, ritual and animal sacrifice had been central to the religious quest. You experienced the divine in sacred dramas that, like a great theatrical experience today, introduced you to another level of existence. The axial sages changed this; they still valued ritual, but gave it a new ethical significance and put morality at the heart of the spiritual life. The only way you could encounter what they called "God", "Nirvana", "Brahman", or the "Way" was to live a compassionate life...All the sages preached a spirituality of empathy and compassion; they insisted that people must abandon their egotism and greed, their violence and unkindness.*

It was during this period that the "Golden Rule" in its various expressions became a prominent tenet in the world's major religions. Theistic religions which are grounded in a conception of god include Judaism, Christianity, Islam, Hinduism, Sikhism and Zoroastrianism. Morality is believed to be emanated from God in these religions. The Hebrew prophets during the axial period (e.g., Amos, Micah, Isaiah, Jeremiah, Trito-Isaiah) took the emphasis off burnt offerings and festivals and stressed instead justice issues, particularly care of the poor and the downtrodden.

Centuries later when Jesus lived, the Sadducees of that time continued to stress temple sacrifices, and the Pharisees stressed picayune rule following. Jesus, however, said what was important was love and justice. He said the most important commandment was to love God, and the second most important was to love one's neighbor as oneself. "On these two commandments hang all the law and the prophets." Jesus' follower, the apostle Paul, said "the whole law is summed up in a single commandment, 'You shall love your neighbor as yourself.'" Centuries later Muhammad said "Love for your brother what you love for yourself." (Hadith 13)

In India Hinduism is the predominant religion, and very important principles are *karma* and *dharma*, which are concerned with moral behavior and righteousness. In ancient Hindu literature Brihaspati, the Vedic era sage says "One should never do that to another which one regards as injurious to one's own self. This in brief, is the rule of dharma. Other behavior is due to selfish desires." Another religion that developed in India was Jainism, and Mahavira has been identified as its founder. Mahavira lived between 599 and 527 BCE during the Axial Age. Jainism is a non-theistic religion that also emphasizes karma. A major tenet of Jainism is *ahimsa*, which is the commitment to not harm *any* life. Verse 151 of Saman Suttam, a Jain religious text, says "Killing a living being is killing one's own self; showing compassion to a living being is showing compassion to oneself. He who desires his own good, should avoid causing any harm to a living being."

Living during the same time period as Mahavira was Siddhartha Gautama (560-480 BCE) who became the Buddha, the "enlightened one". Buddhism originated in India but now has become most prominent in China, Japan, Korea and Southeast Asia. As with Hinduism and Jainism, karma is a basic tenet. Buddhism advocates the "noble Eightfold Way" which is right view, right intention, right speech, right action, right livelihood, right effort, right mindfulness, and right concentration. Chapter 5, verse 18 of the Udanavarga (an early collection of Buddhist writings) says "Hurt not others in ways that you yourself would find hurtful." When traveling and visiting Buddhist temples in India and Sri Lanka I was told on a few occasions that Buddhism can be summed up with "Be good, do good".

Contemporaries of Mahavira and Gautama in China were Lao-tzu (sixth century BCE, traditionally thought to be the founder of Taoism), Confucius (551-479 BCE) and Mencius (372-289 BCE), a disciple of Confucius. These founders of non-theistic Chinese religion stressed compassion and love for one another. Confucius stressed the principles of *li* and *jen*, the latter often being translated as "love," "goodness," or "human-heartedness." Sayings of

Confucius included "Do not do to others what you would not want others to do to you." Mencius said "Try your best to treat others as you would wish to be treated yourself and you will find that this is the shortest way to benevolence."

The primary teaching of all these theistic and non-theistic religions is love, compassion and justice. The core teaching of the great spiritual sages since the Axial Age has been of morality. During the Axial Age self-consciousness and rationality evolved. People began to introspect. Philosophy came into being. Religion began to concern itself primarily with ethical and moral issues. There was movement from *mythos* to *logos* and from *exoteric* teachings which were mythic tales meant for the masses to more *esoteric* teachings which were meant for the transformation of consciousness.

Carl Jaspers said "the old mythical world slowly sank into oblivion, but remained as a background to the whole through the continued belief of the mass of the people (and was subsequently able to gain the upper hand over wide areas)." In other words, although a new consciousness of morality took hold simultaneously in various places in the world, the "mass" of people continued to cling to the old myths and old ways of thinking. The Greek philosophers, the Hebrew prophets, and the Indian and Chinese sages all crusaded for morality, justice, compassion, and love. Their cause was to convert the world to this new way of thinking.

As Jaspers stated, the mass of humanity continued to cling to the old ways of thinking, i.e., taking care of oneself first and foremost and family second. Since that time there have been innumerable atrocities committed in the name of religion. Let us take my own religious tradition of Christianity as an example. Although Christianity began as a pacifist movement, unbelievable violence and cruelty occurred in its ongoing history. Between 1095 and 1208 Christian crusaders mobilized to take back Jerusalem from Muslim Turks. Over one million Muslims and Jews were slaughtered. The world population at that time was about 400 million people, so as a percentage of the world population this massacre was equivalent to the six million Jews massacred in the Holocaust in the mid-20th century. In the 13th century the Cathars of southern France embraced a belief in two gods: a good one and an evil one. In response to this "heresy," the King of France and the Pope in collusion tortured and exterminated all the Cathars, an estimated 200,000 people. From the 5th to the 15th centuries were the *Middle Ages* or *Medieval Period.* Steven Pinker (2010) writes in The Better Angels of Our Nature:

> *Medieval Christendom was a culture of cruelty. Torture was meted out by national and local governments throughout the Continent, and it was codified in laws that prescribed blinding, branding, amputation of hands, ears, noses and tongues, and other forms of mutilation as punishments for minor crimes...Sadistic tortures were also inflicted by the Christian church during its inquisitions, witch hunts and religious wars. Torture had been authorized by the ironically named Pope Innocent IV in 1252, and the order of Dominican monks carried it out with relish.*

Acts of evil were also committed in more modern times and in the United States. Perhaps most noteworthy is America's "original sin" of slavery and ongoing racism. While there were many Christians actively involved in the Abolition movement, many other Christians were strong supporters of slavery. The Southern Baptist Church was formed in 1845 in a split from the Northern Baptists due to their opposition to abolition and black civil rights. Some iterations of the Klu Klux Klan used a burning cross to not only terrorize African Americans but also stress their commitment to what they saw as Protestant Christian values. The Christian churches have also been known for their opposition to civil rights for women and gays as well as African Americans.

Christians are not the only religion responsible for evil acts. Americans certainly are aware of Muslim terrorists, and only just recently has there been attempted genocide of the Muslim Rohingya people by Buddhists in Myanmar.

It is questionable whether religion has overall been more a force for good or a force for evil. While the common plea of the great spiritual leaders has been to love others as ourselves, sadly I do not think that most people think of these values when they hear the word "religion." There is an old Christian hymn that exclaims "They will know we are Christians by our love." Unfortunately, Christianity for many is now more associated with hate, bigotry, selfishness, greed, and xenophobia. Therefore, I suggest we move beyond "religion" and back to the teachings of the great enlightened spiritual prophets and sages, who were generally in agreement about what is goodness. There are many names that might be used instead of "goodness" to reflect these teachings. Some use the term "caring." Others use the term "compassion." Some use the term "love." I will use these terms interchangeably throughout this book.

Psychology

I am approaching the content of this book from the perspective of a psychologist. This is a book about psychology. The term "psychology" means the study of the *psyche* (or soul or spirit). This book is about the soul. It also deals with related subjects such as the nature of reality, the meaning of life and death, and God. Theologians concern themselves with these topics as well, but their conclusions or often derived from unfounded beliefs or preconceived notions learned from past "authorities.' Psychologists learn to base beliefs on evidence. Psychologists are taught to think like scientists. Psychologists are interested in discerning truth. Psychologists who do research such as experimental and social psychologists collect data to help explain truths about our world. Clinical psychologists make diagnoses and treatment plans based on data. Neuropsychologists determine neurological dysfunction based on evidence.

In order to be good, we must embrace truth. Plato said "Truth is the beginning of every good to the gods, and of every good to man." Plato also said "False words are not only evil in themselves, but they infect the soul with evil." For the most part people lie to other people out of selfish self-interest, i.e., for personal gain or to escape consequences. Occasionally people may lie out of altruism, for example to avoid hurting an other's feelings, but most often it is to benefit ourselves at an other's expense. People also frequently lie to themselves to avoid uncomfortable feelings and thoughts. Jesus said, "if you continue in my word, you are truly my disciples; and you will know the truth, and the truth will make you free." A major goal of insight-oriented psychotherapy is to help clients uncover personal truths that may be repressed or suppressed because they are difficult to face.

How do we know what is true? The discernment of truth has been a particularly relevant issue in the last few years in the era of "fake news" and "alternative facts." Although truth may be especially under assault in the United States in the Trump era, this really is not a new phenomenon. Kurt Andersen in his book *Fantasyland: How America Went Haywire* (2017) presents compelling evidence of a long history of America's difficulty with discerning truth. He believes there were two events which made things worse. First was an attitudinal paradigm shift that happened in the 1960s of "Do your own thing, find your own reality, it's all relative." Secondly was the rise of the Internet; "Before the Internet, crackpots were mostly isolated and surely had a harder time remaining convinced of their alternative realities. Now their devoutly believed opinions are all over the airwaves and the Web, just like actual news. Now all the fantasies look real."

I begin with the assumption that objective reality exists, and that we have the capability to ascertain truth through abductive reasoning. In Chapter One of this book, I will address how one can determine what is true and what is reality, particularly in regards to spiritual matters and questions of *belief*. I also will discuss the issues that keep us from wanting to see truth.

Chapter Two is a narrative about reality, as we best know it, using the tools and methods described in Chapter One. It is about seeing reality at its broadest. It is about "big history." Universities typically offer history courses about limited periods of history, such as American history, European civilizations, Michigan history, Ancient Greece, or Ancient Rome. Sometimes special topics of history are offered such as African American history, history of American women, or history of warfare. *Big history* attempts to give a coherent account of the entire 13.8-billion-year history from the big bang to the present day. The International Big History Association says that "big history seeks to understand the integrated history of the Cosmos, Earth, Life, and Humanity using the best available empirical evidence and scholarly methods."

Big history has become a passion of Bill Gates after he heard a lecture series on the topic by history professor David Christian. By studying big history, we are better able to see the forest rather than focusing on individual trees. This is an approach that is multi-disciplinary, integrating knowledge not only from history but also scientific disciplines such as geology, astronomy, physics, chemistry, archaeology, and anthropology. When viewing history with this wide-angle lens, one can get a clearer sense of how humanity and cultures gradually developed. The importance of *evolution* becomes evident, and by this term "evolution" I mean more than just biological evolution as described by Darwin. Evolution has been happening in the universe since the "big bang."

In Chapter Three the focus will be narrowed to evolution of culture and the evolution of humans. Developmental psychology, a branch of psychology, is the scientific study of how humans develop. Most people are aware that infants and children develop in a typical sequence. In addition to physical development, there is a "normal" sequence of emotional, cognitive, moral, and spiritual development. Many people are not aware that development in these areas should ideally continue throughout one's life. When enough individuals attain higher stages of development, cultures move into higher stages of development. Chapter three will especially focus on stages of spiritual development. I will also discuss how these stages contribute to our country's current "culture wars."

Emotional development, cognitive development, moral development, and spiritual development significantly correlate with each other. The great sages and wisdom teachers of history such as the Old Testament prophets, Jesus, the Buddha, Confucius, Mencius, Lao Tzu, Gandhi, the Dalai Lama, and Martin Luther King Jr. were all highly developed in these domains. They all promoted a similar direction for living one's life. They all promoted a similar philosophy which has been known by different names including "love," "compassion," "belonging," "goodness," "agape," and "justice." This is the philosophy taught by the founders of the great religions but seldom reflect the ideologies of the religious followers.

In Chapter Four I will discuss evolution in its broadest sense including the important topic of *emergence*. Evolution is a gradual process, but from time-to-time events happen that are revolutionary and completely unexpected. These emergent events completely change everything. I also will discuss relevant breakthroughs in science that are germane to spirituality and an accurate world view. These topics include the laws of thermodynamics, entropy, classical and quantum physics, Heisenberg's Uncertainty Principle, and "entangled twin" particles. I also will discuss a progressive conception of God.

In Chapter Five I will explore the topics of *consciousness* and *transpersonal psychology*. Transpersonal is about going beyond the self. The prefix "trans" means beyond. It is about transcending the ego, the individual. It is about the realization that we are all connected to and part of all else, including the cosmos. Transpersonal psychology is a branch of psychology that emphasizes human growth which then fosters cultural growth which in turn fosters cosmic evolution. In this chapter I will discuss evidence to support a transpersonal world view and will discuss the implications of this view on how we might live our lives. I will discuss how meaning is to be found in evolution.

In Chapter Six I will present my model of a "Continuum of Morality" and will discuss how all the world's most significant problems are the result of greed, lust for power, and selfishness. I will discuss war, poverty and income disparity, and climate change as examples of this contention. The world's problems can be solved but it will require continuing human evolution. I will discuss a spiritual philosophy which includes, integrates, and goes beyond the traditional religions and brings us closer to solving the ills of humanity.

I also will discuss "church," an institution that I think can be reinvigorated. Instead of representing outdated ideas, it could become a place for human growth. Human beings still do crave community. There is much interest in spirituality, as evidenced by strong book sales on the topic and a growing number of people who describe themselves as "spiritual but not religious."

My overall goal in this book is to advocate for a spiritual philosophy that promotes the intentional evolution of human beings and the entire cosmos. This will require a commitment to truth, reason, education, compassion, and love. The result will be prosperity for all - what Jesus called the "Kingdom of God."

Questions for Contemplation or Discussion
Introduction

1. Why do you think church attendance in the United States is declining? What do you think could be done about this?
2. What do you think is positive about religions, and what are the negatives?
3. Are there any ways that you believe your religion should reform or change?
4. What are your hopes about the future of your religion?

Chapter One

Truth

This is a book about evolution. It is not just about biological evolution, the evolution described by Charles Darwin, but also cosmic evolution, the evolution of human culture, and the evolution of humans as studied by developmental psychologists and evolutionary psychologists. I will even talk about my own individual evolution. In fact, let me start with that. I was born in 1955 in Grand Rapids, Michigan. My early development was typical. I was within the average range in regards to physical growth and developmental milestones. I was told that in my childhood I was rather quiet, shy, and serious. I grew up in a middle-class family. My father was a brick mason, and my mother a homemaker. I think probably my parents' primary life goal was the successful raising of a family. I was the oldest, although sadly before my birth my mother had a miscarriage of their first offspring, a son. A year and a half after my birth, my mother gave birth to a daughter. Three years later another daughter was born, and our family was complete.

My cultural background was heavily influenced by Dutch Calvinism. My maternal great grandmother immigrated to the United States from the Netherlands in the latter half of the nineteenth century with her new husband. I was told that the main reason they left the Netherlands was that while working as a maid for a rich family she was impregnated by the teenage son in the family. It is not known if she was raped or if it was consensual, but regardless she was paid off and moved from the Netherlands to the United States. My great grandparents ended up raising twelve more children after they settled in Grand Rapids.

My paternal great grandparents also immigrated to the United States from the Netherlands around the same time period. They too raised a family of twelve children. West Michigan was a prominent destination for Dutch immigrants in the latter 1800s. Immigrants initially came to flee religious persecution and then later for economic opportunities.

The immigrants from the Netherlands to West Michigan were conservative Protestants and followers of Protestant reformer John Calvin. Calvin University is situated in Grand Rapids. This conservative Dutch religious culture significantly influenced my early life. My family never missed church services on Sunday mornings, which was followed by "Sunday School." Wednesday nights were reserved for catechism where we learned *correct* church doctrines. While in my early childhood, as with all children of that age, I was indoctrinated into what to believe. Children at that age have no ability to critically think. I learned that God was a wise father figure in Heaven. He sent his only son, Jesus, to die on a cross as a sacrifice for the sins of mankind. I grew up believing that the main purpose for this life on earth was to commit to believing this. By making the decision to commit oneself to Jesus one could be assured of eternal life in Heaven. Interestingly it was not particularly stressed to follow the teachings of Jesus and to live the kind of life he modeled and taught, but rather to believe a certain belief, namely that Jesus is the one and only son of God, that he died on the cross to save us from our sins, and that we needed to believe this and to accept Jesus as our personal lord and savior.

From kindergarten to the sixth grade, I went to a public school. My parents switched me from public school to a Christian school in the seventh grade. This was a very difficult transition. I had to make new friends among children who had spent the last six years together and had already formed cliques. This was especially difficult being quiet and introverted, and I think the school was particularly parochial in both senses of the word (being a church school and being narrow in outlook). I was also a bit of a book worm. I recall during the eight-grade selling light bulbs to raise money for my Calvinist Cadet troop (religious version of Boy Scouts). I sold the most light bulbs. There was a cash prize for first place with the stipulation that I had to bring to the troop meeting what I spent the prize money on. My peers expressed mild ridicule that I spent the money on books. My junior high school was run by the Christian Reformed Church, and my family were members of the Reformed Church in America and that alone made me mildly an outcast, although there was little difference between the two denominations. Both were made up primarily of Dutch Calvinists. I also had a growing sense of being different from peers at that time of my life. My junior high years were some of the worst years of my life, but I think that is not unusual for many if not most of us.

There were no people of color in my previous public school, certainly none in my parochial school, and no one in my neighborhood. Racism was a prevalent part of my upbringing. I was born in 1955, so my time from junior to senior high was from 1967 until 1973 when I graduated. This was a period when white people were fleeing to the suburbs because they were worried about black people moving into their neighborhoods and depressing property values. I also remember that during that time there was significant animosity of Protestants for Catholics and vice-versa. I do not remember much appreciation for diversity. In fact, a slogan I remember from that time was "If you ain't Dutch, you ain't much."

As I got older and moved into my teenage years, I began to question many of the beliefs with which I was raised. I questioned where the Bible came from. I was taught it was the "word of God" but I was never given a rationale for this belief. I learned the stories from both the old and the new testaments, but I was never taught how we obtained God's word. Was it found in a cave? I was taught that the famous ten commandments were dictated verbally from God's mouth to the prophet Moses, but where did the rest of the Bible come from? Over the years I was able to find the answer to this, but it was not easy. Although I might have learned the answers to this if I went to a mainstream seminary, most adherents of the Christian faith have no idea where the writings that they venerate came from.

I questioned the portrayal of the almighty in the Bible. Why did God have immature emotions such as jealousy? Why is he "quick to anger"? Why does God love the smell of roasting meat? If

God is all knowing and all powerful, why is he so hypersensitive to slights by clueless people? And why do we refer to God as *he*? Does God have testosterone, an XO genotype, and a penis?

I learned that mankind began with the creation of a man, Adam, and a little later the first woman, Eve. Despite being given only a couple simple rules to follow, they disobeyed. As a result, not only were they punished for the rest of their lives for this indiscretion, but all of humanity would be tainted, and not only mildly. I learned the disturbing term "total depravity" to describe the state of mankind as the result of Adam and Eve's sin. Why did all of humanity have to suffer for their sin? I was taught that God was all knowing and all powerful. So, God made Adam and Eve the way that they were, knowing they were going to do what they did?

I learned about and questioned the Calvinist doctrine of predestination. This doctrine teaches that all human beings are sinful as the result of Adam and Eve's *original sin*, and are incapable of salvation and are deserving of being forever damned. Although no one is deserving of salvation, God saves some nonetheless. These are known as the "chosen." Where is the fairness in this? Why would God create humans to be damned? Why would God create a Hell for people to be forever tormented. How does this fit with the idea of a loving God? If God is supposed to be a "loving father" why would he do this to his children? I certainly would not do this to my own children. I would not even sentence my worst enemies to everlasting torment. Just what is this love that God is supposed to be?

I also questioned the idea of substitutionary atonement, i.e., the belief that God sacrificed his only son to atone for the sins of mankind. How does it make sense that God's son had to die to pay for humanity's sins? Steven Pinker makes the point in his 2011 book *The Better Angels of Our Nature*:

> *Though infinitely powerful, compassionate, and wise, he [God] could think of no other way to reprieve humanity from punishment for its sins (in particular, for the sin of being descended from a couple who had disobeyed him) than to allow an innocent man (his son no less) to be impaled*

through the limbs and slowly suffocate in agony. By acknowledging that this sadistic murder was a gift of divine mercy, people could earn eternal life. And if they failed to see the logic in all this, their flesh would be seared by fire for all eternity.

I questioned the concept of Satan. If mankind is already evil due to original sin, what is the role of a tempter to make people do evil? They supposedly are already evil. If God is omnipotent (all powerful), how can there be a cosmic battle between God and Satan? Is Satan omnipotent too? If Satan makes people do evil things, why should we punish these people if it was Satan's fault? I was taught that Christianity, Judaism, and Islam were monotheistic (believing that there was only one God), and that these religions were very different from the primitive polytheistic religions such as Hinduism. But in reality, Christianity and Judaism also suggested the existence of numerous supernatural beings or lesser gods (like Hinduism) such as angels and demons and the Nephilim (the giant offspring of male angels and human women written about in the book of Genesis).

I was taught in my childhood that our earthly life is unimportant. Although the missionaries sent to third world countries may help people with food and medical needs, what was important was saving their souls, not their bodies. Our earthly existence, I was taught, was a test- a test whether we were going to accept Jesus as our Lord and Savior and as a result live eternity in Heaven, or to reject Jesus which would result in eternity in Hell. As Calvinists we were also taught that we were incapable of making the right decision on our own, and so God made some people make the correct choice. We were taught that we really did not have free will in this regard. I was taught that if small children died before they were capable of making this decision though, they would go to Heaven. I also was taught that abortion was evil. But if the purpose for our earthly life was to gain Heaven, and if small children who died automatically gained Heaven, then isn't it to their benefit to die?

For high school I continued in the Christian school. High school was better than junior high, mostly because at that older age kids are less jerks. I was not a very serious student in high school, but I did plan to go to college. My vocational goal was to become an English teacher due to my love of literature and my interest in the inner life of people. After graduating high school, I began attendance at my local junior college. I went to this school due to financial considerations. My parents could not afford to pay for my college tuition, and so I had to work part-time to pay for classes. I did continue to live with my parents rent-free.

After completing an associates degree, I enrolled into Calvin College. I was just following the expected life course of the culture I was raised in at that time. I really did not consider all the possibilities that were open to me, such as obtaining a college loan and going away to school. Attending Calvin really felt like going back to my Christian high school in regards to a parochial world view. I had really enjoyed my classes at Grand Rapids Junior College and had become a motivated student. I appreciated the more diverse thinking at GRCC. While attending my first semester at Calvin an opportunity arose to open a record store with a friend. Music was a great passion of mine. I personally owned an extensive record collection. I was not happy at Calvin and the thought of being an entrepreneur was attractive, so I quit school. It was not a well thought out plan, and the store was closed after several months.

So, I had to find a job. The economy in the 1970s was not very good. There was high unemployment, but I was able to find a job at a factory. This was the beginning of the worst period of my life. I hated the factory work. I had no idea what to do with my life vocationally. I was struggling to figure out who I was. I was very unhappy. Partying predominated my life at that time.

My struggles primarily were with sexuality. I was beginning to come to grips with being gay. I remember an incident when I was in the sixth grade. At the time I was being bullied by a couple kids from school. One kid called me a "fag." I had no idea what this word meant. I was quite naive and sheltered. I told my father about this and asked him what the word meant. He said he really did not know. When he was in the navy, he said he heard cigarettes being called "fags." I do not know if he really did not know what the word meant in modern parlance, or if he just did not want to acknowledge it or have to deal with it.

I think from an early age I had an ambiguous feeling of being different somehow, and being called a fag at that young age might suggest that some others might have thought that as well. One boy always wanted to fight me. His name was John. I had no idea why he wanted to fight me; we had no relationship at all. I felt terrorized by him and did everything I could to avoid running into him. My parents must have been aware of this, so my father arranged for us to fight to resolve it. When John was near our house my father said to him "I hear you want a fight with Craig. Let's do it right now." So, we commenced fighting with my father refereeing. After it was over, and John left, I heard my father remarking to my mom that I "did okay." I learned later that John had broken his arm in the fight. He showed up at school in a cast. It had become known in school that it happened in a fight between us, but I did not gain in reputation as a tough guy. It was spun by John and his friends that it was an indication of how hard John could throw a punch rather than my ability to take a punch or throw a punch that severely injured him. I found out years later that John had come out as being gay.

In junior high school I felt even more out of sync with my male peers when they talked excitedly at times about female breasts. I just did not get it. They might just as well have been talking about water balloons. I did not let on about my confusion though. I tried to fit in. I pretended. It was an age when above all else you want to fit in and be accepted. Like lions in Africa who spot injured prey, junior high aged kids are ready to pounce on any weaknesses or differences. I made out with some girls, but found nothing exhilarating or enjoyable about the experience.

In high school I became aware of the concept of homosexuality. It was a subject that was taboo to talk about. In 1967 CBS News did a documentary hosted by Mike Wallace entitled "The Homosexuals". Mike begins the documentary by saying "Most Americans are repelled by the mere notion of homosexuality. A CBS poll shows two out of three Americans look on homosexuality with disgust, discomfort, or fear." Gay people that were interviewed on television had their faces hidden to protect their identity. I was in the seventh grade at this time. This was the environment one had to contend with to come out.

As a teenager I learned at church and in my Christian school that homosexuality was sinful and would lead one to hell. In Dante's Inferno we learned what specific level in hell the homosexuals would go. Is it any wonder that so many, like myself, prayed fervently that these thoughts and feelings would go away? Is it any wonder that so many have deep denial about who they are and that it takes time before gays can accept themselves for who they are, if they ever do? Is it any wonder that because of the deep shame so many gay teens have for themselves that they attempt or successfully commit suicide?

In 1990 Kevin Berrill of the National Gay and Lesbian Task Force published research on anti-gay violence at that time. The study sampled 1,420 gay men and 654 gay women in eight U.S. cities. Among those surveyed, 19% reported having been physically assaulted because of their sexual orientation, 44% said they had been threatened with physical violence, and 94% said they experienced some type of victimization (including verbal abuse, physical assault, police abuse, weapon assault, vandalism, being spat upon, being chased, or being pelted with objects).

Berrill summarized results of ten other anti-gay violence/victimization surveys. "All surveys found harassment and violence to be widespread." Berrill stated "52% to 87% of the respondents were verbally harassed, 21% to 27% were pelted with objects; 13% to 38% had been chased or followed; 10% to 20% experienced vandalism; 9% to 24% were physically assaulted; and 4% to 10% experienced an assault with an object or weapon."

My later doctoral dissertation of 1999 titled "The perception of prejudice and discrimination and mental health sequelae" investigated the perception of prejudice/discrimination by minority groups on the basis race, gender, and sexual orientation and what the effects were of this prejudice. Research suggested much psychological distress during the "coming out process" due to societal heterosexist attitudes including a high rate of suicidality. However, once gay people come to acceptance of who they are the research has suggested no differences between gay and straight people in terms of mental health. The most common sequelae of the perception of prejudice for both gay people and people of color is anger.

The most basic need that we humans have after subsistence needs (food, water, oxygen) and feeling/being safe is the need for love and the feeling of belonging. Being gay in that period of American history meant for the most of us feeling unloved. Most of us had great fear of being rejected by family and friends for being who we were. We were rejected by almost all churches. There was an implicit message that we were not loved even by God.

My perception of homosexuals was of very effeminate men like Liberace, Paul Lynde, and Truman Capote. I never had any exposure to gay role models who were my age and attractive. I remember trying to find out information about homosexuality from the library; there was little. A book was published that was very popular titled *Everything You Ever Wanted to Know About Sex (*But Were Afraid to Ask)* in 1969. Apparently, I was not the only one in need of information about sex. It was a New York Times bestseller. It was difficult to get good information about sex in general and homosexuality in particular.

It was not until I went to Florida (including Key West) with a group of friends that I realized that there were attractive gay guys my age that seemed like regular guys, i.e., not flamboyant, and "swishy." When I got back to Grand Rapids, I got up the courage to go to a gay bar. I met people. I joined a gay support group in town called Dignity. I made friends there. The group met weekly and provided education and support. It was basically group therapy. It was the beginning of my coming out journey. I was coming out of shame.

There is a difference between *guilt* and *shame*. Guilt is the negative feelings we feel as the result of what we do or do not do. Shame is the negative feelings we have about who we *are*. It is the deep sense of being flawed or defective. Guilt is about doing bad. Shame is about being bad. Being gay is not so much about behaviors, and it is not a preference. It is an *orientation*. It is about who we are, and the *coming out* process is about coming out of

24

denial and coming to acceptance of who we are. If you are heterosexual, you know that was not a choice, and you know that it is an integral part of who you are. For most gay people the coming out process is difficult, particularly years ago when societal acceptance was much less than it is today.

When I grew up in the 1960s and 1970s there was much concern about the breakdown of the family, and much of the blame for this was placed on the changing roles of women. There was a backlash to the women's liberation movement by evangelical Christians who stressed patriarchal authority and rigid gender roles. The man should be the ruler of the family and women should be subservient. Homosexuality was a threat to this world view. Homosexuality was considered a sickness, although it was removed as a mental disorder in 1973 from the Diagnostic and Statistical Manual of the APA.

Because of shame I spent much of my early life hiding who I was. When I was in junior high school and my peers were talking about their interest in the female physique, I did not share my lack of interest- I played along. I never talked about my feelings with parents either. I dated a girl once in my late teens (whom I had met at work). She was a great person and beautiful (in fact she won the title of Miss Teenage Michigan). Although we made out, I am sure she sensed my lack of sexual interest. In my twenties I remember my mother asking one day if I ever met any girls that I was attracted to (as I did not date). I said "no." She dropped it from there. My parents may have had suspicions that I was gay, but they never asked, and I was sure they did not really want me to discuss it, and so I did not.

When I started visiting gay bars in my late twenties, I did not share this with my straight friends. I went out with friends to bars to hear rock bands and then made excuses to leave early and then secretly go to gay bars. I was miserable and resentful at weddings when there was so much celebration and joy about two people making the commitment to spend their lives together, knowing that if I met someone I wanted to spend my life with, it would be met with disapproval and perhaps even disgust.

I eventually did meet someone who has become my life partner. Mark and I have been together for twenty-five years. We did have a commitment ceremony attended by friends but none of my family. To be fair none were invited. In my defense, why would I invite family who made it clear that they did not approve of homosexuality or gay relationships. Since then, many family members' views on this have evolved.

The process for the institution of marriage is usually straightforward for heterosexuals; a couple begins dating, they fall in love, they get engaged, and they have a wedding where they make a public commitment to share their lives together. This process was not possible for me or other gay people of my age cohort. Mark and I made a commitment to each other to share our lives together (including joint finances). We could not be legally married. Later we had a public ceremony officiated at by our pastor, but it could not be legal. (Because we did not want to make a big deal of this or solicit gifts, we made it a surprise ceremony during a Valentine's Day party at our home). When gay marriage became legal, we had a ceremony in our church chapel officiated at by our pastor with only two witnesses present. This finally gave us the legal protections that come with marriage. I ask you to think about which of these events was most essential to being "married"? Our personal commitment to each other and the joining of our finances, the public ceremony, or the legal recognition?

My father died ten years ago and my orientation was never discussed, although I am sure he knew. I am sharing all this because I know my story is not unusual. It is scary and difficult to "come out," particularly back then before the fairly recent changes in societal attitudes toward gay people. By listening to others, sharing about myself, and introspecting I gained insight into myself. I learned truths about myself. I also learned truths about homosexuality through research and study. Sometimes it is uncomfortable to face truth and reality.

I am quite certain that my struggles with coming to grips with being gay had a significant impact on my spiritual journey. In realizing that my sexual orientation was an immutable and fundamental aspect of who God made me to be, I was faced with a conflict between my experience and scientific evidence on one hand and religious teachings on the other. I concluded that these religious teachings were wrong. It did lead me for a time to agnosticism; I made the mistake of conflating these ignorant religious teachings with a belief in God or the teachings of Jesus. My conflict was not with God but with religious individuals who are at a pre-modern stage of spirituality or consciousness (these stages will be discussed in chapter three of this book). I began questioning other religious teachings as well, which I think was not only because of my coming out process but also because of my personality, which the Myers-Briggs personality test labels INTJ. It is my nature to question the status quo and to use reason to find answers to existential questions. My later training in psychology also gave me further tools in critical reasoning to discover truths (particularly several graduate courses in statistics).

Most of us believe that objective reality exists. Reality does not just exist in our minds; its existence is independent of our thoughts and feelings. Philosophically most of us are *realists*. Yet, there is much debate about what is real, what is *truth*. Is truth subjective? Is truth relative? Is it possible for us all to have our own truths? I do not think so. I believe there exists an objective reality that humans can discover. It does not matter whether one is a geologist, philosopher, physicist, theologian, astronomer, or psychologist. Although each take different approaches to studying reality, they are studying the same one and only reality.

I also believe that many people are resistant to seeing many aspects of reality. Why? There also may be other people open to seeing reality but do not have the tools to make the discernment. Some are unable to make the distinction between opinions and facts, or between thoughts and feelings. I believe that the honest search for truth is of critical importance to ongoing human development.

Humankind made a great leap forward with the Scientific Revolution and the Enlightenment, otherwise known as the "age of reason." Prior to these events of the 17th and 18th centuries people primarily believed what they were told by the monarchies and the church. The Scientific Revolution and the Enlightenment caused a paradigm shift to the use of reason to determine truth and reality. Major events during this time period included the writings of Sir Isaac Newton who delineated the laws of physics, the work of Copernicus and Galileo in astronomy, and the development of systematic experimental methodologies to obtain knowledge, i.e., to discern truth. Who can deny the tremendous impact the Scientific Revolution and the Enlightenment have had on humankind. What would the world be without science?!

The psychologist, Steven Pinker, in his book *Enlightenment Now: The Case for Reason, Science, Humanism, and Progress* (2018) wrote that Immanuel Kant said enlightenment "consists of 'humankind's emergence from its self-incurred immaturity,' its 'lazy and cowardly' submission to the 'dogmas and formulas' of religious or political authority." Pinker wrote "If there's anything the Enlightenment thinkers had in common, it was an insistence that we energetically apply the standard of reason to understanding our world, and not fall back on generators of delusion like faith, dogma, revelation, authority, charisma, mysticism, divination, visions, gut feelings, or the hermeneutic parsing of sacred texts."

Although the Enlightenment brought in a new paradigm of rational thought for many, most still held onto the old paradigm of adherence to the dictates of those in authority. Few were capable then of free thought, and unfortunately few still are. Even now in the 21st century rational thought is a disappointingly rare commodity. In the age of Trump, we have declarations of "alternative facts," and people are at a loss in determining what is "fake news". Tribalism and other misplaced loyalties have become more important than truth. One would think that of all the institutions for which truth should be cherished, it would be religion, but it is not. Evangelicals are a demographic that has been most vulnerable to the wild and baseless conspiracy theories of the Trump era.

Steven Pinker in his 2021 book *Rationality: What It Is, Why It Seems Scarce, Why It Matters* lists some statistics from the first decade of the present century in regards to Americans' beliefs (percentiles indicate the prevalence of the beliefs):

- Possession by the devil, 42 percent
- Extrasensory perception, 41 percent
- Ghosts and spirits, 32 percent
- Astrology, 25 percent
- Witches, 21 percent
- Communicating with the dead, 29 percent
- Reincarnation, 24 percent
- Evil eye, curses, spells, 16 percent
- Consulted a fortune-teller or psychic, 15 percent

Pinker in this book makes the interesting point that people are rational for the most part in dealing with their day-to-day world where there are real world consequences. If I do not pay my mortgage, I will lose my house. If I do not go to work, I will lose my job. This is a "zone of reality."

The other zone is the world beyond immediate experience: the distant past, the unknowable future, faraway peoples and places, remote corridors of power, the microscopic, the cosmic, the counter-factual, the metaphysical. People may entertain notions about what happens in these zones, but they have no way of finding out, and anyway it makes no discernible difference to their lives. Beliefs in these zones are narratives, which may be entertaining or inspiriting or morally edifying. Whether they are literally "true" or "false" is the wrong question. The function of these beliefs is to construct a social reality that binds the tribe or sect and give it a moral purpose. Call it the mythology mindset.

Pinker explains the concept of *motivated reasoning.* "The mustering of rhetorical resources to drive an argument toward a favored conclusion is called motivated reasoning." People tend to form opinions based on emotion and then use rationalization to defend these opinions. "We evolved not as intuitive scientists but as intuitive lawyers." Pinker talks about the "myside bias." Human beings are *tribal* in so many ways: political party, religion, race, ethnicity, university, etc. Our opinions are formed not so much by reason but by tribal affiliation. "In study after study, liberals and conservatives accept or reject the same scientific conclusion depending on whether or not it supports their talking points, and they endorse or oppose the same policy depending on whether it was proposed by a Democratic or a Republican politician." The problem is that the goal for perhaps most people is not to get an accurate understanding of the world but rather to be valued and accepted by one's peer groups or "tribes." This is what I think Jesus was talking about in the fourteenth chapter of Luke when he said that to be his follower one would have to leave their families for "I am the way and the truth and the life" (John 14:6). In other words, one must put truth above one's relationships.

Steven Pinker in his 2021 book makes the point that the core of morality is impartiality; "the reconciliation of our own selfish interests with others", which is a primary tenet of this book as well. Pinker goes on to say that impartiality is also the core of rationality; "a reconciliation of our biased and incomplete notions into an understanding of reality that transcends any one of us. Rationality, then is not just a cognitive virtue but a moral one."

Scripture

John Wesley (1703-1791) was the founder of Methodism. His writings suggest he believed there were four sources for coming to theological truths. This formulation is known as the *Wesleyan Quadrilateral.* I became familiar with this in sermons by my own previous minister, who was brought up a Methodist but then became a minister in the United Church of Christ. The four sources are scripture, tradition, reason, and Christian experience. Of these four, he considered scripture to be the most important. Wesley believed that the books of the Bible were divinely inspired. This has become the "orthodox" position of most Christian denominations. Some Christians believe the Bible is the literal, inerrant word of God. When I have asked various individuals why they believe this, I really do not get adequate answers. I have been told "it is what I have been brought up to believe," "I just believe it," and "it is a matter of faith."

I have found out that while many may have read or even studied the content of the Bible, few have studied the history of the Bible and how it came to be.

I grew up as an evangelical Christian and with a reverence for the Bible. As I got older, I began to wonder where the Bible came from. This was never taught to me in Sunday school or in catechism classes at my church. It even was not taught to me in religion classes at my Christian school. So where did it come from? Who wrote it? I began researching the topic and was able to get my questions answered, and the answers were very interesting indeed. Because I believe this information is critical to an accurate world view, I wrote *Evolution of the Bible* (2016) with the intention of presenting this information to the general public (especially my fellow Christians) in a succinct and easily readable format.

Prior to the Enlightenment what was believed to be the truth was what was taught by authorities. These *truths*, such as the earth being the center of the universe, began to be questioned since the Enlightenment. The Bible also began to be scrutinized, as scholars were no longer willing to accept "by faith" teachings that were passed down by tradition. Biblical studies have become an academic discipline, with courses taught in colleges and universities by professors who have spent their lives studying the Bible and the historical context of the writings. Mainline seminaries also teach scholarship about the Bible. Unfortunately, most in the general public are never exposed to this information.

In my studies I learned that the writings of the Bible were written by dozens of people, and the traditional authorship of many of these writings is believed by scholars to be false. Scholars do not believe that the "books of Moses," i.e., Genesis, Exodus, Leviticus, Numbers and Deuteronomy, were written by Moses for several reasons. It is believed by many that there were 5 principal authors of these books, known as the Pentateuch. The writings from these five authors were combined to become the Pentateuch around 550 BCE. There is some question whether Moses was even a historical figure.

The first writings that were included in the Hebrew canon were written during the time of the divided kingdoms. After the death of King Solomon, the northern tribes seceded from the unified kingdom and formed the Kingdom of Israel. The southern tribes remained in the Kingdom of Judah. This time period was from 900 BCE to 600 BCE, and eighteen books of the Hebrew scriptures were written during this time period.

Israel was conquered by the Assyrians in 722 BCE, and Judah was conquered by the Babylonians in 598 BCE. Two books of the Hebrew scriptures were written during this "Babylonian Period" (600 to 540 BCE).

In 539 the Persians defeated the Babylonians and became the rulers over Israel. During this "Persian Period" (540 to 330 BCE) fourteen books were written.

Around 330 BCE the Greeks conquered the Persians, and Israel came under Greek control. The final three books of the Hebrew scriptures were written during this period (330 BCE to 170 BCE).

As one would imagine, being ruled by foreign invaders for centuries would have had a significant effect on Jewish culture, and indeed this was the case. During the time of Jesus of Nazareth, the land of Israel was ruled by the Romans. There were no "orthodox" beliefs that the Jews needed to subscribe to. There was much diversity of thought. There were four major sects (or schools of thought) at that time. One sect were the Sadducees whose scripture consisted only of the Torah (the five books of Moses). They were mostly concerned with sacrificial worship at the temple. Another sect were the Pharisees who were primarily concerned with strictly following the laws of Moses. A third sect were the Essenes who expected an imminent end of times, an apocalypse in which there would be a final battle between the forces of good and evil. The final sect was known as the Fourth Philosophy, and these nationalists were intent on overthrowing Roman rule.

There continues to be much diversity of thought within modern day Judaism. There are three major branches of Judaism in the United States: Reformed, Conservative and Orthodox. The Orthodox are the oldest of the three branches, and they believe that the Pentateuch and the *oral tradition* which explicates it are the revealed word of God, given to the Jewish people by God to Moses on Mount Sinai. Most Americans Jews are *non*-orthodox and do not see the writings of the Hebrew scriptures as being the literal word of God. All three branches see their scripture as being exclusively for the Jews and not for Gentiles or humanity. The Talmud, the primary source for Jewish theology, prohibits gentiles from studying the Torah. Such gentiles are considered "thieves." Judaism is non-creedal; there are no specific beliefs that one must subscribe to. Also, all three branches put little emphasis on any type of afterlife after one dies.

Christianity, on the other hand, has interpreted the writings of the Old Testament very differently. It is seen as the story of God and God's relationship to *all* of humanity. The *New Testament* is seen as a continuation of the Old. Throughout history there has been much blending of religious ideas, known as "syncretism." I wonder how much the religion Zoroastrianism has impacted both Judaism (particularly the Essenes) and especially Christianity. Zoroastrianism was the religion of the Persians, who liberated the Jews from their Babylonian captors. Cyrus "the Great," King of Persia was described in the Hebrew scriptures as the Lord's anointed and as Yahweh's shepherd. It is arguable, I think, which religion has most impacted Christianity: Judaism or Zoroastrianism. The following are religious ideas found in Zoroastrianism. They are not ideas found in Judaism. The information comes from Mary Boyce (1979), British scholar of Iranian language and Zoroastrianism.

- There is an evil entity that is opposed to God and is not under God's control.
- This evil entity has subservient beings.
- The present world will have an end that will be heralded by the coming of a cosmic savior who will help bring it about.
- Heaven and Hell exist.
- At death each soul is judged by God and sent either to Heaven or Hell.
- At the end of time there will be a resurrection of the dead and a Last Judgment, with annihilation of the wicked.

- The kingdom of God will then be established on earth and the righteous shall enter this paradise and will live in happiness there eternally with God.
- These souls shall be immortal in body as well as soul.

The early Christians were very diverse in their beliefs, particularly in regards to beliefs about the nature of Jesus. One group of early Christians (Ebionites) believed that Jesus was human and not divine. Another group (Marcionites) believed Jesus was divine and not human. In 325 CE a council was convened in the city of Nicea to make decisions about what were *correct* beliefs. It was decided that Jesus was "of one substance" with God and that Jesus was both human and divine. A creed was also developed at this council to outline what was considered correct belief; it is known as the Nicene Creed. This did not end disputes about the nature of Jesus, however. These disputes were taken up at further ecumenical councils in 381, 431, 451, 553, and 681 CE. Pay attention to these dates! It took centuries for decisions to be made about what were "orthodox" beliefs.

There also were many different writings in early Christianity that were used as scripture. In addition to the gospels of Mathew, Mark, Luke, and John, there also were the Gospel of Thomas, The Gospel of Judas Iscariot, the Gospel of Peter, and the Gospel of Mary. None of these were believed to have been written by disciples or even of eyewitnesses of Jesus' life, including the canonical gospels of Mathew, Mark, Luke, and John. These four gospels were written in Greek, not Aramaic the language of Jesus and his disciples. They were believed to have been written decades after the life of Jesus. In fact, none of the writings of the New Testament are believed by Biblical scholars to have been written by eyewitnesses or associates of Jesus. Beginning in the fourth century lists of scriptures began to be formulated that were considered canonical. Different Christian communities had different canons. The list of Athanasius (300-375 CE) appears to be the first that lists the exact 27 books that are in our current New Testament.

As I have previously stated, John Wesley as well as today's evangelical Christians, believe that scripture is the primary source for authority about God and what to believe. But how did scripture come to be canonical, i.e., determined to be truth? It was determined by "authorities." Various men wrote "scriptures," and it was other men who determined what should be believed and kept and what should be discarded. These men who made these decisions lived centuries after the time of Jesus.

I want to make clear that I believe there is much value in the writings of the Old and New Testaments, but I do not believe that these writings are the literal word of God, and there is no evidence that they are. Most Christians who believe this believe it because they were told to believe it when they were very young. Additionally, Muslims who believe the Quran is the literal word of God likely believe this because they were taught to believe this when very young. Mormons who believe the Book of Mormon is a revelation from God, likely believe this because they were told to believe this when very young. Mainline Christian denominations often put it this way: "I take the Bible seriously, but not literally." The Bible gives us invaluable information about the evolution of religion and the development of morality. Just because something has been accepted as truth over long periods of time does not automatically make it true.

Tradition

There is a well-known story about a man who is sent to the butcher by his newlywed wife to buy a ham. He comes home with the ham and is asked by his wife why he did not have the ends of it cut off by the butcher. The man asked why the ends should be cut off. His wife replied that her mother always had the ends cut off, and her mother was the best cook that she had ever known. It just so happened that the bride's mother was coming over for dinner, and so they had the opportunity to ask her about this. The mother explained that she did it that way because it was what her own mother had always done. They decided to telephone grandma to get her explanation. Grandma said she cut the ends off so that it would fit into her small roaster. This is a story about tradition. People often do things because "that's how it's always been done."

Many people believe that a valid reason for belief is tradition. We believe that Moses wrote the Pentateuch because this has been the traditional belief for centuries. The fact that a belief has existed for such a long period of time seems to give it credence. In actuality, however, length of time that something is believed has nothing to do with its validity. For ages it was believed that the sun revolved around the earth. Just because this was the accepted belief for centuries did not make it correct.

Let us look at two examples of traditional practices and beliefs that were accepted for thousands of years: slavery/racism and the inferiority of women. Defenders of slavery had argued that since slavery existed throughout history it was a natural state of humankind. Slavery was referred to in the 4,000-year-old Code of Hammurabi from ancient Mesopotamia, the first human civilization. It was well known among the ancient Egyptians. It was common in the ancient Greek and Romans civilizations. Heroes of the Bible had slaves, for example Abraham. It is mentioned in the Ten Commandments: we should not covet thy neighbor's manservant or maidservant. The Bible (both old and new testaments) do not speak out against the practice. Slavery was a prominent institution in the early history of the United States. John C. Calhoun, former vice president, senator, and secretary of state, said this about slavery in a speech in 1837.

> *I hold that in the present state of civilization, where two races of different origin, and distinguished by color, and other physical differences, as well as intellectual, are brought together, the relation now existing in the slaveholding states between the two, is, instead of an evil, a good-a positive good. I feel myself called upon to speak freely upon the subject where the honor and interests of those I represent are involved. I hold then, that there never has yet existed a wealthy and civilized society in which one*

portion of the community did not, in point of fact, live on the labor of the other. Broad and general as is this assertion, it is fully borne out by history.

John Calhoun makes the case that slavery is a good institution and is justified by history and tradition. Judge Leon Bazile was the judge who presided in the case of Loving v. State of Virginia (Richard Loving and Mildred Jeter were charged with violating the state's ban on interracial marriage). Bazile argues for the marital tradition that marriage is between a man and a woman of the same race.

Almighty God created the races white, black, yellow, malay and red, and he placed them on separate continents. And but for the interference with his arrangement there would be no cause for such marriages. The fact that he separated the races shows that he did not intend for the races to mix.

Just because a belief has existed for eons does not mean it represents truth. We now know, through evidence, that all our homosapien ancestors originated in east Africa and migrated to different parts of the world. Early members of our species likely had dark skin due to the climate of Africa. Our ancestors settled in various parts of the world in societies that grew larger and larger. Because of separation from other societies, these group developed unique genetic characteristics, and those living in tropical climates developed increased skin pigments to better deal with the hot sun. There is no such thing as separate races; it is just that some of us may have more genetic similarities with some people than with others.

Another traditional belief that has been prevalent since the beginnings of history is that women are inferior to men. Some fundamentalists cite the story of Adam and Eve to support this belief. Many brilliant men including religious leaders have supported this belief. Here are some examples:

"It is the law of nature that woman should be held under the dominance of man" Confucius

37

Women with their two-fingered wisdom, have a difficult time understanding what I teach." Buddha

"A proper wife should be as obedient as a slave" Aristotle

"Any woman who does not give birth to as many children as she is capable is guilty of murder." Augustine

"Nature intended women to be our slaves. They are our property." Napoleon

"The words and works of God are quite clear, that women were made either to be wives or prostitutes" Martin Luther

When I was growing up it was commonly asserted that women were physically incapable of doing many jobs such as construction, police work, serving in the military, or competing with men in sports. We now have ample evidence that this assumption was not true. Since the 1970s, the "religious right" has made well known the concept of *traditional values* and the opposition to abortion, homosexuality, contraception, sex education, and feminism. There was particular emphasis on *traditional marriage*. Conservapedia is an online conservative encyclopedia, and they say "traditional values refer to those ideals and values held to be true because of their long history and proven success." A traditional marriage is thought of as a lifelong commitment between a man and a woman of the same race who love each other. But this does not reflect what the true history of marriage is. In actuality, the tradition of marriage throughout most of history had nothing to do with love. The purpose of marriages, which were often arranged, were primarily for economic or political reasons. Women were considered property and had few rights. This is still reflected in many current marriage ceremonies when it is asked "Who gives this woman to be married to this man?" Tradition has it that the woman is going from being the property of the father to being the property of the husband. Also, traditional marriage was the union between one man and one or more women. Polygamy was common.

Let us look at the tradition of marriage in the Hebrew scriptures. Abraham had three wives: Sarah (who was also his half-sister), Hagar and Keturah. His grandson, Jacob, married two sisters who were also his first cousins. King David had at least eight wives, and his son Solomon had seven hundred wives and three hundred concubines. This harem was considered part of Solomon's wealth. Tradition alone is not a good reason for doing or believing anything. Traditions can be beneficial for providing a sense of security and stability, but they are not evidence for truth.

Experience

Jennifer was devastated to hear that her 34-year-old husband, Nate, was diagnosed with stage 4 cancer. The melanoma was inoperable and had spread to lymph nodes. The couple were told they should start planning for Nate's inevitable death. The couple had not been involved in a church in the ten years that they had been married. This crisis made them start confronting their mortality, something at their young age they had given barely a thought to. Both Nate and Jennifer had been baptized as infants and did have church involvement in their childhood. Their preoccupation had been on their careers, and recently they had been thinking of trying to have a child. Nate began wondering whether he was saved. Although baptized, he never made a commitment to accepting Christ as his personal savior. A coworker of Jennifer's had invited the couple to her church in the past, and so Nate and Jennifer began attending. They felt very welcomed by the church members, and the pastor was truly a comfort. The whole congregation began praying for Nate, and both Nate and Jennifer made profession of faith and joined the church. Nate was dumbfounded at his next oncology appointment to hear that his tumors have been shrinking. Over the next few months, they continued to shrink until Nate's cancer was declared to be in remission. The entire congregation rejoiced with Nate and Jennifer that God had answered their prayers and provided this miracle.

Personal experience is another source for determining truth according to the Wesleyan Quadrilateral. Nate and Jennifer learned from their experience that God takes care of his children when they are faithful to him. However, people inexplicably recover from cancer and other ailments whether they are religious or not, whether they are prayed for or not. How do we know where to attribute the reason for an event? Research by psychologists has suggested that something called *confirmation bias* strongly influences our perceptions. Human beings tend to interpret events and information in such a way that it confirms preconceived ideas, values and beliefs. We tend to disregard data when it contradicts our preconceptions. So, for example, if I have a strong belief that God will reward me financially if I am faithful to him, any financial gains I have I attribute to God, and any financial misfortunes I tend to minimize, to attribute to something else, or to attribute to a wrong that I had committed. Similarly, if I am uncritically loyal to my president or political party, I tend to attribute stock market gains or low unemployment to my president, and market losses or unemployment spikes to other factors.

This brings me to another cognitive bias. People tend to incorporate beliefs because other people have these beliefs. Terms to describe this phenomenon include "group think," "herd behavior", and "bandwagon effect". Because many people have difficulty with critical thinking, or they are too lazy to put in the work of critical thinking, they simply incorporate the beliefs of the groups they value, for example social groups, neighbors, church, or political party. This is a major reason for the current crisis of political polarization in the United States at the time of this writing. People become loyal to individuals or groups rather than to principles, which would require critical thinking.

"Thinking is the hardest work there is, which is probably the reason why so few engage in it."

Henry Ford

There are several other pitfalls to using personal experience for discerning truth. First, our early life experiences greatly color our perceptions. If I grew up in a family with parents who could not be trusted, were not loving, and maybe were abusive or neglectful, my tendency is to generalize distrust and wariness to all people. My two parents are a small sample size to base a belief onto all humanity. Humans commonly do generalize based on the small sample of people we come across rather than large data studies. For example, during the current Covid-19 pandemic that is occurring at the time of this writing, I have heard people say that they think the pandemic is being greatly exaggerated (some even maintaining that it is a "hoax") as they do not know personally anybody has died from the virus.

Experiences are also colored by faulty memories. Our recall of events in our life, research has shown, is not as accurate as we might believe, even for traumatic events. We generally trust our perceptions and experiences, but research on the accuracy of memory would suggest that we should not be so confident. Research has shown evidence for malleability of long-term memories (e.g., development of "false memories" in individuals reporting recovery of repressed memories of childhood abuse). Research has also shown frequent errors in eyewitness testimony in court cases. We tend to think that the most damning evidence for the guilt of a criminal defendant is someone witnessing the commission of a crime. However, with the advent of DNA analysis in the 1980s, hundreds of people who had been convicted and sentenced to death based on eyewitness testimony have been exonerated. The reader is referred to the research of psychologist, Elizabeth Loftus.

Experiences are also colored by various feelings. Human beings (unlike Vulcans, if you are a Star Trek fan like me) do not interpret personal experiences in a completely reasoned manner. Emotions such as anger, sadness, fear, joy, and disgust significantly affect our perceptions of experiences and what we perceive as reality. Psychologist Jonathan Haidt makes the point in *The Righteous Mind* (2012) that individuals frequently make judgments based on instinct and gut feelings. The use of reason comes into play only to justify the judgments already made. Here is an example: an acquaintance related a story in which another acquaintance greeted his mother with a kiss on the lips. The acquaintance who was relating this story was repulsed by this noting "That is just wrong." However, I think he might have struggled to give a reasoned explanation of why this was "wrong."

Humans frequently conceive of reality based on their personal experiences rather than objective data. If nobody that I am acquainted with are affected by a coronavirus pandemic, and my acquaintances are cavalier about the virus and do not wear face masks, the tendency is to become less concerned ourselves, despite what the virologists and epidemiologists say and what the data suggests. My attitude might then change when a close friend or family member succumbs to the disease. Although my personal experience may have changed my view of reality, reality itself did not change.

There are numerous examples where empirical evidence has refuted stereotypes and prejudices. Unfortunately, too few people base their beliefs on evidence but rather base beliefs on personal experience, which is usually highly affected by confirmation bias. Over the last decade the American public's perception of GLBT people has significantly become more accepting and positive. Why? I don't think it is because people have become more reasoned. I think it is because more and more gay people "came out" and have become known to others. Through personal experiences the American public came to see that gay people are just normal people. Personal experience is a source for determining truth, but only when it is accompanied by reason.

Authority

Although not discussed in the Wesleyan Quadrilateral (other than scripture), authorities are probably the main source that people have used for determining truth. In prehistoric times shamans and chieftains were believed to have had special access to the spiritual realm, and they were seen as the arbiters of ultimate truth. Later, priests, prophets and kings took on that role. After scripture was established and canonized in the Christian church, the Roman

Catholic Church did not feel that the Bible should be made available to the general public as they felt the public could not properly interpret the readings, and that the educated authorities (clergy) were required to convey the correct meanings of the writings. It was during the Reformation that scripture took on the importance that it has now for Protestants. But as I previously have stated, it was early church authorities that made the decisions about what writings would be authoritative and which would not. These decisions were in no way unanimous, but rather quite contentious.

As far as beliefs about ultimate truths, I believe that people still primarily incorporate their beliefs from authority figures. As children, these beliefs are from parents. As adults we incorporate beliefs from clergy, teachers, professors, and politicians. Too few are questioning, and too few think critically. Fundamentalists believe the Bible is the literal word of God because their pastor tells them this. Progressive Christians say they take the Bible "seriously but not literally," because their minister tells them this. Few educate themselves enough to be able to make decisions about such issues on their own. It is the same with political issues; rather than studying the pros and cons of issues, too many are content to just follow the dictates of their chosen political party. For example, a couple years ago I posted on Facebook my support for a ban on assault weapons. A cousin of mine responded in anger over not only this issue but the assumption that I also then was endorsing other political issues, including support for abortion. She assumed that because I held this position, I automatically would hold the other positions of what she perceived as the "other side".

Journalist Ezra Klein in his book *Why We're Polarized* (2020) makes an interesting point about political parties. He points out that both the Republicans and the Democrats used to be diverse in terms of ideology; there were liberal Republicans and conservative Democrats. Klein said "The parties used to be scrambled, both ideologically and demographically, in ways that curbed their power as identities and lowered the partisan stakes of politics." Voters were therefore required to be more knowledgeable about issues and candidates than they are now. Voters now tend to pledge loyalty to a political party that they think represents a particular ideology.

Although that ideology may change in a party, subservience, and loyalty to the authority of the party may continue. Take the Republican party under Ronald Reagan as an example. He and the party stood for free trade, openness to immigration, smaller federal government, strong support of NATO, and opposition to deficit spending. Under Donald Trump the party is advocating protectionism, hostility to immigrants, hostility toward NATO, and a ballooning national deficit. Despite touting that he was presiding over the greatest economy the U.S. has ever known, instead of paying down the national debt, he added another trillion dollars to the deficit for a tax break that primarily benefited corporations and the uberwealthy.

There is a phenomenon known as *groupthink*, in which members delegate authority to a group in order to conform. Ezra Klein says:

> *The human mind is exquisitely tuned to group affiliation and group difference. It takes almost nothing for us to form a group identity, and once that happens, we naturally assume ourselves in competition with other groups. The deeper our commitment to our group becomes, the more determined we become to make sure our group wins. Making matters worse, winning is positional, not material; we often prefer outcomes that are worse for everyone so long as they maximize our group's advantage over other groups.*

Fealty to authority is perhaps most pronounced in a phenomenon known as *cult of personality*. Political and religious leaders who are charismatic and crave power, fame and money can utilize propaganda techniques that promote themselves rather than principles or an ideology. This is not something most of us want in a political or a religious leader, i.e., someone who is primarily interested in promoting themselves rather than a country, an ideology such as democracy, or a faith. Such leaders have been common throughout history. In ancient Egypt the pharaohs were gods. Roman emperors were venerated also as gods. Augustus was known as the son of god (Julius Caesar) and as a god himself. Mass media in more recent times has provided further tools for such leaders to use, giving rise to Benito Mussolini, Adolf Hitler, Joseph Stalin, and Mao Zedong, and to even more recent leaders as Donald Trump. Mass media has also been used by charismatic religious leaders for tremendous financial gain, e.g., Kenneth Copeland (net worth of $760 million), Benny Hinn ($42 million), and Joel Osteen ($42 million).

There have been religious cult leaders with more nefarious intent than just scamming money out of their followers. The self-proclaimed messiah, Jim Jones, attracted hundreds of followers by promising utopia if they would follow him. Charismatic and narcissistic, he increasingly became paranoid and led 900 followers to mass suicide in Guyana; 276 of them were children. David Koresh, another charismatic narcissist, considered himself the "final prophet" who convinced his followers to stockpile weapons and to become the "army of God." An FBI raid of his compound in Waco, Texas, resulted in six dozen of his followers' death. Marshall Applewhite declared himself the messiah and was the leader of the Heaven's Gate religious cult. He too led his followers to mass suicide.

There are times that we do need to depend on authorities. We do not have the time or ability to become fully knowledgeable about every subject that becomes important. If I am diagnosed with cancer, I need to rely on an oncologist to figure out my treatment plan rather than educating myself in order to make these decisions for myself. When my car will not run, I need the expertise of a mechanic to fix it. The key to relying on an authority, however, is that the authority makes decisions based on education, and that their education is based on empirical evidence. To be licensed as a physician a person must complete prescribed education in medical school and in internships. Throughout the process testing is employed to make sure the student is gaining the knowledge necessary to be a competent physician. The successful passing of the licensing exam assures the public that the person has the requisite empirical knowledge to be a physician. Likewise, a certification in auto mechanics also assures the consumer that the mechanic has the knowledge and ability to fix their car.

Too often individuals may be treated as an authority on a certain subject who in fact are not expert and do not have the requisite education. Also, one needs to beware of "ulterior motives" even if an individual is an expert in a particular field of study. Let me give you a few examples:

Larry is a 31-year-old married man who over the past year has had significant difficulties with mood. At times he is severely depressed with suicidal thoughts, and over other periods of time he is feeling on top of the world with wonderful energy. His wife thinks he may have bipolar disorder, which does run in his family. He is referred by his family physician to a psychiatrist who does diagnose the patient with Bipolar II disorder and prescribes the patient a new drug that has FDA approval for mood stabilization. In this case Larry has been evaluated by a valid authority, a board-certified psychiatrist. He is prescribed a medication that has been researched and approved for his diagnosed disorder. What Larry does not know, and probably has no way of knowing, is that the psychiatrist is paid to do educational dinners by the drug manufacturer of the medication that was prescribed. The doctor has a vested interest in the prescribed medication. So, was the doctor's choice of the medication for Larry biased? When I have attended psychopharmacology meetings for continuing educations the presenters are required to disclose any potential conflicts of interest.

Lisa was a local talk show host in the 1990s. She asked two experts to appear on her show to debate the topic of whether homosexuality was a choice. One expert had a doctorate in neuroanatomy and specialized in research on human sexuality. The other was a Pentecostal minister who was a well-known national opponent to LGBT rights. Now the disparity between "expertise" about human sexuality here might appear obvious, but I do remember such debates over the past decades. In a desire to be "fair and balanced" about an issue in which the scientific evidence was quite clear, it was felt important to present some opposing view. This created controversy where really none existed. The general public then perceived that there were no clear answers, and they could just choose which "authority" they wanted to believe.

At the time of the writing of this book when the coronavirus pandemic is raging, people are choosing which "authority" to believe about the seriousness of the crisis and whether to wear face masks in public. Public health experts, virologists and epidemiologists who follow empirical data agree that the pandemic is a crisis and that the wearing of face masks in public are critical for lessening spread. On the other hand, are politicians, most notably the president, who downplays the pandemic and does not encourage the wearing of face masks, and in fact discourages their use. Who here is an expert? What type of authority should we follow in regards to a disease? Who should we listen to for treatment of a disease? A physician, or a politician who recommends hydroxychloroquine (a medication used for the treatment of lupus with no scientific evidence supporting its use for Covid) or Ivermectin (an animal deworming medicine)? Likewise, who should we listen to as an authority on global warming or the impact of fracking? A politician or a scientist? The key questions here are who is knowledgeable about the empirical evidence, and who is motivated to get at the truth, rather than to lie for personal gain or to be swayed by preconceived ideological beliefs.

We now can "fact check" like we never have before, thanks to the advent of the internet. We can "google" information. However, the internet is full of false information as well as accurate information. How do we decide what is valid and reliable information? How do we know what is fake and what is real? As a former university professor who graded research papers, "sourcing" was an important issue for students and for me who critically evaluated their papers. Just where were the students getting their information from? Wikipedia is not an appropriate source for a college research paper, as it is not a *primary* source of information. A primary source has firsthand information which would include eyewitness accounts and original research. A good source for primary academic research articles is Google Scholar. Academic articles are not only a primary source of information by genuine authorities, but usually are also peer reviewed by other authorities. Wikipedia is a *secondary* source; we do not know who inputs the information into articles. Wikipedia does have benefit, however, for finding primary sources of information.

When evaluating the validity and reliability of information on the internet we should assess the author's credentials. Are they well educated in the topic in which they are writing? Are conclusions backed up by data including statistics? Is the website reputable and a well-known source of reliable information? For example, I would trust medical information from the websites of the Mayo Clinic or the Cleveland Clinic, but would be skeptical of information from some random blogger. Might there be ulterior motives by the authority such as financial incentives? Are there other reasons they might be biased? For example, if I want accurate information about reliability of automobiles a better source would be Consumer's Reports rather than the website of Ford Motors.

Another authority sometimes cited for a belief is God himself. Some people believe that God imbues in us innate knowledge about certain things, including the existence of the Almighty. One such person is C.S. Lewis, the English professor, writer, and well-known lay theologian. There was a very interesting book written by psychiatrist Armand Nicholi titled *The Question of God* (2002) which compares the lives and views of Lewis with Sigmund Freud. There were several similarities as well as dissimilarities between these two famous men. "The early life experiences of Freud and Lewis shows a striking parallelism. Both Freud and Lewis, as young boys, possessed intellectual gifts that foreshadowed the profound impact they would make as adults. Both suffered significant losses early in life. Both had difficult, conflict-ridden relationships with their fathers. Both received early instruction in the faith of their family and acknowledged a nominal acceptance of that faith. Both jettisoned their early belief system and became atheists when in their teens. Both read authors that persuaded them to reject their nominal childhood beliefs" (Nicholi, 2002). Freud remained a lifelong atheist. Lewis had a conversion experience at the age of 31.

Freud argued that a belief in God is the result of projection of a childish wish for a loving all-powerful parent who could protect us from the terrible vicissitudes of life. The only conception of God that Freud argues against, however, is the idea of a superman in the sky, not a more transcendent formulation such as that of Baruch Spinoza or Paul Tillich.

Lewis in contrast argues that his desire for God makes it likely that there is a God. "Creatures are not born with desires unless satisfaction for these desires exists. A baby feels hunger; well, there is such a thing as food. A duckling wants to swim; well, there is such a thing as water. Men feel sexual desire; well, there is such a thing as sex. If I find in myself a desire which no experience in this world can satisfy, the most probably explanation is that I was made for another world." (Lewis, 1952). Freud (and I) would argue that a loving, powerful, and protective parental figure is something human beings have a natural inclination to desire. The orthodox conception of God as a loving father is not something beyond our comprehension, but rather a most basic human need.

Lewis also argues that the fact that humans have a conscience is evidence for God. "We have two bits of evidence about the Somebody [behind the Moral Law]. One is the universe He has made. If we used that as are our only clue, then I think we should have to conclude that He was a great artist (for the universe is a very beautiful place), but also that He is quite merciless and no friend to man (for the universe is a very dangerous and terrifying place). The other bit of evidence is that Moral Law which He has put into our minds. And this is a better bit of evidence than the other, because it is inside information. You find out more about God from the Moral Law than from the universe in general just as you find out more about a man by listening to his conversation than by looking at a house he has built." (Lewis, 1952). Lewis believes that God gave us a conscience that causes us to feel guilt when we do wrong, and the knowledge of right and wrong was imparted to us by God.

Lewis does not reconcile this idea with evolution. When did God put this moral law into our minds? Did God put it in the mind of our hominid ancestors such as homo erectus? Did God put it in the mind of the common ancestor of humans and chimpanzees? Did God put it in the mind of the earliest mammals? Invertebrates?

Just what is this moral knowledge that we are supposed to know instinctively? Do people always feel guilt for transgressing the "moral law"? Did the Christians and the Muslims feel guilty about killing each other for religious reasons during the Crusades of the Middle Ages, or were their actions just not wrong? Did the officials of the Roman Catholic Church who brutally tortured and killed Jews, Muslims and other "heretics" during the Inquisition feel guilty, or were their actions just not wrong? In our own country, did the slave traders and the slave owners feel guilty about their actions, or did they feel that what they were doing was just not wrong? I do not think there really was consensus and there still is not consensus about what is right and wrong. Some people seem to be more prone to feeling guilt than others.

Freud saw conscience as something that is developed. "He believed that during a child's development, 'at about the age of five,' an important change takes place. The child internalizes the part of his parents that tells him what to do and what to avoid doing, and this internalized part of the parents becomes his conscience, a part of what Freud calls the superego." (Nicholi, 2002). I mentioned above that some people are more guilt-prone than others; this is what some psychoanalytic therapists call an overly harsh superego. At the other extreme are *psychopaths* who completely lack a conscience. Psychologist Lawrence Kohlberg has extensively researched moral development and has outlined how morality develops in stages. Research does not suggest that morality is instinctual or innate. Rather morality evolves in both individuals and cultures. The higher stages of moral development require education and reason.

Reason and Evidence

In March of 2019 Donald Trump began touting a medication called hydroxychloroquine for the treatment of Covid 19. It has FDA approval for the treatment of malaria, and it is also used for the treatment of lupus, for which there is clinical evidence. Trump said that he heard of instances in which critically ill Covid patients had taken the drug and recovered. "What do you have to lose?" So, does

Trump have a point? Why not try it if there are reports of patients getting well while being administered the drug?

Well, there are several problems with this. One problem is the maxim that one cannot infer causation from a correlation. Just because two variables correlate with each other does not mean that one causes the other. Height and weight strongly correlate, but increasing weight in childhood does not make one taller. Just because one thing comes after another does not mean that the one thing caused the other. This is known in logic as the *post hoc fallacy*. Just because patients begin to recover while taking a medication does not mean it was the medication that made the difference.

Another problem is the lack of controlled randomized studies for this drug with Covid 19. In 2010 a 25 year-long study was published in the journal Pediatrics that found that lesbians may make better parents than heterosexual parents. In their study they found that the children of lesbian mothers rated significantly higher in social, academic, and overall competence and rated lower in social problems, rule breaking and aggressive behaviors. However, this was not a controlled randomized study. What this means is that the children were not randomly assigned to being raised either by the heterosexual parents or the lesbian parents. Perhaps there are other factors that caused the children of lesbian parents to function better. Perhaps the two groups are different in other ways than the sexual orientations of the children's parents, for example the size of family, or socioeconomic status. One major difference between the two groups that I see is the motivation for having children. The lesbian parents as a group had to go to significant expense and trouble for one of the partners to get pregnant. These children, as a group, were *really* wanted. The heterosexual controls, however, would have included not only parents who really wanted to have children, but also parents who unintentionally got pregnant. Many of these children may not have been wanted.

Methodologies have been developed for the acquisition of knowledge. This is science. Science is less about being a body of knowledge than it is a methodology for determining truth. With knowledge about scientific methodology, I know that I cannot just conclude in the above study that lesbian mothers are superior to heterosexual mothers, or that having two mothers make for better outcomes than having only one mother, or that there are better outcomes for children by not having men involved in their upbringing.

There are numerous designs for scientific experimentation, and one of the best is known as a double-blind placebo-controlled study. As a psychologist and psychopharmacologist, this methodology is very important in my line of work, as this is the method for determining efficacy and safety for medications. In these studies subjects are given either the medication being studied or a placebo. A placebo contains an inert substance only, such as a pill that contains no active ingredients. Placebos can have powerful effects. If a patient has the expectation that a medication or a procedure is going to be effective, it usually will be...at least for a while. If a new medication is given approval by the FDA, let us say for example an antidepressant, it must be more effective than a placebo in alleviating depression. Placebos also surprisingly can have negative effects, i.e., "side effects" such as GI upset, decreased libido, weight gain, weight loss, headache, etc. In "double-blind" studies neither the subjects nor the experimenters know which subjects get the placebo and which get the drug under investigation. This eliminates the bias that comes with having expectations.

Beliefs should be based on evidence. When an individual is charged with a crime, the arrest should be based on evidence. When a jury convicts that individual, it should be based on evidence "beyond a reasonable doubt." We should not arrest people or convict them based on gut feelings, and hopefully evidence comes from multiple sources such as DNA, eyewitness testimony (although this is often unreliable), finger prints, tire tracks, etc. My occupation as a clinical psychologist is to make judgments about people. I am asked to make psychological diagnoses, to make treatment recommendations, to make recommendations about psychotropic medications, to assess veracity and malingering (whether a patient is faking symptomatology for financial gain or other reasons), and to determine neurological problems (such as dementia, ADHD, post-concussion syndrome, traumatic brain injury, etc.). My conclusions need to be based on evidence- not feelings or instinct. One method for obtaining objective data are various psychological and neuropsychological tests.

Also, just as detectives try to discern motives for individuals under criminal investigation, psychologists need to keep in mind motives as well for examinees. I expect some degree of minimization and defensiveness in child custody evaluations, for example. You would expect that a parent who is trying to get custody of his or her children would try to present themselves in the most positive light and would tend to minimize faults. On the other hand, I would anticipate some degree of embellishment or exaggeration for individuals who are being evaluated for disability. Because he or she wants to be deemed "disabled," I would expect them to over-emphasize any problems that they have.

Over the past few years, the most common referral I receive is from pain physicians for determining level of risk for individual patients to get prescriptions for narcotic pain medications. I assess for psychopathology (particularly personality disorders), history of substance use disorders, and most importantly veracity and forthrightness. Patients may tell me they never use illicit drugs, but their urine drug screen may show otherwise. Patients may maintain that they take their prescribed medications regularly, but their negative urine drug screens for the drug may suggest otherwise. Patients may report that they are recovering alcoholics and that they have been maintaining abstinence for years, but their urine drug screens may show the presence of alcohol metabolites (which can show up for 80 hours after last use). Patients who report being recovering alcohol/drug addicts who are regularly involved in Alcoholics Anonymous or Narcotics Anonymous may not be telling me the truth if they have little knowledge of these programs or the twelve steps. In answering questions patients may be inconsistent in their facts, vague or evasive. They may tend to minimize or rationalize. All of this, as well as validity scales of psychological testing, may suggest the patient is not being completely open and forthright.

Occasionally I get referrals for independent medical evaluations (IMEs). My referrals usually come from auto insurance companies who want a neuropsychological evaluation to determine such questions as what are the patient's deficits and conditions (such as problems with short term memory or concentration), are the deficits the result of the motor vehicle accident, were there premorbid issues which contributed to the deficits, has treatment been appropriate, and what is the prognosis? The conclusions of my assessments are of significant consequence, as it can influence whether a patient continues to get wage loss, whether auto insurance needs to continue paying for medical treatments, and who may be the beneficiary of a large monetary settlement if there is litigation.

There are three types of reasoning I would like to briefly discuss: deductive reasoning, inductive reasoning, and abductive reasoning. Deductive reasoning can be best illustrated by a syllogism, which is an argument in logic based upon a major premise, a minor premise, and a conclusion based upon the two premises. For example, a major premise might be that all living humans breathe oxygen, the minor premise is that John is a living human, and so therefore the conclusion is that John breathes oxygen. For the conclusion to be valid, the major and minor premises must be accurate. So, if we change the major premise to be "all humans breathe oxygen" our conclusion would not be correct if John died two weeks ago.

For inductive reasoning we develop hypotheses based on observations. In other words, from observations we generalize. Then we might do experiments to test the validity of our hypothesis. This is the basis of the scientific method. For example, observations were made for hundreds of years that water containing the element lithium had psychiatric benefits. This led to a hypothesis that it could treat bipolar disorder (what used to be called manic depressive disorder). Experiments were done to determine the safety and efficacy for its use. Through testing it was discovered that lithium has a very narrow therapeutic window, i.e., too little is inefficacious, but too much can be lethal. It now is perhaps the gold standard for treating bipolar disorder, although we know now the importance of regular blood tests to make sure that blood levels remain within the narrow therapeutic window.

A third type of reasoning is called *abduction* or *Bayesian reasoning*. This type of reasoning involves gathering all the facts we have in regards to a question and then weighing all that knowledge to determine the most likely explanation. This would be the type of reasoning used by a jury. The prosecution presents evidence that a person is guilty, the defense presents evidence that the person is not guilty, and it is up to the jury to weigh the evidence and decide. This is also the type of reasoning I use as a psychologist to make decisions about examinees.

Successful abductive reasoning is contingent upon good information. The acquisition of knowledge is a prerequisite for valid conclusions based on reasoning. In the case of a jury, for them to make a good decision the prosecution must have convincing evidence to make their case. It is the job of detectives to uncover the evidence. The defense attorneys in the case must do their own investigation to prove the defendant's innocence and to dispute the presented evidence by the prosecution. In my work as a clinical psychologist, I try to obtain other information other than that which I gather in a clinical interview. This might include medical records, school records, urine drug screen results, various psychological or neuropsychological testing results, and interviews with family members.

Abduction is also the type of reasoning that is the basis of this book. It is the type of reasoning one might use to determine religious or spiritual beliefs and to develop a world view. I strongly believe it is the method one *should* use to form such beliefs and opinions. In order to develop a valid worldview, knowledge is required, and from various disciplines including history, philosophy, psychology, and all the various scientific disciplines. Abductive reasoning is required to determine meaning and purpose for life. Abductive reasoning is needed to answer questions of *metaphysics* and *ontology* (determining the nature of reality and being, mind and matter), *cosmology* (determining the origin and evolution of the universe), *phenomenology* (the study of consciousness), and *ethics* (determining what is morally good and bad and why).

Abductive reasoning is important in theory formation including in the development of a theory for the nature of reality. An important question to consider is what is the most *plausible* explanation for reality. When looking at all available empirical evidence, what is the explanation that is most likely? It is *possible* that all of reality is just a product of my mind (like in the film *Total Recall*) and that I am the only conscious being in existence, but how plausible is this? It is *possible* that the world is only 6,000 years old and that the world was created with very old artifacts such as old dinosaur bones and ancient rocks (as some fundamentalists believe) just to make us believe that the earth is 4.5 billion years old, but how likely is this? It is *possible* that the earth is only two years old and that all of humankind's memories were implanted into our minds, but how plausible is this?

There are various obstacles in our search for truth through empirical evidence. One such obstacle is a construct known as *paradigms*. This is a topic written about by Thomas Kuhn in *The Structure of Scientific Revolutions* (1962). A paradigm is a pattern for seeing reality. We tend to readily perceive things that we expect to see, and we have difficulty perceiving the unexpected. I viewed a video years ago (the fact that it was a video tells you how long ago it was) that demonstrated a concept known as *paradigm paralysis*, which refers to the inability to comprehend things outside of the current framework of thinking or perceiving. The film flashed cards from a playing deck very quickly. The viewer is asked to identify the cards that are shown. A few are recognized only. Then cards are flashed again at half the speed. Again only a few are identified. The cards are then flashed at one-quarter of the speed of the first administration. One then might recognize that there is something different about this deck of cards. The deck contains red spades and black hearts. What the narrator correctly explains is that subjects can quickly and easily recognize cards that are "correct" (i.e., black clubs and red diamonds) but unable to recognize the cards that are "wrong" (i.e., black spades and red hearts). The unexpected cards just do not register.

The film then gives some real-life examples of this phenomenon of paradigm paralysis. One example was the development of the quartz clock, which was much more accurate and cheaper to produce than the mechanical watch. The Swiss completely dominated the watchmaking industry at the time of this invention. Although the Swiss were involved in the development of the quartz watch, they did not recognize that it was the future for watchmaking. It did not fit their paradigm of what a watch should be. The Japanese were open to this new paradigm, and as a result they took over dominance of the watchmaking industry. This is an example of a *paradigm shift*, which is a revolution which causes a dramatic shift in thinking or ways of doing things. Paradigm shifts not only occur in business but in all aspects of society and culture. The film stated that paradigms can be very useful in that they provide a foundation to work from. However, the lesson to be learned is that we can fall into paradigm paralysis, that is, believing the way we are doing things or thinking about things is the only way for doing or thinking about things. Paradigms can be a hindrance to innovation and creativity. Paradigms can keep us from seeing new realities.

Another obstacle are defense mechanisms. This is an issue that psychoanalytic psychotherapists work to confront and minimize in psychotherapy. Many of us do not want to see certain truths because it is too painful or scary, and so we employ unconscious psychological mechanisms to reduce these difficult feelings. For example, an alcoholic might employ the unconscious defense mechanism of *denial* in order to avoid facing the fact that he has this disease. A young woman might employ the unconscious defense mechanism of *repression* to avoid memories of being sexually molested by her father in her childhood. A young man may employ the unconscious defense mechanism of *rationalization* to avoid feelings of guilt over a past transgression. The goal of insight-oriented psychotherapies is to uncover and work through truths. As Jesus said, "The truth shall set you free." As Socrates said, "the unexamined life is not worth living." Another famous saying is "We are only as sick as the secrets we keep."

Defense mechanisms are not only employed to defend against personal problems or traumas, they are also employed to protect against ideas that one finds threatening, particularly when the new ideas threaten cherished core beliefs or paradigms, such as those one often holds with religion or politics. Much of the content of this book will be uncomfortable and even distressing for many readers because the ideas presented will conflict with such cherished beliefs. The ideas will be based on evidence, however.

Human beings have a long history of believing things that have no empirical evidence at all. Examples include the beliefs in witchcraft, ghosts, alien abductions, demons, and astrology. Kurt Andersen in his book *Fantasyland: How America Went Haywire* (2017) suggests that Americans might have been and still are particularly susceptible to screwy, unfounded beliefs.

This disease perhaps has never been as virulent as it has been in the era of Trump whose political aspirations began with an unfounded assertion that Barack Obama was born in Kenya and was an illegitimate president. Polls in 2011 suggested most Republicans believed in birtherism despite no evidence whatsoever.

When Covid 19 began infecting the world the president said not to worry and that it would just disappear. It then was labeled a "hoax," and then later that it was the creation of a "deep state" in a plot to hurt Trump's reelection chances or that it was exaggerated despite mounting deaths. In July of 2020 perhaps one-third of Americans believed Covid-19 was a hoax despite 3.5 million reported cases and 136,000 reported deaths.

For the first time in America's history a defeated presidential candidate refused to concede, alleging widespread voter fraud despite zero evidence. The election results were challenged in dozens of court cases which were quickly dismissed because there was no evidence. Despite the lack of evidence, a November 2020 Reuters poll suggested that half of Republicans believed that Trump had won the election. Many congressmen and senators encouraged this disinformation for political gain.

In October of 2017 an anonymous user known as "Q" posted on 4chan for the first time, predicting the imminent arrest of Hillary Clinton and a violent nationwide uprising. Although the predicted arrest on October 30 never happened, more ominous predictions ensued. Several other conspiracy theorists promoted Q, and there are now thousands of adherents. The "Qanon" beliefs are that a cabal of world leaders are Satanist pedophiles and cannibals, they are part of a "deep state" in the federal government, and they are working against Donald Trump, who is tirelessly working to defeat them. Many followers are evangelical Christians who look forward to a coming battle between good and evil with the forces of good being led by Trump. Of course, there is no evidence for any of this, just as there was not in the 1980s when there were widespread allegations of Satanic ritual abuse, or that in the late 1600s Salem, Massachusetts was beset by a cabal of witches.

Entrepreneur P.T. Barnum famously said "There's a sucker born every minute" and "Nobody ever lost a dollar by underestimating the taste of the American public." Author H.L. Mencken said "No one in this world, so far as I know...has ever lost money by underestimating the intelligence of the great masses of the plain people." Carl Sagan opined,

> *Both Barnum and H.L. Mencken are said to have made the depressing observation that no one ever lost money by underestimating the intelligence of the American public. The remark has worldwide application. But the lack is not in intelligence, which is in plentiful supply; rather, the scarce commodity is systematic training in critical thinking.*

I contend that the *only* means for ascertaining truth is through empirical evidence and reasoning, and I believe that education in how to think critically is essential for a healthy democracy, for a functioning society, and for human development. Not only do I believe that learning how to reason is the most important goal of a liberal arts college education, but I believe it also should be taught in K through 12th grades.

Extracurricular debate clubs are an excellent way to learn about the perspectives of others and to learn critical thinking skills. In debate clubs, kids learn to argue both sides of a controversy. We do not really understand a dispute unless we know all sides of the argument.

An important technique in marital/relationship counseling is to have one member talk uninterrupted about his/her thoughts and feelings about a dispute. Then the other member of the couple is to repeat back what their partner said to make sure they heard correctly and completely. Then it is the other partner's turn. First, we need to come to agreement about the facts of a dispute before we then discuss opinions about what to do with those facts.

We also need to come to agreement about the meaning of definitions before we can discuss the pros and cons of a hotly debated issue. For example, we need to have working definitions of terms such as "liberal" or "conservative" or "socialism" or "religious" or "Christianity." If we are going to debate the pros and cons of the above, we need to know what we are really arguing about. We do not possess a clear understanding of an issue until we understand exactly what our terms mean.

The remainder of this book is based on the contention that the only way to truth is by empirical evidence and reason. If you do not buy this, you are unlikely to buy most of the other ideas presented. Former senator Daniel Patrick Moynihan once famously quipped that "Everyone is entitled to his own opinion, but not his own facts." Having a shared set of facts is a critical principle of the enlightenment and is crucial to a working democracy and to a functional society. Facts are discoverable if we have the inclination to find them. We can discover truth if we are not afraid.

I wrote earlier in this chapter about *confirmation bias*, which is the human tendency to recognize data that supports our preconceived beliefs and to disregard data that is in contradiction to our beliefs. It really is the opposite of critical reasoning in that with confirmation bias we manipulate or disregard facts to conform to our beliefs, while with critical reasoning we change our beliefs as new facts come to light. Confirmation bias is not an insignificant phenomenon, as evidenced in the current American political climate. A major premise that I am advocating in this book is that we live our lives and base our beliefs on empirical evidence and reason- even our religious beliefs. Our religious beliefs are perhaps our most cherished beliefs. In fact, we hold them "sacred" in both senses of the word, i.e., having to do with God but also being something so ingrained and deep that they are unquestioned. Challenges to these beliefs often cause significant emotional consternation.

What would religion look like if we based our beliefs on evidence and reasoning rather than unfounded purported revelations from ancient peoples? That is what this book is about.

The next chapter presents knowledge that we presently know about the universe from evidence we have learned from numerous disciplines including history, archaeology, astronomy, chemistry, physics, geology, and biology. The chapter is about "big history;" looking at the history of the universe in its entirely. What does big history have to teach us about God and reality?

Questions for Contemplation or Discussion
Chapter One. Truth

1. Do you believe that objective truth and reality exists, or is truth relative?
2. Do you agree with theologian John Wesley that the most important source for information about God is scripture?
3. How important is tradition in learning about God and ultimate realities?
4. How important is personal experience in learning about God and ultimate realities?
5. What is your belief about how a conscience develops? Do you believe we are we given innate knowledge of right and wrong by God?
6. Do you agree with the author that the only way to ascertain truth is through empirical evidence and reason?

Chapter Two

Time and Space

Historicity

Most people have some familiarity with the story about the elephant and the blind men. This group of blind men had never come across an elephant before. They try to figure out what this animal is all about by gathering around it and touching it. Each, of course, are touching a different part of the elephant. One is touching the tail, another the mid-section, another the trunk, another the tusk, etc. They then each describe their conceptions of the animal, and their conceptions are completely different from each other, as you would imagine. They argue with each other about the true nature of the animal. The moral of the story is that, like these blind men, we all tend to conceptualize truth based on our own limited subjective experiences, and we tend to denigrate others' conceptions and experiences. To learn about reality, we need to integrate information from a variety of sources. To understand the universe, we need to integrate knowledge from various disciplines including history, archeology, astronomy, chemistry, physics, geology, and biology. This is the goal of "Big History." The International Big History Association says that "big history seeks to understand the integrated history of the Cosmos, Earth, Life, and Humanity using the best available empirical evidence and scholarly methods." The goal of big *history* is to be able to see the big *picture*.

Currently there is a new space race going on between billionaires Jeff Bezos, Richard Branson, and Elon Musk. In interviews they all said that they wanted to go to space because they heard from those who had been there that it forever changes a person. One gets a new perspective on life when one can see the big picture. That is true too of "Big History." It helps us to put everything in perspective.

I grew up unconsciously conceptualizing a 6,000-year history of the universe. This was the paradigm I accepted in my childhood and early teen years, and this is probably the paradigm that most fundamentalists and evangelicals unconsciously or consciously subscribe to, despite probably learning conflicting information in science classes.

On the left side of the timeline on the next page (figure 2.1). is the six-thousand-year-old history described in the Biblical book of Genesis. This is a history of myths. There is no scientific evidence for a great flood or of a great exodus of Israelites out of Egypt.

4,000 BCE is a point of time that does have much significance though, not because it was the time that God created Adam and Eve and the rest of the universe, but because of two other momentous events. For one thing, this is the time that history began due to the advent of writing. All of time prior to this were *prehistoric* times. The only way that we know about prehistoric times is through archaeology; the study of artifacts and skeletons- the remnants of these humans' existence. But with the advent of writing, people became able to tell us about themselves. Writing likely first developed with the Sumerians in Mesopotamia (present day Iraq) and shortly after that with the Egyptians. Amazingly, we can decipher the languages of both civilizations, the latter due to the famous Rosetta Stone.

The other significant event of this time period was the development of agrarian civilization. For more than 99 percent of human existence our species were hunters and gatherers. We migrated in small groups seeking game and nutritious vegetation. But then around 10,000 BCE a revolution took place known as both the *Agricultural Revolution* and the *Neolithic Revolution*. Humans began settling down and domesticating animals and cultivating crops. Humans began living in larger and larger groups. The first

FIGURE 2.1

TIMELINE OF HISTORICITY

TIMELINE OF GENESIS

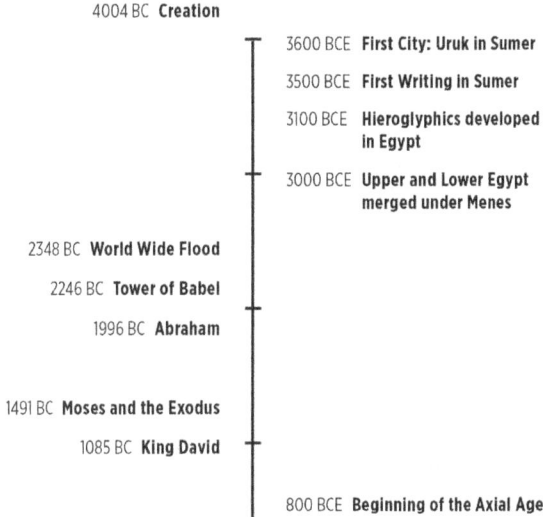

4004 BC **Creation**

3600 BCE **First City: Uruk in Sumer**

3500 BCE **First Writing in Sumer**

3100 BCE **Hieroglyphics developed in Egypt**

3000 BCE **Upper and Lower Egypt merged under Menes**

2348 BC **World Wide Flood**

2246 BC **Tower of Babel**

1996 BC **Abraham**

1491 BC **Moses and the Exodus**

1085 BC **King David**

800 BCE **Beginning of the Axial Age**

BIRTH AND LIFE OF JESUS

300 CE **Conversion of Constantine**

571 CE **Birth of Muhammad**

1440 CE **Gutenberg's Printing Press**

1500 CE **Copernicus**

1600-1800 CE **The Enlightenment and Scientific Revolution**

1760-1830 CE **Industrial Revolution**

1859 CE **Darwin "On the Origin of Species"**

1990 CE **Development of the World Wide Web**

© Craig R. Vander Maas

town was likely Jericho in the 9th century BCE in Palestine. Towns continued to proliferate and got larger and larger. Finally, we had the first large cities in Mesopotamia. Around 3600 BCE we had the beginnings of the great ancient city of Uruk in Sumer. By 2800 BCE it covered 617 acres and probably had 50 to 80,000 residents. At that time, it was the largest city in the world.

What I would like to do now is highlight what I think are some of the most important events in the history of the last six thousand years, particularly in regards to spiritual development. Then we will move on to subsequent timelines. Each subsequent timeline opens to a larger period of time which includes at the bottom a shaded space which shows the time span of the previous timeline.

The Sumerians were considered the first civilization. Civilizations are large (usually over 20,000 people) complex societies that are usually made up of multiple cities and have centralized political and social organization. By 2500 BCE there were also civilizations in Egypt and the Indus Valley. To the north of the Sumerians in Mesopotamia were another civilization, the Akkadians. Their ruler, Sargon, established rule over their neighbor Sumer around 2300 BCE. This is considered the first *empire*. The middle east then was controlled by a succession of empires: Babylonian empire, Assyrian empire, Chaldean empire, Persian empire, Greek empire, and then the Roman empire.

The religion of the early Israelites primarily involved making sacrifices, which the Israelites had in common with all other religions at that time. The books of Exodus, Leviticus, and Deuteronomy of the Hebrew scriptures are replete with such laws, including the famous Ten Commandments. This innovation of law codes was not unique to the Israelites. In Mesopotamia several law codes were written many centuries before the laws of the Israelites, including the *Code of Hammurabi*, a document very similar to the writings in the Hebrew Torah. Law codes were necessary at this time period because societies grew from small bands and tribes of people who were related to each other into larger societies known as *chiefdoms*. People were now living with strangers, and we are less likely to be kind and considerate to strangers than we are to kin. Laws were required to keep order.

Religion continued to consist of sacrificial worship and laws for many centuries until there was a further evolution in religions. This revolution and paradigm shift occurred between 800 BCE and 200 BCE and is known as the Axial Age. Now for the first-time religion began to be concerned with morality. Religion began to be concerned about the welfare of the poor and the weak and the downtrodden. Amazingly this shift in thinking occurred simultaneously in several parts of the world by the spiritually enlightened. These enlightened thinkers included the Hebrew prophets, Greek philosophers (including Parmenides, Heraclitus, Pythagoras, and Plato), Confucius and Lao-tse in China, Zarathustra in Persia, and Buddha in India. Although this evolution of moral development occurred for more spiritually developed individuals, most of the populations continued in the old paradigm, with little concern about morality.

The various books that make up the Hebrew scriptures were written over a period of 700-800 years. The earliest writing is believed to be from the *Yahwist source* (one of the four sources believed to have contributed to the Torah, the first five books of the Bible) which could have been written as early as 950 BCE (during the reign of King Solomon). The last of the Hebrew scriptures to have been written was the book of Daniel. Hebrew scholar Michael Coogan (2011) said the "scholarly consensus" was that the book "was written during the difficult years immediately preceding the revolt of the Maccabees in 167 BCE" during the years of the Greek Empire.

It was during the time of the Roman Empire that another very significant event took place- the birth and life of Jesus of Nazareth. It was so significant that the measure of time now centers on his birth: time prior to his birth is designated B.C. (before Christ) or BCE (before the common era), and time after his birth is designated A.D. (anno domini which is Latin for "in the year of our Lord") or CE (common era). Perhaps even more significant than the life of Jesus was the conversion of the Roman emperor Constantine to Christianity in 313 CE. Constantine convened over an ecumenical council in Nicaea that made decisions about what was orthodox Christian beliefs. Constantine also significantly moved the capital of the Roman Empire from Rome to Byzantium, renamed Constantinople (present day Istanbul). As a result of Constantine's conversion, Christianity quickly grew. New Testament scholar Bart Ehrman (2012) said "the Christian church grew quite slowly in its early years. At the end of the first century, far fewer than 1 percent of the empire's population of 60 million was Christian." In 380 CE Emperor Theodosius I made Christianity the official state religion and made paganism illegal. As a result, at the end of the century half of the Roman empire had become Christian.

Another very significant event took place in 571 CE, which was the birth of the prophet, Muhammed, who reported spiritual visions that became the basis of a powerful religious movement. Adherents aggressively sought converts, and by the time of Muhammed's death in 632 a substantial part of Arabia was under Muslim control. By 637, Syria, Palestine, and all of Mesopotamia had fallen to Islam. By 661, Egypt, much of North Africa and Persia fell. Several Hindu kingdoms of northern India were conquered in 711, and Islam moved into Spain by 718. At this time the Islamic world covered more than 5 million square miles. This contrasts with the Roman Empire which at its height covered 2.2 million square miles. By the year 1500, Islam had spread to Turkey, across Central Asia and into China, and into what is now Malaysia, Indonesia, and the southern Philippines. Currently Islam is the world's second largest religion (after Christianity), but many estimate that it will become the largest religion in the second half of this century.

Around the same time period that Islam was developing, the western Roman Empire was fragmenting into a series of competitive regional kingdoms. The eastern Roman Empire, however, remained stable and strong and became the Byzantine Empire. This was the beginning of the "Middle Ages" which began with the fall of the western Roman Empire in 476 CE and ended in 1500 CE. The early centuries of the western empire came to be known as the "dark ages" due to cultural, demographic, and economic deterioration. In contrast, in the Byzantine empire classical knowledge and science continued to flourish, and the era became known as the "Islamic

Golden Age" in the Muslim world. Classic written works of antiquity were translated into Arabic and Persian. Mathematical progress was made in algebra, geometry, calculus, and trigonometry. Scientific progress was made in astronomy, physics, chemistry, and biology.

The late Middle Ages (1300-1500 CE) had its ups and downs. In the beginning of the 14th century climates began to cool, and as a result famines became more common. Europe underwent the *Great Famine* from 1315 to 1317 in which 15 percent of the population may have died. Then the European population fell victim to the *Black Death*, a plague that killed up to a third of the European population. The plague's peak was from 1347-1351. But the 15th and 16th centuries also brought the *Renaissance*, a time of rebirth to classical scholarship and innovative thought after the stagnation of the Middle Ages. It was a period of transformation to the Modern Age.

Another very significant event happened in 1440. Johannes Gutenberg invented the printing press. With the Gutenberg printing press, 3,600 pages could be printed per day, compared to only a few by hand copying. Literacy rates significantly grew during the Renaissance. The printing press made written materials available for the first time to the general public. One of the first books to be mass produced was the Bible. Gutenberg published a two-volume version of the Vulgate in 1455. Now people could read the Bible rather than just hear portions recited at mass. Just think about how revolutionary this was. Prior to the availability of books, knowledge could only be obtained by word of mouth.

Another significant event in this time period was the revolutionary model proposed by mathematician and astronomer Nicolaus Copernicus in the early 1500s. Everybody believed at this time that the earth was the center of the universe. Copernicus proposed instead that the planets, including the earth, revolved around the sun. You might think, so what is the big deal? Well, this completely rocked people's paradigm about the importance of human beings- that everything in the universe was created for their benefit, and that their home, the earth, was the center of all existence.

There were three great interrelated revolutions that marked the transformation to the Modern Age: The Scientific Revolution, the Enlightenment, and the Industrial Revolution. The Scientific Revolution perhaps began with the writings of Francis Bacon (1561-1626) and Rene Descartes (1596-1650). Both stressed the importance of questioning long held beliefs by past philosophical and religious authorities and relying instead on the careful exploration and study of physical phenomenon employing inductive reasoning. It was the beginnings of the scientific method. Another key figure of the Scientific Revolution was Isaac Newton (1642-1726), English physicist and mathematician, who outlined the basic principles of modern physics. His *Mathematical Principles of Natural Philosophy* was one of the greatest compositions in the history of science. The Enlightenment arose from the Scientific Revolution and the Age of Reason in the 17th century and is conventionally placed in the last two thirds of the 18th century. The Enlightenment thinkers stressed the importance of reason, science, humanism, and the idea that humanity could be improved through rational change. British historian, David Wootton, in his book *The Invention of Science: A New History of the Scientific Revolution* (2015) reminds us just how backwards people were prior to the Scientific Revolution. He writes that the typical well-educated European in 1600 (let me stress here he means the well-educated, not most people who were not educated) believed the following:

- Witches exist, and they can summon up storms that sink ships at sea.
- Werewolves and unicorns exist.
- Circe really did turn Odysseus's crew into pigs.
- Mice are spontaneously generated in piles of straw.
- A murdered body will bleed in the presence of the murderer.
- There is an ointment which, if rubbed on a dagger which has caused a wound, will cure the wound.
- The shape, color and texture of a plant can be a clue to how it will work as a medicine because God designed nature to be interpreted by mankind.

- It is possible to turn base metal into gold.
- Rainbows are a sign from God.
- Comets portend evil.
- Dreams predict the future.

Wootton then contrasts an educated Englishman a century and a quarter later in 1733. Such a person has familiarity with telescopes and microscopes. Instead of owning a dozen books, they have hundreds or maybe even thousands.

- "He does not know anyone (or at least not anyone educated and reasonably sophisticated) who believes in witches, werewolves, magic, alchemy or astrology.
- He thinks the *Odyssey* is fiction, not fact.
- He is confident that the unicorn is a mythical beast.
- "He does not believe that the shape or color of a plant has any significance for an understanding of its medical use."
- "He believes that no creature large enough to be seen by the naked eye is generated spontaneously- not even a fly."
- "He does not believe in the weapon salve or that murdered bodies bleed in the presence of the murdered."
- He believes the earth goes around the sun, rainbows are produced by refracted light, comets have no significance for our lives, and the future cannot be predicted."
- "He believes that science is going to transform the world and that the moderns have outstripped the ancients in every possible respect. He has trouble believing in any miracles, even the ones in the Bible."

The Enlightenment above all was about reason in determining truth. It also was about humanism, human rights, and morality. The United States government was founded on Enlightenment ideals. The Declaration of Independence states that we are endowed by our Creator with certain inalienable rights which includes life, liberty, and the pursuit of happiness. The Bill of Rights were developed to limit government and to protect the rights of people, a key idea of John Locke. Democracy grew out of the Enlightenment. Enlightenment thinkers such as John Locke, Charles Montesquieu, and Jean-Jacques Rousseau all advocated democratic ideas for government.

The Industrial Revolution was responsible for the biggest change in society since the Agricultural Revolution 10,000 years earlier. Due to fossil fuels (first coal made from fossilized trees, then crude oil from fossilized one-celled plants and animals, and then natural gas composed mostly of methane produced by fossilized organisms), vast new sources of energy became available. Machines replaced human and animal energy. Just look around and imagine what life would be like without fossil fuels. There would be no cars, trains, airplanes, power boats, gas to heat your home or cook your food, electricity, or factories to make all the products you find around your home.

Throughout most of human history were cycles in complex societies in which the size of populations would rise and fall due to food production. Thomas Malthus, an English pastor and economist, argued that human populations would increase at a faster rate than would food supplies, causing times of famine and rapid declines of populations. These population cycles are now called *Malthusian Cycles*. The greatly increased energy from fossil fuels broke these Malthusian cycles. David Christian in *Big History: Between Nothing and Everything (2014)* said "The world in 2012 extracted huge resources to support 7 billion people; in 1700 the traditional sources of energy could support a population of only 670 million. Thus, the Industrial Revolution has produced in just over 300 years enough food to support more than a 10-fold increase in world population." The control of energy is a defining characteristic between humans and other animals. Physicist Eric Chaisson in *Cosmic Evolution: The Rise of Complexity in Nature (2001)* has calculated that about 20,000 ergs per second per gram flow through large animals such as apes, and in contrast humans use on average 25 times as much energy.

Nobel prize-winning chemist, Paul Crutzen, has argued that early in the nineteenth century as the result of the industrial revolution our planet has entered a new geological epoch called the

Anthropocene. For the first time in our planet's history, a species (homo sapiens) has the power to change earth's climate. We have gone from being just another species on the planet to the species that is totally dominating the planet. Most of us have been brought up with a very anthropocentric world view, i.e., the belief that everything centers on us, the human being. Many think of the whole universe as being created for the benefit of humans, rather than seeing us as being part of the universe. There was a time though that Homo sapiens were just another species- maybe more evolved than other species, but no more prevalent and with no more impact on the planet than many other species.

Two additional world changing events were the publishing of *On the Origin of Species by Means of Natural Selection* by Charles Darwin in 1859 and the development of the World Wide Web in 1990. The former further degraded an anthropocentric world view. Not only did Copernicus and Galileo demonstrate that the Earth was not the center of the universe or even the solar system, but now Darwin was giving evidence that humans evolved from animals and in fact were animals. Of course, now with research from molecular biology and the sequencing of genomes, there is overwhelming evidence that animals, including humans, evolved from other animals and in fact that all of life on earth is related and originated from the same source.

The Internet was as revolutionary as was the printing press. The printing press made possible the acquisition of books and newspapers to the general public for the first time. The internet has made possible the acquisition of almost unlimited information-and making it accessible to us right in our own homes almost instantly! I cannot imagine doing the research that I have done for the books that I have written without benefit of the internet. Unfortunately, along with the tremendous advantages come problems. Along with access to information comes access to misinformation and disinformation, the difference being wrong information by accident with the former, and wrong information on purpose with the latter. Disinformation, in particular, is a very significant threat to the pursuit of truth and to democracy. Richard Stengel in his book *Information Wars: How We*

Lost the Global Battle Against Disinformation & What We Can Do About It (2019) writes:

> *There is indeed an information war going on all around the world and it's taking place at the speed of light. Governments and non-state actors and individuals are creating and spreading narratives that have nothing to do with reality. Those false and misleading narratives undermine democracy and the ability of free people to make intelligent choices. The audience is anyone with access to a computer or a smartphone- about four billion people. The players in this conflict are assisted by the big social media platforms, which benefit just as much from the sharing of content that is false as content that is true...As Thomas Jefferson said, information is the foundation of democracy. He meant factual information.*

To be able to discern truth using the internet requires some sophistication and reasoning abilities. We need the abilities to fact check, to be able discern who is an authority on a topic and who is not, and we need the willingness to try to be objective. We need the ability to remain open to information that may conflict with preconceived ideas. I have heard more than once someone saying that certain information must be true because it was on the internet. That is like saying certain information is true because it was written down.

I have discussed events over the past six thousand years that I believe are especially important to human development. This six-thousand-year period of time is significant in that fundamentalist and evangelical Christians frequently believe that this represents the sum total for the existence of time. They believe that approximately six thousand years ago God created the universe, and that prior to this nothing at all existed other than God. We now know through science that the universe is much older than this, and even the history of our species, homo sapiens, is much older. The history of our species is the subject of the next timeline (figure 2.2). You will notice that six thousand years is only .03 percent of the 200,000-year history of homo sapiens.

Homo Sapiens

Our species originated in East Africa in the vicinity of modern-day Ethiopia. The species began to look like modern humans about 100,000 years ago. Contrary to popular belief, evolution is not a linear line going from one species to another, such as an ape evolving into a human. Our genetic family tree is much more complicated than this. Humans did not evolve from chimpanzees; rather, both species have a common ancestor.

When Homo sapiens first began to appear around 200,000 years ago there were two other human species in existence at the same time: Homo erectus and Homo neanderthalensis (you probably have heard of Neanderthals). Both Homo neanderthalensis and Homo sapiens are species believed to be descended from Homo heidelbergensis, while Homo erectus is believed to be descended from Homo ergaster. Homo sapiens lived in east Africa, Homo Neanderthals were in Europe and western Asia, and Homo erectus lived mostly in Asia.

A momentous event happened somctime prior to 100,000 years ago- perhaps 160,000 years ago as noted on my timeline, and perhaps much earlier than this. Nobody really knows, but it was very significant and very important. Humans (probably both Homo neanderthalensis as well as Homo sapiens) developed symbolic language. Many animals have some form of simple communication, for example particular noises to warn others of danger. However, humans alone developed symbolic language. David Christian in *Big History: Between Nothing and Everything* explains:

> *Rather than using sounds or gestures to refer to one particular thing, we can use sounds as conceptual parcels that refer to whole categories of ideas and things. Furthermore, through syntax, or the careful arrangement of words according to grammatical rules, we can convey multiple possible relationships between different people,*

things, and ideas. (We can tell the difference between "I kicked you" and "I was kicked by you.") The result is that we share so much information that the amount of shared information in each community begins to accumulate from generation to generation. That sustained increase in shared knowledge is the foundation of human history because it ensures that, as a general rule, later generations will have more knowledge than earlier generations so that their behaviors will slowly change over time.

Progress as a species is impossible without symbolic language. Stories, myths, and songs were a good method for passing information down from one generation to another. Although as a species this was a major leap forward, we were still limited by the constraints of our collective memories. When writing was developed, we had a much more effective and accurate way for storing and conveying knowledge. We now were able to store vast amounts of information. When the printing press was developed, we were able to readily reproduce and disseminate all the information we have been accumulating. And with the World Wide Web we are now able to store unlimited information, and we can access it almost immediately!

Around 50,000 years ago another very significant event occurred: our species, Homo sapiens, left Africa. It is believed by geneticists that our ancestors shrank to a population size of as few as 5,000 people between 60,000 and 40,000 years ago due to a dry climate that shrank the forests and dried the savannas. It is believed that our ancestors originated in what is now Ethiopia, or at least somewhere in East Africa. Geneticists believe there was a single immigration of our ancestors out of Africa, and the number of people leaving may have been as small as 150 individuals.

FIGURE 2.2
TIMELINE OF HOMO SAPIENS

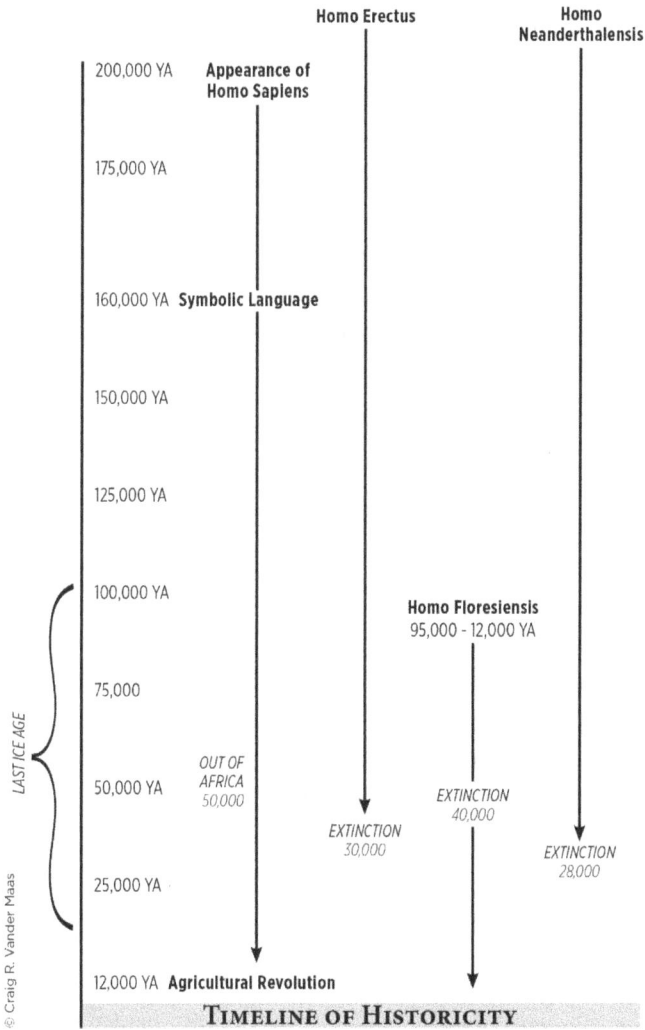

Homo Erectus

Homo
Neanderthalensis

200,000 YA — **Appearance of
Homo Sapiens**

175,000 YA

160,000 YA — **Symbolic Language**

150,000 YA

125,000 YA

100,000 YA

Homo Floresiensis
95,000 - 12,000 YA

75,000

LAST ICE AGE

50,000 YA — *OUT OF
AFRICA
50,000*

*EXTINCTION
40,000*

*EXTINCTION
30,000*

*EXTINCTION
28,000*

25,000 YA

© Craig R. Vander Maas

12,000 YA — **Agricultural Revolution**

TIMELINE OF HISTORICITY

The legendary anthropologist Margaret Mead was reportedly asked by a student years ago what she considered to be the first sign of civilization in a human culture. The student expected she would say possibly the use of tools, the use of clay pots or grinding stones, or the use of fish hooks. Instead, Dr. Mead said it was evidence of a healed femur bone. In the animal world a broken femur is a death sentence as one cannot escape predators or take care of oneself. Evidence of a healed femur in a human suggests that other humans cared for that person. Mead said that helping someone else through difficulty is where civilization starts.

Our ancestors were hunter-gatherers and did not settle down, and so they continued to cover significant distances. They initially went from Africa to the Arabian Peninsula. They likely often followed coastlines. While some people continued to push on into new territories, others remained in various geographical locations, and so the population of the world from this small group of people appeared to be quite orderly. From the Arabian Peninsula the migration moved to India. From there some migrated into Asia, and some continued to the Australian land mass, China and Japan. Others went Northwest into present day Iran and Turkey and probably eventually met and maybe combated the Neanderthals.

By about 30,000 years ago the Neanderthals went extinct. It is surprising that the earliest fossils of Homo sapiens outside of Africa have been found (thus far) in Australia, and so the migration which likely followed shorelines went fast. Homo sapiens did not appear to get to North and South America until 14 to 15,000 years ago, although once they were able to cross the Bering land bridge the migration all the way to the tip of South America appeared to go quite quickly.

Remarkably, at around 50,000 years ago it also is believed that four separate human species lived simultaneously. Homo neanderthalensis were in Europe, Homo erectus were in East Asia and Africa, Homo floresiensis were on the island of Flores in Indonesia, and Homo sapiens were in Africa and were migrating out of Africa to the rest of the world.

Although Neanderthals and Homo sapiens were of different species, there is DNA evidence of some interbreeding. Interbreeding between species is not unheard of. For example, female horses can breed with male donkeys, which results in a mule. Mules are unable to reproduce. Male lions have reproduced with female tigers; offspring are known as ligers. DNA evidence has suggested that 1% to 3% of DNA in present-day people of European and Asian descent comes from Neanderthals. This is not found in present-day people of African descent.

If you have ever had genetic testing done from companies such as *23 and Me*, you might have found out that you have some Neanderthal DNA. That is what I found out from my own testing. Now I should note here that dates about hominid ancestors are approximations and there is dispute among scholars about dates. The dates I am referencing in this book is from anthropologist Alice Roberts in her publication *Evolution: The Human Story*. Our knowledge about the story of early hominids continues to unfold, and undoubtedly new knowledge will continue to be discovered, particularly due to research with DNA.

Humans (Genus Homo)

While our species has been in existence only for about 200,000 years, our genus (Homo) has been around for 2.5 million years. Currently only our species, sapiens, are members of this genus, although in the distant past there have been numerous other species, and as I recently mentioned there were periods of time in which more than one species lived concurrently. All our hominid ancestors lived in Africa. A major event occurred around 1.8 million years ago; hominids started migrating out of Africa. Likely they were from the species Homo ergaster and Homo erectus, although it is possible that individuals from Homo habilis also migrated. It is from these species that Homo heidelbergensis, Homo neanderthalensis, Homo floresiensis, and Homo sapiens evolved.

"Homo" is Latin for "man." Timeline 2.3 suggests that "mankind" has been in existence for 2.5 million years.

FIGURE 2.3

TIMELINE OF HUMANS (GENUS HOMO)

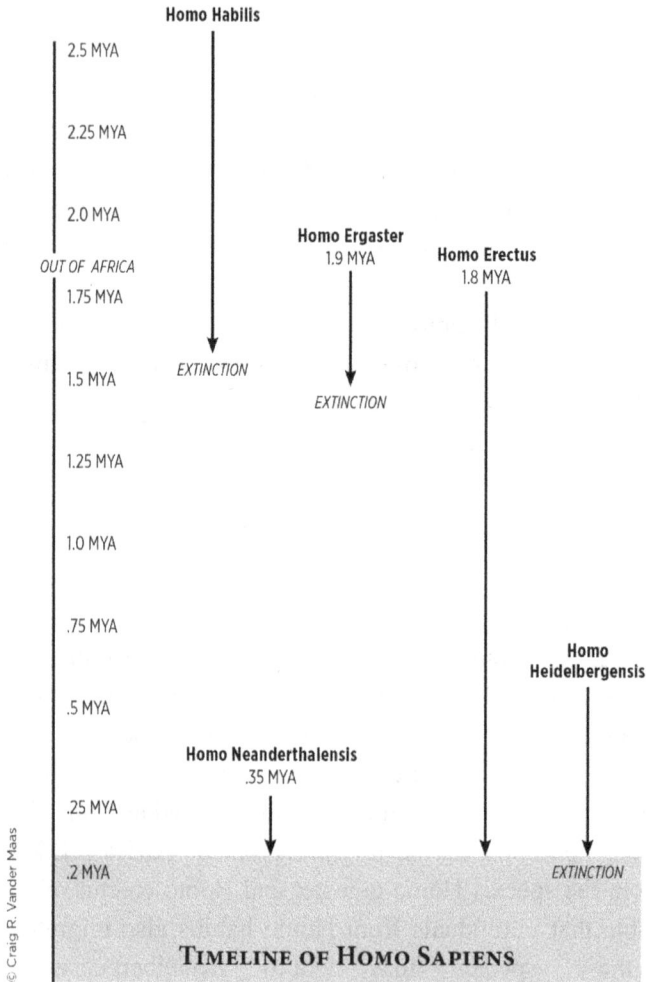

Homo Habilis

2.5 MYA

2.25 MYA

2.0 MYA

OUT OF AFRICA

1.75 MYA

1.5 MYA — *EXTINCTION*

1.25 MYA

1.0 MYA

.75 MYA

.5 MYA

.25 MYA

.2 MYA

Homo Ergaster
1.9 MYA

EXTINCTION

Homo Erectus
1.8 MYA

Homo Heidelbergensis

Homo Neanderthalensis
.35 MYA

EXTINCTION

TIMELINE OF HOMO SAPIENS

© Craig R. Vander Maas

Primates

While our genus Homo has existed for 2.5 million years, the larger category (order) of primates has existed for 65 million years. Contemporary primates include lemurs, lorises, monkeys, apes, and man. The early primates lived in tropical rain forests. Today there are more than 400 species of living primates, the majority of which still live primarily in trees. Around 40 million years ago we have evidence for the first *anthropoids*, i.e., animals with a human/ape/monkey-like appearance. Figure 2.4 below shows the timeline for divergence of monkeys and apes, and then the divergence between the various great apes which includes us humans.

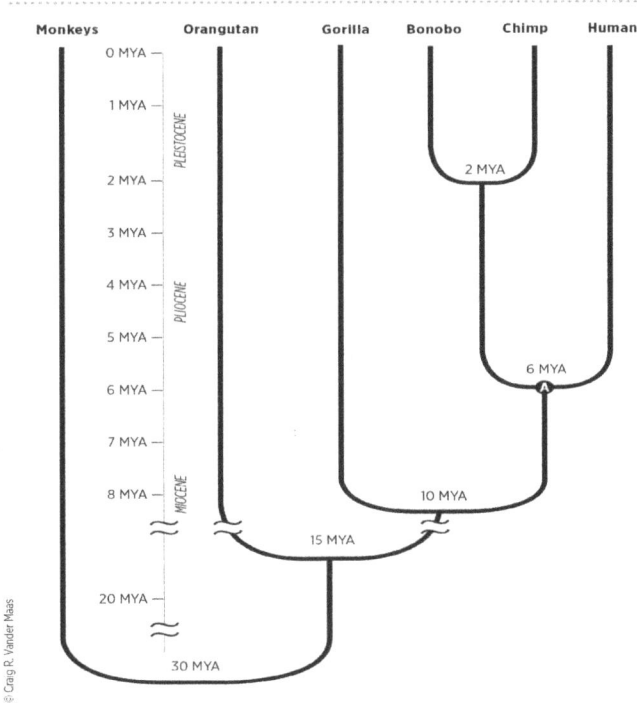

FIGURE 2.4
TIMELINE OF PRIMATES

© Craig R. Vander Maas

© Craig R. Vander Maas

FIGURE 2.5

TIMELINE OF PRIMATES

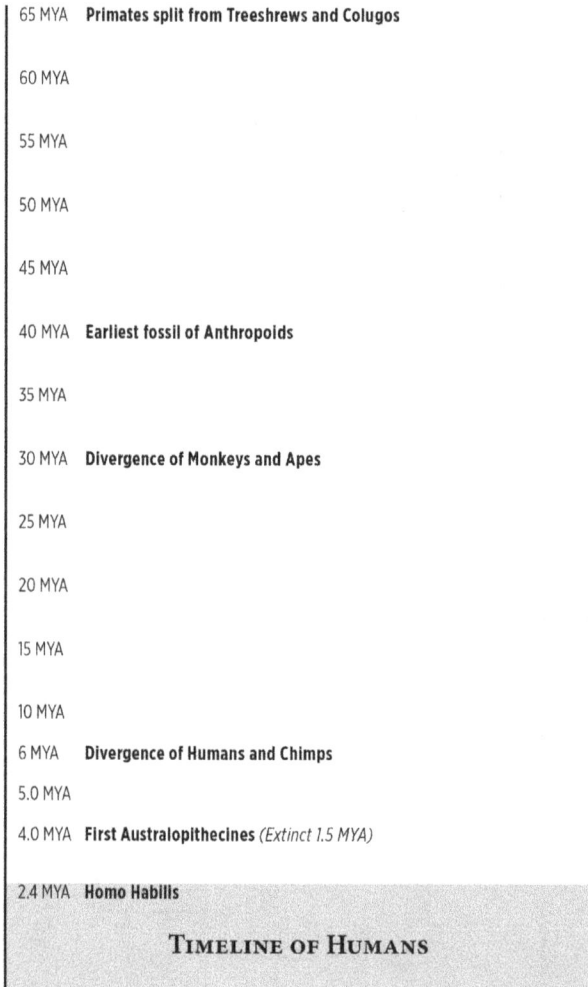

65 MYA	Primates split from Treeshrews and Colugos
60 MYA	
55 MYA	
50 MYA	
45 MYA	
40 MYA	Earliest fossil of Anthropoids
35 MYA	
30 MYA	Divergence of Monkeys and Apes
25 MYA	
20 MYA	
15 MYA	
10 MYA	
6 MYA	Divergence of Humans and Chimps
5.0 MYA	
4.0 MYA	First Australopithecines *(Extinct 1.5 MYA)*
2.4 MYA	Homo Habilis

TIMELINE OF HUMANS

An important genus of hominids that predated our own genus of Homo was Australopithecus which is dated between 4.2 million years ago and 1.78 million years ago. All the species from this genus were believed to have walked upright on two legs. The famous fossil "Lucy" belonged to the species Australopithecus afarensis.

Mammals

The timeline of mammals is seen in figure 2.6. Mammals have been around on this earth for a very long time. In fact, they predated the dinosaurs. But the first mammals 250 million years ago were nothing like most of the mammals we think of today. The earliest mammals were tiny, furry rodents about the size of an adult thumb. Nevertheless, they are the ancestors of humans. The animals that really dominated the time period from 250 million years ago to 65 million years ago were the dinosaurs.

Around 252 million years ago there was a great extinction, which colloquially has been known as "the Great Dying" and whose formal name is the Permian-Triassic extinction. It was the greatest mass extinction event up until that point; 95 percent of all marine life and 70 percent of terrestrial species died out after volcanic eruptions poisoned the oceans and atmosphere. It was after this event that mammals and dinosaurs evolved. The first dinosaurs appeared around 230 million years ago.

Another great extinction event occurred 200 million years ago, known as the Triassic-Jurassic extinction. Crocodile-like reptiles (known as crurotarsians) predominated during the Triassic period. Most species of crurotarsians died out during this extinction due to toxic gas in the atmosphere from volcanoes and skyrocketing temperatures. As a result, the dinosaurs began to flourish in the Jurassic period. Animals from this period included brachiosaurus and stegosaurus.

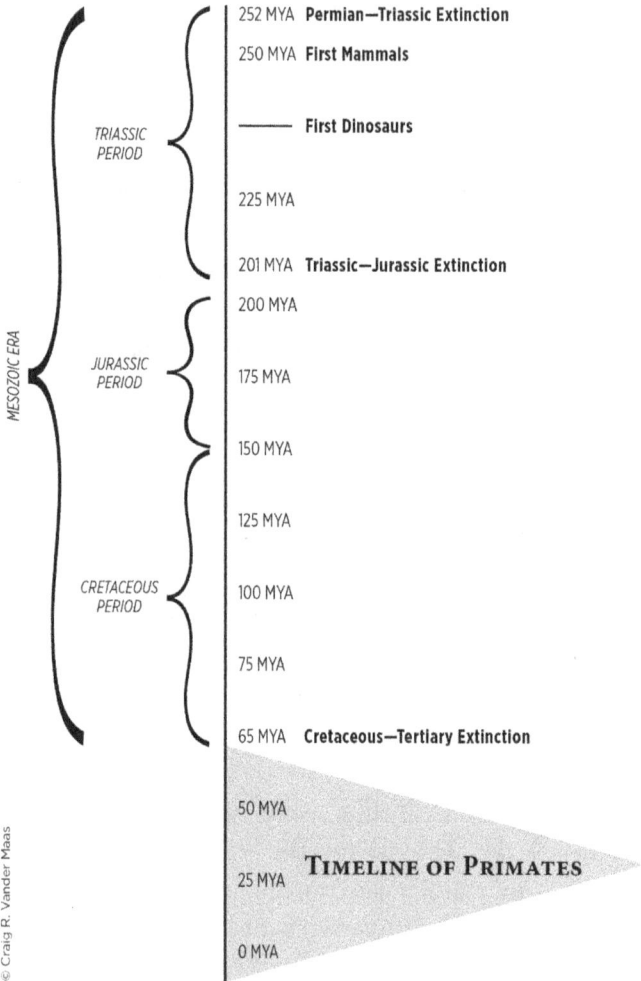

FIGURE 2.6

TIMELINE OF MAMMALS

During the Cretaceous period which began 150 million years ago dinosaur evolution reached its pinnacle. The most well-known dinosaurs lived during this period, including tyrannosaurus, velociraptor, and triceratops. During this period birds also evolved from dinosaurs. Dinosaurs ruled the planet until 65 million years ago when a meteor hit the earth in the Yucatan Peninsula in Mexico killing 75 percent of plant and animal species, including most dinosaurs. As the Triasic-Jurassic extinction allowed the dinosaurs to evolve and flourish, the Cretaceous-Tertiary extinction allowed mammals (and birds) to evolve and flourish.

Life on Earth

During its early history, the earth was under constant threat from asteroids, meteors, and remnants of failed planets. It is believed that there may have been a period of a significant increase in this barrage from 4.5 to 4 billion years ago which has been called the *Late Heavy Bombardment*. This would of course be a hindrance to the development of life on earth.

It is believed that life made its first appearance on earth 3.8 billion years ago. There are three main theories about how life began. The traditional explanation throughout most of history was that God (or gods) supernaturally intervened. Another theory (whose most well-known proponent possibly has been cosmologist Fred Hoyle) is that life (or at least constituents of life) was transported to earth on meteors and comets during the bombardment. Of course, this does not explain how life started elsewhere in the universe. Most scientists subscribe to a theory of chemical evolution, i.e., that in an appropriate atmosphere of methane and ammonia (and without free oxygen, as earth's atmosphere was at that time), the basic chemicals of life (amino acids, nucleotides, and phospholipids) could spontaneously develop life. This has been demonstrated in laboratories.

FIGURE 2.7

TIMELINE OF LIFE ON EARTH

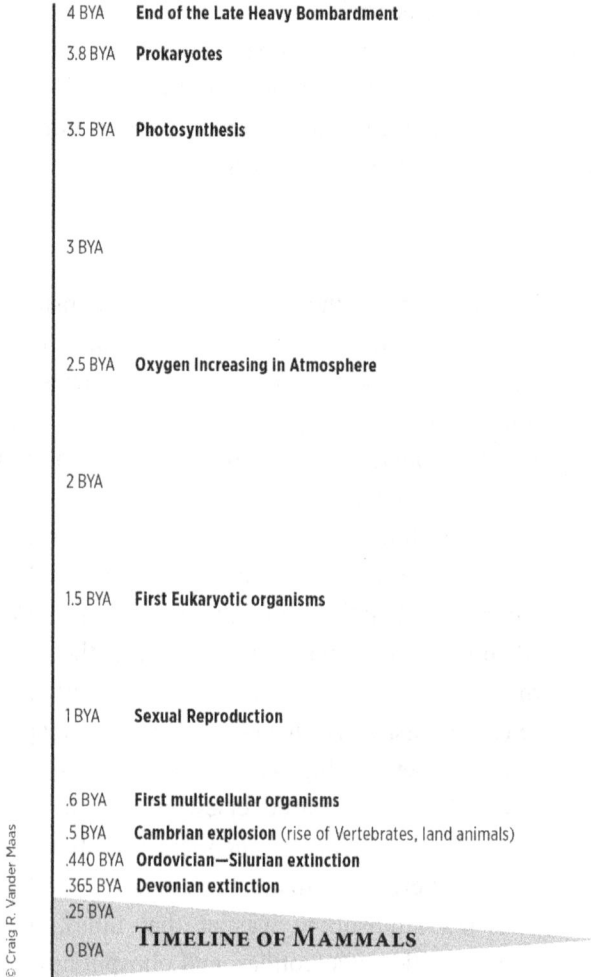

4 BYA	**End of the Late Heavy Bombardment**
3.8 BYA	**Prokaryotes**
3.5 BYA	**Photosynthesis**
3 BYA	
2.5 BYA	**Oxygen Increasing in Atmosphere**
2 BYA	
1.5 BYA	**First Eukaryotic organisms**
1 BYA	**Sexual Reproduction**
.6 BYA	**First multicellular organisms**
.5 BYA	**Cambrian explosion** (rise of Vertebrates, land animals)
.440 BYA	**Ordovician—Silurian extinction**
.365 BYA	**Devonian extinction**
.25 BYA	
0 BYA	**TIMELINE OF MAMMALS**

© Craig R. Vander Maas

The history of the earth has been divided into four eons by geologists. The first eon is the Hadean eon from 4.5 to 3.8 billion years ago. It was called *Hadean* after the Greek Hades. The earth was indeed "hotter than hell." It had no free oxygen in its atmosphere, the sky appeared red due to the predominance of carbon dioxide in the atmosphere (80 percent), the surface of the planet was constantly bombarded by meteorites and comets, and there was continuous volcanic activity. The land was barren and molten.

In the *Archean* eon (3,800 to 2,500 million years ago) the earth had cooled enough for continents to form. It was also during this eon that a truly momentous event occurred; life first appeared. Most of us instinctively believe that there is a dichotomy between the living and the nonliving. Yet defining life is rather difficult. Three attributes are usually given to the living but not the nonliving:

1. Living creatures take in energy from the environment. Plants take in energy through photosynthesis. Animals take in energy by eating.
2. Living creatures reproduce.
3. Living creatures change to adapt to their environments. Giraffes can grow longer necks to reach leaves, zebras develop stripes to camouflage, insects develop poisons to kill prey, other insects develop resistance to poisons, etc.

The first living entities were single-celled microorganisms with no nucleus that ate simple molecules (called *prokaryotes*). New forms of prokaryotes gradually evolved that could obtain nourishment from deceased prokaryotes and from compounds produced by prokaryotes. These evolved into microorganisms that were able to make food from sunlight (photosynthesis). Not only was it an amazing evolutionary development to be able to get nourishment from sunlight and carbon dioxide, but the equally amazing side benefit was the conversion of this to oxygen. This caused the atmosphere of the earth to change over millions of years from an atmosphere of predominantly carbon dioxide to an atmosphere primarily of oxygen.

The third of four eons, the *Proterozoic*, covers the time period from 2,500 million years ago to 541 million years ago. This eon is ushered in by the oxygenation of the earth. There was an *oxygen revolution*. Bacteria evolved to live off this oxygen. In photosynthesis bacteria use carbon dioxide and discharge oxygen. In this new process called *respiration*, other bacteria use oxygen and discharge carbon dioxide. This created a wonderful balance for the biosphere. Also, about this same time a new organism developed known as a *eukaryotes*, which were significantly more complex than prokaryotes. This brought in a new era of life.

The prokaryote era was from four billion years ago to two billion years ago, and the eukaryote era began two billion years ago and continues to this day. Another development occurred when organisms began consuming other living organisms for nourishment. Organisms began *eating*. Another major change occurred with the development of meiosis, i.e., the development of sex. The last major development of the Proterozoic eon was the development of multicellular organisms 700 to 600 million years ago.

The most recent eon began with the Cambrian explosion around 541 million years ago. During a period of 15 to 20 million years there was a remarkable explosion in organism diversity. Some animals developed backbones. Some animals moved onto land from the oceans. Some animals developed central nervous systems. These type of developments in animals and plants is what people generally think of with the term "evolution." Charles Darwin theorized that organisms that have traits that allow them to flourish in any environment are better able to survive and pass on their genes to offspring than organisms that do not have such traits. The theory does not suggest that evolution is progressive. Rather, organisms simply change to meet present circumstances.

Sometimes dramatic changes occur in animal and plant evolution due to catastrophic events such as mass extinctions. There have been at least five major extinction events. The most famous is probably the extinction that occurred at the end of the cretaceous period that was responsible for the demise of the dinosaurs and the rise of mammals. Prior to the extinction the earth was inhabited by plesiosaurs, tyrannosauruses, brontosauruses, and triceratops. After this extinction event these animals were eventually replaced by mammals such as horses, elephants, rodents, dogs, cows, lions, and primates.

Although in this early atmosphere of the earth life may have arisen in more than one place (and likely under the seas near hydrothermal oceanic vents), I find it fascinating that all of life currently on earth has been determined to have come from only one common ancestor. This ancestor is known as the *last universal common ancestor* (LUCA). So not only do humans and chimpanzees have a common ancestor, but humans and potatoes have a common ancestor as well!

The Universe in Time

It is believed that the universe came into being 13.8 billion years ago. The event has become known as *The Big Bang*. The term ironically was popularized by a critic of the theory, astronomer Fred Hoyle, who believed in a universe that had no beginning and no ending and was in a "steady state." Evidence now suggests that there was a beginning to the universe and that the universe is expanding. The further away objects are, the faster they are moving. Further evidence for an expanding universe was the discovery of "cosmic background radiation." This faint radiation which fills the entire universe is a remnant of an ancient tremendous flash of energy. *Astrophysicist Eric Chaisson in Epic of Evolution: Seven Ages of the Cosmos (2006) writes:*

FIGURE 2.8

TIMELINE OF UNIVERSE

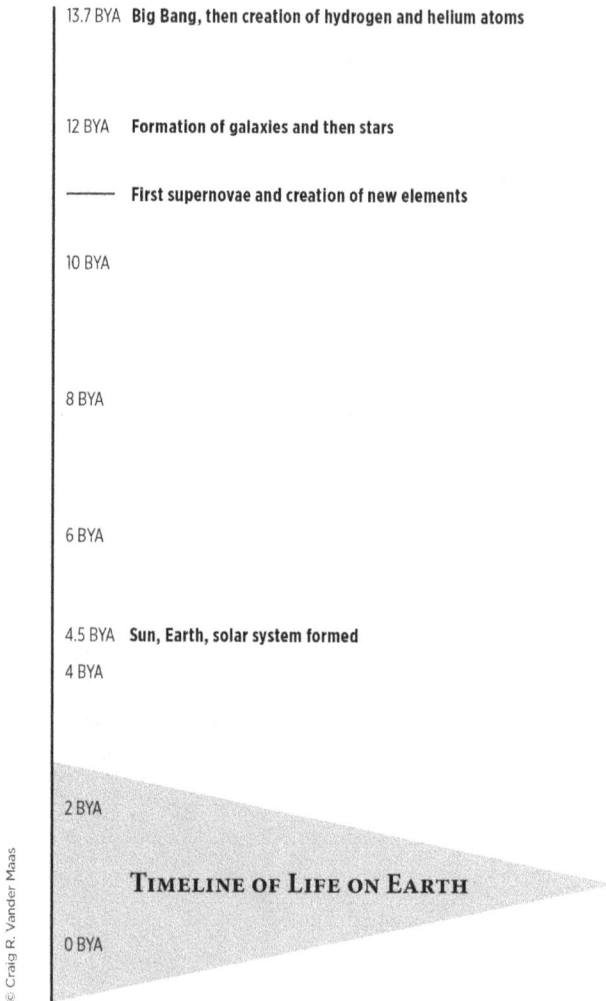

13.7 BYA **Big Bang, then creation of hydrogen and helium atoms**

12 BYA **Formation of galaxies and then stars**

——— **First supernovae and creation of new elements**

10 BYA

8 BYA

6 BYA

4.5 BYA **Sun, Earth, solar system formed**
4 BYA

2 BYA

TIMELINE OF LIFE ON EARTH

0 BYA

© Craig R. Vander Maas

The galaxies are simply the debris of a primeval "explosion," a cosmic bomb whose die was cast long ago. The word explosion is in quotes above because, technically, most astronomers don't like that description. Since there was no preexisting space, nor any matter per se at the start, that word can be misleading. Yet if we keep this bomblike interpretation in mind as merely artistic license- here with energy initially expelled into time, rather than matter into space- then the analogy serves a useful purpose.

At the beginning of the creation of the universe (following the "big bang") in what has been called the *radiation era* there was only one thing: energy. All the energy that would ever exist in the universe came into being in a split second during the big bang. As the universe cooled, it expanded allowing for something new to come in existence: matter. Energy and matter are the same. Matter can become energy, and energy can become matter. Einstein's famous mathematical equation of $E=MC2$ posits that matter and energy are different forms of the same thing. Humans have learned how to convert matter to energy; this is demonstrated with nuclear reactors and atomic bombs. We do not know yet how to convert energy into matter, but that is what happened shortly after the Big Bang.

Initially it is believed that subatomic particles were the first instances of matter. In the first half of the twentieth century the only subatomic particles known were protons, neutrons, photons, and electrons. Since then, hundreds of other particles have been discovered, and the way that they have become known has been through technology to cause collisions between atoms or particles to discover their constituent parts. The largest particle accelerator in the world is the *Large Hadron Collider* at the CERN laboratory on the French-Swiss border.

Scientists believe that the first particles created were *quarks* and *gluons* which are constituent parts of neutrons and protons. "Soon thereafter, yet still only about a microsecond after the big bang, heavy, strongly interacting elementary particles such as protons and neutrons…became the most abundant types of matter." (Chaisson, 2006) Within a millisecond electrons and neutrinos came into being. Although the beginnings of matter had now come into being, pure energy or *radiation* continued to reign for the first hundred centuries of the universe.

Scientists believe that between the first few millennia and a million years after the big bang subatomic particles began clustering into atoms through electromagnetic forces. This began what has sometimes been called the *Matter Era*. It began the era of the emergence of *things*. From a universe of pure energy only, we now have *stuff* coming into existence. Atoms came to proliferate throughout the universe. Initially the only types of atoms that existed were helium and especially hydrogen atoms.

Somehow during time these two atomic elements evolved into metals, rocks, plants, stars, planets, oceans, hummingbirds, pizza, and you and me. Amazing! The universe expanded from something a million billion billion times smaller than a single atom to its current size of an estimated one hundred billion galaxies and about 93 billion light years in diameter. Astounding!

When looking at the universe along its 13.8-billion-year timeline it is indisputable to me that the universe has evolved, and that there is a direction to this progression. For me this is evidence of God. God is the force behind the growing complexity of the universe. God is the entity that encompasses all and is responsible for the progression of all- the whole that includes everything. This process of the evolution of the universe has been called *cosmic evolution*.

Scientists have no idea how or why the universe popped into existence out of nothingness. We also cannot discount the possibility that there are other universes out there that also popped into existence. We are not able to say where the Big Bang occurred, as it occurred everywhere. Prior to this event there was no space, and there was no time. Hard to get one's head around this!

The universe continued to be nothing more than huge clouds of hydrogen and helium for perhaps 200 million years. Then a mysterious new force appeared in the universe now known as *gravity*. This force was responsible for gas and dust clumping together and eventually forming galaxies and stars. Before gravity did its magic, the universe was a very boring entity; it consisted of nothing but diffuse energy.

Electromagnetic and nuclear forces bind elementary particles within atoms, and it is gravity that binds together atoms into giant clouds that were the beginnings of galaxies. The formation of galaxies started occurring about a billion years after the big bang, and it is believed that there has not been any further development of galaxies in the universe in the past ten billion years.

All galaxies are believed to contain generally comparable amounts of matter and seem to average about a hundred billion stars. Stars continue to be born and to die, but galaxies do not. The specifics of galaxy formation continue to be somewhat of a mystery to cosmologists.

Stars live for millions to billions of years. Eventually they die. It is in the death of stars that other chemical elements came into existence. Stars die when they start running out of hydrogen. In very large stars the shrinking of its core causes such high temperatures that helium atoms begin to fuse to cause carbon, a critical element for the development of life.

The largest stars have still higher temperatures at their cores causing carbon to start fusing creating oxygen and silicon. At seven billion degrees Fahrenheit stars start producing large amounts of iron. A second process also occurs in the deaths of very large stars called *neutron capture* (the details of which are beyond the scope of this book) causing the creation of still other new heavy elements (up to number 83 in the periodic table which is bismuth).

The very largest stars end their lives in a stupendous explosion called a *supernova*. It is in this event that the remaining chemical elements of the periodic table are created.

Periodic Table of the Elements

These explosions caused all the known elements to be scattered throughout the universe. So, everything that exists on this earth (except for hydrogen and helium) came into being as the result of the death of stars. Hydrogen and helium do continue to be the most prevalent element in existence, i.e., 98 percent of all atoms.

Further complexity came to the universe when various elements began to combine with other elements to create completely new substances. For example, hydrogen atoms combined with oxygen atoms to create water. Carbon atoms combined with oxygen atoms to produce carbon dioxide. Sodium atoms combined with chloride atoms to create salt. Chemistry is responsible for the universe becoming more and more diverse, and more and more complex.

Many stars have lived and died prior to the birth of our own star, the sun. The sun was formed in the same way that all stars are formed- dispersed matter being pulled together by gravity. Using radiometric dating techniques, researchers have determined that our solar system is precisely 4.568 billion years old. Planets began forming due to a process called *accretion*. Particles would collide and coalesce together. As gravitational fields became stronger and stronger, more and more debris were swept up into the growing planetary bodies. It is believed that 1 to 2 million years after the formation of the sun an influx of iron came into our solar system as the result of a nearby supernova. Therefore, the inner planets of our solar system are rocky (Mercury, Venus, Earth, and Mars) and the outer planets (Jupiter, Saturn, Uranus, and Neptune) are gaseous.

I believe that most of us grow up with the perception of human life on earth as being about six thousand years- the amount of time that we have had written language. This is far from reality. If we were to convert our actual 13.8-billion-year history to a year's time we might get a better conceptualization of the big picture of time. The Big Bang would have occurred at midnight on January 1st. Our solar system, including the Earth, would not come into existence until September. The planet would oxygenate in October, and multi-cellular life would evolve in December. Amphibians would evolve on December 22, reptiles on December 23, and mammals on December 26. Dinosaurs went extinct on December 30, and mammals took over. Humans (who walk upright) would finally make their appearance on the last day of the year, December 31, at 9:25 pm. The agricultural revolution and the beginning of written history occurred at 30 seconds before midnight. Jesus Christ was born 4 seconds before midnight, and Columbus arrived in America 1.5 seconds before midnight.

The Universe in Space

Not only can we be overwhelmed with the immensity of time in the universe, we can also be blown away by the immense size of the universe. Even our own solar system is much larger than most of us conceptualize it. In elementary school we saw models of our solar system that looked like the model below.

This is certainly not to scale. If our earth were the size of a pinhead, the sun would be the size of a grapefruit (6 inches in diameter). Our sun is not a particularly large star. "Red giant" stars can be 1500 times as large as our sun. So, with the above scale, that would make a red giant 9,000 inches in diameter (which would be 250 yards, the size of 2.5 football fields put together).

The above model also certainly does not accurately represent the distance between our sun and the planets. Using the above scale, the earth would be just under four inches from the sun, Jupiter would be 20.5 inches from the sun, and Pluto would be almost thirteen feet from the sun.

One of the nearest stars to our sun is Alpha Centauri. Using our scale this star would be 2,734 miles away (about the same distance as New York is from Los Angeles)! This is typical of the density of stars in this part of our galaxy, the Milky Way (i.e., about five light years between stars). A *light year* is the distance one can go when traveling at the speed of light (186,282 miles per second).

As I said, we live in a galaxy known as the *Milky Way*. It covers over 100,000 light years across. Estimates about the number of stars in our galaxy range from 100 billion to 400 billion. There are an estimated 100 billion galaxies in the universe, and the universe is estimated to be 93 billion light years in diameter and continues to expand.

The nearest spiral galaxy to our galaxy (the Milky Way) is called Andromeda. Chaisson said "Roughly two-and-a-half million light-years distant, this galaxy's radiation takes some twenty-five thousand centuries to reach us- meaning that Andromeda's light left that galaxy well before Homo sapiens emerged on planet Earth. And yet it is the nearest major galaxy to us!"

The number of stars in the universe is believed to be more numerous than every single grain of sand on the planet earth! And we now know, thanks to the Hubble telescope, that many stars have planets orbiting them. As incomprehensible as all of this is, we cannot rule out the possibility also that ours is not the only universe in existence!

I believe the study of history is very germane to spiritual development, particularly "big history." By understanding the history of our universe in its entirety we gain perspective. And by studying science we have been gaining ongoing knowledge about the nature of reality using the best evidence that is currently available.

What science does not address, however, is ultimate meanings about this reality. That has been the purview of philosophy and religion. What is the meaning of life? Does life have a purpose? What happens after death? What is morality. Does it matter if I am good or bad? Is there a god? What is the nature of God? These are topics I will address in the next and following chapters.

Questions for Contemplation or Discussion

Chapter Two. Time and Space

1. Looking at the history of the universe in its entirety, do you see any themes that predominate? How would you characterize the history of the universe?
2. What is the reason for the existence of the universe?
3. What is the reason for the existence of humans?
4. What does scientific knowledge about the universe have to tell us about God?
5. Do you think knowledge of "big history" is important for spiritual development?
6. Has your worldview changed over the course of your life? In what ways, and why?

Chapter Three

Human Development

After dropping out of Calvin College and closing my record store, I began working for Knape and Vogt Manufacturing (KV). I started out as a "racker" in their plating department. It was a terrible job. I had to hang greasy metal drawer slides on racks that were on a traveling conveyor belt. It was hot, dirty, physical work. It was not the first unpleasant job I had. I worked a summer job at Keebler (the cookie company) in the factory which was probably the job I had that I hated the most (although it was a union job that paid extremely well). I also worked as a stock boy (my first job at age 16 other than cutting lawns), dishwasher, and bricklayer tender with my father. At KV after several months I got a better job as a hoist operator. Then later I got a new position at KV as lab technician and managing their waste treatment plant on second shift.

It was during this period that I was going through the "coming out" process. This was a time of crisis for me and a significant turning point in my life. My family and the culture I grew up in made clear what was considered a good life: graduate from high school, possibly get additional education to get a good job, make a decent living, get married, raise a family, retire when you are able, and above all accept Jesus as the son of God so that upon death one could live forever in Heaven. At an earlier age this was the life I assumed I would have. Part of the coming out process was coming to terms with acceptance of not raising a family.

I also realized I wanted more for my life than working at a factory. I needed more meaning in my life than that. I was very fortunate that KV had a college tuition reimbursement program. If I got at least a grade of C in classes, they would reimburse me 80 percent of the cost of classes.

I enrolled back in school, this time at Aquinas College, a small Catholic college in Grand Rapids. I continued to major in English but also added a second major: Psychology. I enjoyed attending Aquinas. I was a good student and attended full-time while still working full-time at KV. I graduated in two years and then decided to go on to obtain a master's degree. I enrolled at Western Michigan University in the industrial psychology program but later changed programs to counseling psychology. KV continued their tuition reimbursement.

While working on this degree I got fired from KV for excessive absence. They had a point system for absence/tardiness, and I exceeded the number of points allowed. I had often called in sick to study for tests or to write papers. I did not intend to be fired. I had a house that I was buying as well as other bills. I was panicked. Looking back, however, it really was fortuitous. It made me leave the security of this job and to find work in the occupational field that I was studying for. I got a job as a counselor at an inpatient chemical dependency program. I worked there for a year and then got a job at an outpatient counseling center (that primarily dealt with substance abuse issues) as a therapist. I continued working on my master's degree and finished this in 1990.

I worked as a therapist for AOS and then Arbor Circle (which the agency merged into) for sixteen years and it was a very good period of my life. I continue to have contact with many of my ex-coworkers. I discovered during my time there that I really had interest in psychological assessment. Psychologist John Holland developed expertise in personality and career choice. Holland's theory suggests that there are six occupational personality types:

- Realistic (Doers). These are people who like to work with things. It includes occupations such as carpenter, mechanic, surveyor, farmer, and fire fighter.

- Investigative (Thinkers). These are people who like to figure things out. They like working with data. It includes occupations such as psychologist, lawyer, chemist, and veterinarian.

- Artistic (Creators), These people are imaginative and includes occupations such as composer, artist, architect, and interior decorator.

- Social (Helpers). These are people who like to work with people. Occupations include counselor, speech therapist, nurse, clergy, and teacher.

- Enterprising (Persuaders). These people are acquisitive, entrepreneurial, and ambitious. Occupations include business and sales.

- Conventional (Organizers). These are people who enjoy clerical work. Occupations include bookkeeper, tax auditor, and web developer.

People can be combinations of these personality types. My most prominent occupational type was *investigative* followed by *social*. My job as a counselor was primarily working with and helping people, which I did enjoy, but what I really found fascinating was figuring people out. So, I went back to school to study clinical psychology. I was accepted at the Illinois School of Professional Psychology which was situated in Rolling Meadows, Illinois (the west suburbs of Chicago). I attended school full-time in Chicagoland but continued to live and work in Grand Rapids. It was a three-and-a-half-hour commute to school each week. My sister Jan lived in Geneva, Illinois (a forty-five-minute commute from the school). I was able to arrange my classes in two consecutive days and then spent a night at my sister's house in-between these two days. While still working almost full time I was able to obtain a master's degree and doctorate degree in clinical psychology in three years.

I focused on psychological assessment in my doctoral studies and attended a total of seven psychological assessment classes, including personality and intellectual assessment. I also discovered a new area of assessment- neuropsychological assessment. This involves assessment of cognitive functioning following traumatic brain injuries and assessment of degenerative diseases such as Alzheimer's Disease. I found it fascinating and decided to make a detour in my vocational course. I completed two practicums, my doctoral internship, and post-doctoral training in neuropsychology. I was continuing to also work at AOS during this time and began to integrate psychological and neuropsychological assessments into my practice there.

In 2001 while reading the APA Monitor, a monthly magazine of the American Psychological Association, I noticed in the want ads a job opportunity in Grand Rapids for a psychologist at a pain clinic. Because psychological evaluations were a major part of the job I applied and was hired. I knew nothing about chronic pain but was taught the things I needed to learn for that part of the job. Not only did I learn about various chronic pain conditions, but I also learned how to do biofeedback.

It might have been in the APA Monitor again that I saw an advertisement for training in psychopharmacology. The advertisement that I saw was for a two-year postdoctoral Master of Science degree from Nova Southeastern University. It was a "fly in program" requiring students to fly to the school from around the country for one week every two months for two years. It was particularly attractive in that the place we would be flying into was Ft. Lauderdale, Florida. After completing coursework, a psychopharmacology practicum was required which I did with a psychiatrist at an inpatient psychiatric hospital unit. The practicum required 100 write ups on patients with diverse psychiatric conditions with discussion about pharmacological treatments. I graduated with my M.S. in 2004.

I have now been working for Michigan Behavioral Consultants for over twenty years and do only psychological and neuropsychological evaluations and still very much enjoy this work. The travel on my career path was serendipitous; I took roads that I never knew were there when I began the trip. My interest in the workings of people led me to major in English and Psychology for my undergraduate degree. I found an interest in insight-oriented psychotherapies and started work as a counselor. I discovered even more interest in psychological assessment and completed degrees in Clinical Psychology. I discovered neuropsychology and completed training in this. I stumbled into pain psychology. I took an interest in psychopharmacology and completed training in this. The diversity of this training has helped me to evolve as a psychologist and as a person. It also allowed me to do something else I enjoyed doing- teaching. I taught as an adjust professor at Western Michigan University for fifteen years teaching Tests and Measurement as well as some other graduate courses and at Monmouth University for six years teaching an online graduate course in psychopharmacology.

There are a couple points I wish to make by sharing my vocational history here. The first is that all our lives are a journey, and that along the way there will be unexpected challenges and opportunities. We have choices to make about whether to alter our trip itinerary or to rigidly maintain our original plans. The life plan, I believe, for most individuals is to complete a certain amount of schooling (for some 9th grade might be enough and for others it is considerably more depending on vocational objectives), to obtain a good job, to find a significant other and get married, to raise a family, and to accumulate wealth to be able to buy things. This is the road many if not most travel. Robert Frost reminds us in his poem *The Road Not Taken* that we have other options. "I took the one less traveled by, and that has made all the difference."

There is a misconception by many that we as individuals stop developing when we reach adulthood. Many think the time for development is only childhood and adolescence. We all know that childhood is a process with typical developmental milestones. Crawling typically happens between 5.2 and 13.5 months. Walking alone typically happens between 8.2 and 17.6 months. At age 2 years a child can typically put two to three words together. Most 3-year-olds can ride a tricycle. Most 4-year-olds can catch a bouncing ball. Most 5-year-olds can jump rope. At age 6 to 7 permanent teeth come in. Puberty happens between ages 11-15. By age 16 most kids have stopped growing in height. At age 18 individuals are usually considered adults. At this point many think that human development is complete, although additional education is often required for vocational reasons; to get good jobs, make money, and to accumulate wealth to buy things. However, psychologists know that this is not the case. Even biological development is not fully complete. The frontal lobes of the brain continue to develop until the mid-twenties.

Ken Wilber in *Integral Psychology (2000)* writes:

The traditions often divide life's journey into the "Seven Ages of a Person," where each age involves adaptation to one of the seven basic levels of consciousness, and each of the seven stages is said to take seven years. Thus, the first seven years of life involve adaptation to the physical realm (especially food, survival, safety). The second seven years involve adaptation to the emotional-sexual-feeling dimension (which culminates in sexual maturation or puberty). The third seven years of life (typically adolescence) involves the emergence of the logical mind and adaptation to its new perspectives. This brings us to around age twenty-one, where many individuals' overall development tends to become arrested. But if development continues, each seven-year period brings the possibility of a new and higher level of consciousness evolution.

Psychiatrist M. Scott Peck wrote a bestselling book (over seven million copies sold) titled *The Road Less Traveled (1978)* whose purpose was to encourage ongoing spiritual growth, which is the purpose of this book as well. Growth comes as the result of continuing education and contemplation. It comes as the result of honestly and sincerely seeking truth, rather than just blindly incorporating information passed to us in our early years. Peck writes:

For truth is reality. That which is false is unreal. The more clearly we see the reality of the world, the better equipped we are to deal with the world. The less clearly we see the reality of the world- the more our minds are befuddled by falsehood, misperceptions and illusions- the less able we will be to determine correct courses of action and make wise decisions. Our view of reality is like a map with which to negotiate the terrain of life. If the map is true and accurate, we will generally know where we are, and if we have decided where we want to go, we will generally know how to get there. If the map is false and inaccurate, we generally will be lost.

While this is obvious, it is something that most people to a greater or lesser degree choose to ignore. They ignore it because our route to reality is not easy. First of all, we are not born with maps; we have to make them, and the making requires effort. The more effort we make to appreciate and perceive reality, the larger and more accurate our maps will be. But many do not want to make this effort. Some stop making it by the end of adolescence. Their maps are small and sketchy, their views of the world narrow and misleading. By the end of middle age most people have given up the effort. They feel certain that their maps are complete and their Weltanschauung is correct (indeed, even sacrosanct), and they are no longer interested in new information. It is as if they are tired. Only a relative and fortunate few continue until the moment of death exploring the mystery of reality, ever enlarging and refining and redefining their understanding of the world and what is true.

My roadmap has had many detours along the way but I have gotten to the main destinations that I have sought: making a good living with work that I find meaningful, wonderful relationships including especially my life partner of 25 years, traveling the world, and fulfilling my lifelong thirst for knowledge and growth. Although I have four graduate degrees, I have spent even more time engaging in informal education than I have in formal. Primarily my interest has been in human development and spiritual development. Long ago I discovered that what I had been taught about the meaning of life was inadequate, and so I pursued a program of study to work at seeing the "big picture," to getting a clearer idea of God, to discover the purpose for life, and to come to peace about death. I have sought to develop an accurate map of reality. I have found satisfactory answers for myself. The purpose of this book is to share what I have discovered.

Spiritual growth is a topic for study in psychology. The word "psychology," after all, comes from the Greek word psyche which means spirit or soul. Psychology is the study of the spirit. In this chapter I will discuss human development starting first with looking at human development in its broadest; the history of our development as a species. This is an area of study by evolutionary psychologists. Then I will narrow the focus to research about individual human development in the present. This is an area of study by developmental psychologists.

Evolutionary Psychology and the Big Picture

I remember hearing a story years ago about a woman who lived in the California desert. A rare cold front came through the area and the temperature went below freezing. She found a rattlesnake outside that was frozen stiff. She felt pity for the creature and brought it inside and placed it near the fireplace to warm. She then went to get a dish of water. As she was placing it near the snake the animal sprang at her and bit her. The woman exclaimed "How could you do this to me! I saved your life!" As the venom spread through the woman's body the snake replied, "What are you wining about? You knew I was a poisonous snake when you brought me in. How did you expect me to act?" This story was related to me in the context of a discussion about relationships, in that individuals frequently fall in love and seek relationship with an individual whose history suggests a poor outcome for a lasting and meaningful relationship. In other words, love is blind. We should not get into relationships expecting to change the other person. Not only does this story teach us a lesson about relationships, it also teaches us a lesson about reptiles.

Few of us keep reptiles such as snakes and alligators as pets. They seem to have no feelings, empathy, or love for us. Dogs and cats are popular pets because we feel an emotional connection to them. An explanation for this difference between reptiles and mammals that has become popular is that of the *triune brain,* a model developed by German anatomist Ludwig Edinger and American neuroscientist Paul MacLean and made popular by astronomer Carl Sagan in his best-selling book *The Dragons of Eden* (1977). Edinger suggested a triune brain to explain the evolution of brain *structure*, while MacLean suggested a triune brain to explain the evolution of brain *function*.

The inner and most ancient part of the brain includes the spinal cord, the medulla, the pons, and the midbrain. This part of the brain is referred to by MacLean as the *neural chassis*. It is the part of the brain that controls the heart, breathing, blood circulation and reproduction.

MacLean's model suggests three levels of brain development above this. Surrounding the midbrain are the olfactostriatum, corpus striatum, and the globus pallidus. These structures MacLean refers to as the reptilian brain or the R-complex. Sagan writes "MacLean has shown that the R-complex plays an important role in aggressive behavior, territoriality, ritual and the establishment of social hierarchies." It corresponds to Fraud's conception of an *id* and the *pleasure principle*.

Surrounding the R-complex is the limbic system which includes the thalamus, hypothalamus, amygdala, pituitary, hippocampus, and cingulate gyrus. The limbic system evolved perhaps one hundred and fifty million years ago and was an innovation that evolved in mammals. Sagan writes:

> *There are reasons to think that the beginnings of altruistic behavior are in the limbic system. Indeed, with rare exceptions (chiefly the social insects), mammals and birds are the only organisms to devote substantial attention to the care of their young- an evolutionary development that, through the long period of plasticity which it permits, takes advantage of the large information-processing capability of the mammalian and primate brains. Love seems to be an invention of the mammals.*

Surrounding the limbic system is the *neocortex* (that is, the new cortex as opposed to the paleocortex or old cortex, also known as the cingulate gyrus) which probably evolved tens of millions of years ago. The evolution of the neocortex particularly accelerated a few million years ago with the dramatic increase in the size of brains in humans. Our large complex brains have enabled increased memory, self-awareness, symbolic thought and language, introspection, abstract thought, and deeper levels of consciousness.

The triune brain model suggests that the R-complex developed in vertebrates first, that the limbic system later developed in mammals, and that the neocortex evolved in the more advanced mammals, particularly primates, and especially homo sapiens. New systems developed on top of older systems. Sagan makes the point that this sequence corresponds to fetal development in humans. He cites the German anatomist Ernest Haeckel: "Haeckel held that in its embryological development, an animal tends to repeat or recapitulate the sequence that its ancestors followed during their evolution. And indeed, in human intrauterine development we run through stages very much like fish, reptiles and non-primate mammals before we become recognizably human."

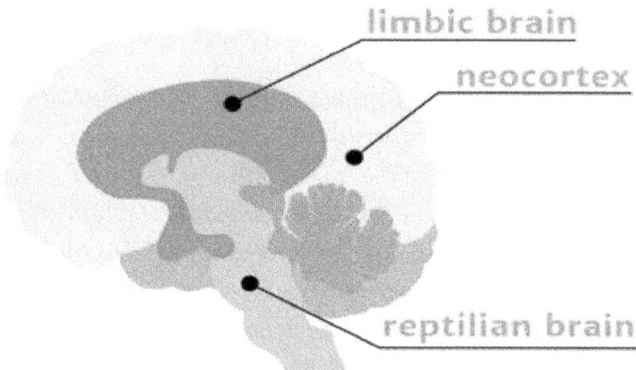

limbic brain

neocortex

reptilian brain

Neuroscientists now cite research that show the triune brain model does not reflect evolutionary brain development quite as simply as the model would suggest. Nevertheless, there was a significant evolutionary leap from reptiles to mammals resulting in the development of a very important new quality: empathy, which is the capacity to understand the point of view of another person so that one vicariously shares the other person's feelings, perceptions, and thoughts. Bekoff and Pierce in *Wild Justice: The Moral Lives of Animals* (2009) conclude "there's mounting scientific evidence that animals, even rodents, have the capacity to feel empathy." They also conclude that "empathy is an ancient capacity, probably present in all mammals." They report that the evidence for empathy in animals comes from several fields of research, especially ethology, psychology, and neuroscience."

Mammals also developed the capacity for *sympathy*, which is an expression of understanding and care for someone else's suffering. Dutch primatologist and ethologist Franz De Waal said in The Bonobo and the Atheist (2013) "Empathy can be quite passive, reflecting mere sensitivity, whereas sympathy is outgoing. It expresses concern for others combined with an urge to ameliorate their situation." "Chimpanzees rescue each other from leopard attacks. Squirrels give alarm calls that warn others of danger. Elephants try to lift fallen comrades." Bekoff and Pierce also give numerous examples of animals showing sympathy for members of other species, including dolphins protecting humans from a great white shark.

Mammals also developed the capacity for *altruism*, which is putting others' interests before one's own sometimes to the point of sacrificing one's own interests or life in the process. De Waal in *Good Natured: The Origins of Right and Wrong in Humans and Other Animals* (1996) said "Altruism is not limited to our species. Indeed, its presence in other species, and the theoretical challenge this represents, is what gave rise to sociobiology- the contemporary study of animal (including human) behavior from an evolutionary perspective. Aiding others at a cost or risk to oneself is widespread in the animal world."

Evolutionary psychology along with cognitive psychology and evolutionary biology deal with human development from an evolutionary perspective over millions of years. I now would like to zero in on evolution (i.e., development) in our own species and in the present time. People vary in regards to their cognitive, emotional, moral, and spiritual development. This is the purview of the sub-discipline of psychology known as Developmental Psychology. But before doing this I would like to take a short detour to discuss something that does not evolve or develop over one's lifetime: intelligence.

Intelligence

You might have heard it said that people go to school to get "smarter." This would be a true statement if what is meant is that people get more educated. School does not help people to be more intelligent, however. The definition of intelligence has been rather controversial. Some believe it is not a unitary construct but rather that there are various types of intelligences. Psychologist Howard Gardner is the most well-known proponent of this view. The more traditional view of intelligence, however, is that it is a unitary construct. In 1904 English psychologist Charles Spearman proposed that there existed an entity that was general intelligence. He referred to this as "g." Although he agreed that people have individual strengths and weaknesses, he said that all tests of various mental abilities correlate very strongly with each other. To account for this, he said that there must be some underlying construct that all these tests are tapping into.

I had taught a class entitled Tests and Measurement for years for graduate counseling students at Western Michigan University, and I think probably the most controversial topic in the class was intelligence, particularly the idea that it was a single construct, that it was relatively stable throughout one's life, and that heredity plays a significant role in one's level of intelligence. Students disliked the hierarchical implications of intelligence as a single construct, and that some people were higher or lower on this. They preferred the idea that we all have strengths and weakness and that there are various types of intelligences.

Did you ever notice in high school that the stars of the baseball, basketball and football teams seemed to be the same individuals? Could it be that these individuals had more of a construct called *athleticism* than others? Most of my students did not have difficulty in believing that some individuals are more athletic than others, but the idea that some are more intelligent than others was repugnant. Most developmental psychologists and neuropsychologists do accept the idea of "g." When administering a battery of neuropsychological tests my expectation would be that all cognitive abilities (such as attention, memory, cognitive processing speed, and visual spatial abilities) would all correlate significantly with each other. A significant weakness in a certain area could be indicative of pathology. For example, a significant deficit in the ability to encode new information in an older individual could be indicative of the beginning of a progressive dementia such as Alzheimer's Disease. A significant deficit in visual spatial abilities in a person who had a head injury could indicate brain damage.

It is rare for people to have a cognitive ability that is significantly different from overall cognitive abilities. There is a rare condition called *Savant syndrome* in which persons with serious mental disabilities, particularly autistic disorder, have remarkable genius abilities in some circumscribed area which is incongruous to their overall handicap. For example, Kim Peek, whom the film *Rain Man* was based on, memorized over 12,000 books in his lifetime. Leslie Lemke could hear a piece of music once and then perform it flawlessly in the future by memory. Daniel Tammet could recite Pi from memory to 22,514 decimal places.

Intelligence (IQ) tests were developed to measure "g," although their purpose is to do much more than to simply categorize or label. For example, they are important for developing treatment plans for individuals with psychological disorders or learning disabilities. Probably the most widely used intelligence tests are the Wechsler scales which have a mean of 100 and a standard deviation of 15. What this means is that the average IQ in the population is 100, that 68 percent of the population have IQs between 85 and 115, and that 96 percent of the population have IQs between 70 and 130. Individuals with IQs below 70 are considered *intellectually impaired*, (what we used to call *mental retardation*).

It is unfortunate that general intelligence ("g") cannot really be increased, just like athleticism cannot really be increased. However, despite not being very athletic I could become proficient in athletic activities such as shooting free throws or golfing- it may just not come as naturally to me as it does to others, and I need to work at it more to achieve skill. However, no matter how much I practice, I might not have the athleticism to become a pro athlete. It is the same with intelligence. Some learn quickly and easily. Their minds are quicker than others. Although we are all able to learn, some regrettably do not have the innate intellectual abilities to be able to achieve certain occupations such as doctor or lawyer. One needs an IQ of at least 83 to be allowed to serve in the U.S. military.

So much for what we cannot change. The good news is about what we can change. For one thing we can obtain knowledge, and we can do it on an ongoing basis for the rest of our lives. Secondly, partly as the result of knowledge, we can continue to evolve and develop as individuals in several different ways. This is the focus of developmental psychology.

Developmental Psychology

Initially the subfield of psychology dealt primarily with child and adolescent development, but now it also addresses adult development. It is adult development that I focus on in this book. Perhaps the most famous developmental psychologist was Jean Piaget who studied cognitive development in children. Piaget's research led him to conclude that children's cognitive abilities developed in stages. He believed these stages were biologically determined rather than influenced by culture or environmental factors. For example, between the ages of eighteen and twenty-four months a child should learn *object permanence*, i.e., grasping the notion that just because an object is covered up and is not in view that it still exists. The last stage of Piaget's model is called the *formal operational stage*. It includes the ability to think and reason hypothetically, abstractly, and deductively. Deductive reasoning is the ability to develop hypotheses and then to systematically test (through observation) the validity of our hypotheses. It is the basis for the *scientific method*. This ability might develop as soon as the early teens or into adulthood, but for some individuals this never develops. *Inductive reasoning*, which is the ability to generalize based on specific observations, is also important in the scientific method. It is the ability to develop hypotheses. This ability develops in grade school.

Another very famous developmental psychologist was Lawrence Kohlberg who developed a model of moral reasoning. Like Piaget, Kohlberg's research suggests that moral reasoning develops in stages, and like Piaget he believed the stages were directional, i.e., that when one reaches a certain stage of development they do not regress or go backwards. Kohlberg described six stages of moral development. The first two stages are based on reward and punishment. What is "right" for a child at this stage is whatever brings reward, and what is "wrong" is whatever causes punishment. Kohlberg called this *preconventional morality*. The next two stages involve *conventional morality* which emphasizes adherence to social rules. It is a law-and-order mentality. What is good or bad is what authorities say is good or bad, such as the church, religious scripture, or law makers. Many people never develop further than this in their moral development.

The fifth and sixth stages of Kohlberg's model involve *postconventional morality*. In order to reach this stage, one must have the ability to reason (formal operational stage of Piaget). Morality is based on reasoned principle. It is not about rewards or punishments, or even about what others think. At this stage one follows their own ethical principles which usually involve reverence for truth, fairness, justice, human rights, and liberty. If I am a soldier in the military and I receive an order to kill some people, I will likely follow orders without question if I am at the conventional morality stage. However, at the postconventional morality stage I am likely to question or refuse an order that is against my ethical principles.

Kohlberg's theory is based on research he did on males. American psychologist Carol Gilligan researched moral development in females. Her results were very similar to Kohlberg's, although she found that while males emphasized the importance of justice and independence, females emphasized more the importance of caring and taking care of the needs of others.

The conflictual world views of those in the conventional morality stage and those in the postconventional morality stage we can see played out in the current culture wars. More about this later in this chapter.

Spiritual Development

Several theorists have developed models about stages of spiritual development, although these models go by various names such as faith development, ego development, world views, or stages of consciousness.   So, what is this construct we might call "spiritual," and how is it different from religion? The title of this book suggests that we go *beyond* religion. By religion I mean institutional dogmatic beliefs established by authority figures. Whereas by spirituality the definition by E. R. Canda is a good one: "Spirituality relates to the person's search for a sense of meaning and morally fulfilling relationships between oneself, other people, the encompassing universe, and the ontological (metaphysical) ground of existence, whether a person understands this in terms that are theistic, atheistic, nontheistic, or any combination of these." A well know refrain these days by many is "I am spiritual, not religious."

I will list here some prominent developmental theorists of spirituality and encourage the reader to investigate their individual models.

- Abraham Maslow was an American psychologist who developed a model of hierarchy of needs.
- Jean Gebser was a German philosopher who theorized about structures of consciousness/world views.
- James Fowler was an American psychologist who developed a model of stages of faith development.
- Ken Wilber is an American philosopher who developed a model of stages of consciousness.

- Jane Loevinger was an American psychologist who developed a model of stages of ego development.
- Robert Kegan is an American psychologist who developed a model of stages of development.
- Susanne Cook-Greuter is an American psychologist who developed a model of levels of ego development.

There are great similarities between all these models in terms of what spiritual/ego/faith/consciousness development looks like. The differences primarily are in what we choose to call this construct and how we conceptualize the levels of the construct. So, for example with the construct of depression, a classification system might be devised to determine whether patients have no depression, mild depression, or significant depression. Another classification system might have more categories, such as no depression, mild depression, moderate depression, severe depression, and severe depression with psychotic features. The classification system we choose to use is completely arbitrary.

Ken Wilber uses the example of temperature. How many degrees is it from freezing to boiling? It depends on what scale you use. For the centigrade scale it is 100 degrees (0 to 100). For the Fahrenheit scale it is 180 degrees (32 degrees for freezing to 212 degrees for boiling). Jean Gebser has five stages in his model. Ken Wilber has ten levels in his model.

I would like to make a comment briefly about James Fowler's model of faith development. The term *faith* often refers in general vernacular to one's religion. What is his faith? Hindu. The term was also used in my youth to discourage me from analyzing too much. I was told to "just have faith." In other words, just believe what I, the Bible, or the church is telling you to believe. Fowler's use of the term faith is very similar to the previous definition of spirituality I shared. Fowler in *Faithful Change: The Personal and Public Challenges of Postmodern Life* (2000) writes regarding faith as being:

> *an integral, centering process, underlying the formation of beliefs, values, and meanings that (1) gives coherence and direction to people's lives, (2) links them in shared trusts and loyalties with others, (3) grounds their personal stances and communal loyalties in a sense of relatedness to a larger frame of reference, and (4) enables them to face and deal with the limited conditions of life, relying upon that which has the quality of ultimacy in their lives.*

All the above models are hierarchical, meaning that certain levels or stages are higher than other levels or stages. This does not mean that people in one stage are *better* than those in lower stages. The idea of a hierarchy is objectionable to a great many people. Ken Wilber addresses this in *The Integral Vision* (2007):

> *Well, perhaps we should stop right here and deal first with the enormous misconceptions surrounding the word "hierarchy." For so many people, this has become a very dirty word, and for understandable reasons. But there are at least two very different types of hierarchy, which researchers call oppressive hierarchies (or dominator hierarchies) and growth hierarchies (or actualization hierarchies). A dominator hierarchy is just that, a ranking system that dominates, exploits, and represses people. The most notorious of these are the caste systems East and West. Any hierarchy is a dominator hierarchy if it subverts individual or collective growth.*
>
> *Actualization hierarchies, on the other hand, are the actual means of growth itself. Far from causing oppression, they are how you end it. Growth or developmental hierarchies classically move, in humans, from egocentric to ethnocentric to worldcentric to Kosmocentric waves.*

The scale that I am going to use now is the one used by Steve McIntosh in *Integral Consciousness and the Future of Evolution* (2007) and by Paul R. Smith in *Integral Christianity* *(2011)*. In this model there are six stages of spirituality-consciousness: Tribal, Warrior, Traditional, Modern, Postmodern, and Integral.

Tribal Consciousness

When our human descendants were hunter-gatherers, they originally lived in small groups of people called bands, usually between thirty and fifty people who were mostly related. Later, larger groups formed known as *tribes* who shared an ethnicity. The level of spirituality or consciousness of tribal people can be characterized as having strong belief in magic. The main goal for tribal religion is to please god(s) in order to earn rewards and to avoid punishments. The primary method for pleasing god(s) is to give offerings and praise. Offerings in tribal religions have included food items, incense, sacrificed animals, and even sacrifice of people (including one's own offspring). If catastrophes happen, such as floods, droughts, eruptions of volcanoes, or earthquakes the belief is that it must be because of something my tribe did or did not do.

This is the level of spiritual development that we see in young children. Cognitively, children are at this level between the ages of two and seven according to Piaget. At this stage children believe in Santa Claus and the Easter bunny. Children believe that their thoughts and actions can have magical effects on others and the world. If you step on a crack, you may break your mother's back. Children at this age often believe they are at fault if their parents divorce. Young children's prayers may include bargains, e.g., if you give me this, I will do that. "I promise I'll be good from now on."

This level of development also corresponds to Lawrence Kohlberg's *preconventional* stage of morality. Kohlberg said that the primary motivation for children up to around the age of seven is to avoid punishment and to receive rewards. *Right* is what rewards me, and *wrong* is what punishes me. Morality is as simple as that.

In this stage of consciousness there is concern for the members of ones' tribe and not for others. This is progress, though, from those who have concern only for oneself or for ones' immediate kin. The circle of compassion and care is larger... although still small. It is estimated that five to ten percent of the world's adult population are centered in this stage of development.

In regards to stages, do not think of them as being completely distinct entities, i.e., that you move into one stage and completely leave the previous stage behind. Rather, think of these stages as being directional (and hierarchical), but that they are diffuse. Just as in a rainbow the colors meld gradually from one into another, so it is with these stages. Individuals usually have a center of gravity though, i.e., a stage that predominates. In regards to the Tribal stage, this is the center of gravity for children and for those in primitive societies. However, individuals whose center of gravity is usually at a higher stage may become *tribal* at times. These individuals may have excessive allegiance to an ethnicity, race, political party, etc.

Warrior Consciousness

The Warrior stage of consciousness is characterized by allegiance to authorities, laws, and a desire for domination. Roughly twenty percent of the world's population is at this spiritual stage. At this stage authority is absolute and may come from a king or other ruler, a priest/minister/pope or from religious scripture. Scripture such as the Bible or Quran are taken literally. This stage corresponds to Kohlberg's *conventional* stage of morality. There is no distinction between moral principles and legal principles. The emphasis is on following rules. Good and bad are thought of in black and white terms. What authority says is right and wrong is what is right and wrong. In western societies, individuals frequently enter this stage about the time they are entering their teens. The focus is on being a good person and living up to expectations of society. Kohlberg believed that many people remain in this stage for the rest of their lives.

Christians in this stage often believe there is a battle between God and Satan for our souls. The good are rewarded in Heaven, and the evil are punished in hell. Rather than stressing the love and justice teachings of Jesus, the emphasis is on a warrior Jesus who will put into action God's wrath against sin and Satan.

This is the Jesus reflected in the old popular hymn Onward Christian Soldiers.

1. Onward, Christian soldiers!
Marching as to war,
With the cross of Jesus
Going on before.
Christ, the royal Master,
Leads against the foe;
Forward into battle,
See his banners go!

[Chorus]
Onward, Christian soldiers!
Marching as to war,
With the cross of Jesus
Going on before

2. At the sign of triumph
Satan's host doth flee;
On, then, Christian soldiers,
On to victory.
Hell's foundations quiver
At the shout of praise;
Brothers, lift your voices,
Loud your anthems raise.

3. Like a mighty army
Moves the Church of God;
Brothers, we are treading
Where the Saints have trod.
We are not divided;
All one body we:
One in hope and doctrine,
One in charity.

4. Onward, then, ye people;
Join our happy throng.
Blend with ours your voices
In the triumph song:
Glory, laud, and honor
Unto Christ, the King.
This through countless ages
Men and angels sing.

Warrior spirituality was the religion of the Roman Catholic Church when they initiated the "holy" Inquisition during the Middle Ages. This was a period in which incredible violence and torture were inflicted on people who were considered heretics. Hundreds of people were executed in the name of God for having "incorrect" beliefs. Warrior stage religion is not interested in freedom of religion or freedom in general. It is coercive. It wants to impose its beliefs and rules onto others. They have an absolute belief in their own rightness and the divine right to impose their version of truth onto others.

Warrior spirituality was the religion of Christians and Muslims during the "holy" wars of the Middle Ages known as The Crusades. Western European Christians were involved in military expeditions against Muslims to check the spread of Islam and reconquer former Christian territories and to regain control over the "Holy land." It was a war between two religions. The warrior church sees the world as a battle between correct religion and heresy.

Warrior spirituality was the religion of the Islamic terrorists who were responsible for the September 11, 2001 attacks that included the World Trade Center in New York resulting in almost 3,000 deaths. Osama bin Laden had declared a holy war against the United States. This is the worldview of lesser jihad which is the armed struggle against the enemies of Islam.

Warrior spirituality is the religion of many current American Christian evangelicals. For example, take this interview on November 21, 2020 of Franklin Graham, son, and successor of televangelist Billy Graham, by evangelical radio host Eric Metaxas (as reported by Baptist News): Metaxes

> *asked Graham about the "very bizarre situation to be living in a country where some people seem to exist to undermine the president of the United States."*
>
> *"Well, I believe it's almost a demonic power that is trying ..." Graham elaborated before being cut off by Metaxas.*
> *"It's not almost demonic," the interviewer interjected. "You know and I know, at the heart, it's a spiritual battle."*
>
> *"It's a spiritual battle," Graham conceded, steering the conversation to the nation's low unemployment rate and a booming economy.*

Traditional Consciousness

The Traditional stage of consciousness is the most prevalent stage of spirituality in the world, estimated at between 40 and 55 percent of the world population. This stage of consciousness evolved during what has been labeled the Axial Age (800 BCE to 200 BCE). It represents a shift from a focus just on adherence to laws to a focus on morality. I have written much about the Axial Age previously in this book, so I will not belabor the point here. This increased level of consciousness represents a shift from self-centeredness and caring for one's family and tribe to others in one's own culture. There is movement from egocentrism to ethnocentrism, i.e., care for others "like me." There is, however, distrust, fear, and prejudice towards "the other" such as people of other ethnic groups, races, and homosexuals. Churches at this stage are authoritarian and patriarchal and have been resistant to women in leadership positions. There is attraction to strong, alpha male leaders. Gender roles are "traditional;" women are expected to be feminine, and men are expected to be masculine. God and country are intertwined into a Christian nationalism.

The concern at this stage is for conformity and fitting in. This worldview remains within Kohlberg's conventional stage of morality. Much from the previous stages of consciousness remain in this stage including reliance on authority for truth, literal interpretation of scripture, intolerance for those who are different, moralism and legalism. In the Christian church there is emphasis on having relationship with God and his son, Jesus. God, however, is both personal but also distant, i.e., being "out there" and separate rather than being of substance with us. We can communicate with God in prayer. God will intervene in human affairs when asked in prayer. God is loving but also a disciplinarian. The ultimate goal is eventual communion with God somewhere else, i.e., Heaven. The hymn *What a Friend We Have in Jesus* is reflective of a traditional worldview.

What a friend we have in Jesus,
all our sins and griefs to bear!
What a privilege to carry
everything to God in prayer!

Are we weak and heavy laden,
cumbered with a load of care?
Precious Savior, still our refuge,
take it to the Lord in prayer.

O what peace we often forfeit,
O what needless pain we bear,
All because we do not carry
everything to God in prayer.

Do your friends despise, forsake you?
Take it to the Lord in prayer!
In His arms He'll take and shield you;
you will find a solace there.

Have we trials and temptations?
Is there trouble anywhere?
We should never be discouraged;
take it to the Lord in prayer.

Blessed Savior, Thou has promised
Thou wilt all our burdens bear
May we ever, Lord, be bringing all to
Thee in earnest prayer.

Can we find a friend so faithful
who will all our sorrows share?
Jesus knows our every weakness;
take it to the Lord in prayer.

Soon in glory bright unclouded there
will be no need for prayer
Rapture, praise and endless worship
will be our sweet portion there.

Modernist Consciousness

Modernist consciousness arose as a result of the Enlightenment of the 17th and 18th centuries, also known as the "Age of Reason". This marks a change from relying on authority and purported revelations for truth to scientific investigation and reason. It is estimated that 15-30 percent of the world population is at this stage of spiritual development. Although the developed western world is mostly of a modernist world view in regards to such fields as medicine, technology, and science, it is less prevalent in religion where traditional consciousness is still more prevalent. Modernist consciousness welcomes questioning, free thinking and individuality.

It is not infrequent in this stage of development for individuals to become (at least for a period) agnostic or atheist. For others it is movement from an anthropomorphic god to a much more transcendent god, to deistic beliefs rather than theistic, or movement to pantheism or panentheism. Many of you might question the idea that a movement from faith to agnosticism or atheism is progress. It represents progress because it reflects progression from just blind acceptance of teachings to thinking and questioning of what one really believes. Can one truly believe something if one never gave it any real thought?

This stage of consciousness is to be found commonly in "mainline" Protestantism, i.e., in such denominations as the Presbyterian Church USA, Episcopal Church, Disciples of Christ, Methodist Church, the United Church of Christ and the Unitarian Universalist Church. It is also the stage of consciousness of Reformed Judaism, whereas Orthodox Judaism is at the traditional stage. Modernists generally do not believe that religion was *revealed*, but rather that religion has *evolved*.

The *historical-critical method* is an outgrowth of this stage of consciousness. Rather than a reliance on tradition and authority to understand ancient scriptures, modern scholars critically investigate the sources of sacred texts, examining the historical context of the writings. An example of this scholarship is the *Jesus Seminar*. The purpose of the seminar was to gather Biblical scholars together to determine what is historically known about Jesus and his teachings. The founder of the Jesus Seminar, Biblical scholar Robert Funk, notes that the fellows of the seminar came to a consensus on the following conclusions which I think demonstrate some stark differences between the traditional worldview of Jesus and the Modernist view.

Jesus of Nazareth did not refer to himself as the Messiah, nor did he claim to be a divine being who descended to earth from heaven in order to die as a sacrifice for the sins of the world. These are claims that some people in the early church made about Jesus, not claims he made about himself.

At the heart of Jesus' teaching and actions was a vision of a life under the reign of God (or, in the empire of God) in which God's generosity and goodness is regarded as the model and measure of human life; everyone is accepted as a child of God and thus liberated both from the ethnocentric confines of traditional Judaism and from the secularizing servitude and meagerness of their lives under the rule of the empire of Rome.

Jesus did not hold an apocalyptic view of the reign (or kingdom) of God—that by direct intervention God was about to bring history to an end and bring a new, perfect order of life into being. Rather, in Jesus' teaching the reign of God is a vision of what life in this world could be, not a vision of life in a future world that would soon be brought into being by a miraculous act of god.

Modernist consciousness embraces reason and science. *Miracles* are seen not as supernatural events but as consistent with the laws of physics. For example, in Matthew 14 there is a story about a crowd of 5,000 people. It was getting dark, and the disciples worried about the need for them to eat. All they could muster up to feed them was five loaves of bread and two fishes. They passed this food out, and amazingly all the people had enough to eat. The modernist would interpret this not as food magically appearing out of thin air, but rather that this was a story of unselfish sharing. The people in the crowd shared what they had, and all were fed.

An example of a hymn that might reflect a modernist world view is *All Are Welcome*:

Let us build a house where love can dwell
And all can safely live
A place where saints and children tell
How hearts learn to forgive
Built of hopes and dreams and visions
Rock of faith and vault of grace
Here the love of Christ shall end divisions

All are welcome, all are welcome
All are welcome in this place

Let us build a house where prophets speak

And words are strong and true
Where all God's children dare to seek
To dream God's reign anew

Here the love of God, through Jesus
Is revealed in time and space
As we share in Christ the feast that frees us

All are welcome, all are welcome
All are welcome in this place

Criticisms of the modern church and modern consciousness include cultural materialism. As a result of the modern age and the industrial revolution, people are used to having a lot of *stuff*. For most people throughout history the focus was on just getting basic needs met, i.e., food, shelter, safety, family and friends. Now, in our society, the focus is on having fancy cars, trips, trendy clothes, and the latest technological innovations. Money, possessions, and power have become a god for many. The Oxford dictionary defines materialism as a tendency to consider material possessions and physical comfort as more important than spiritual values. This growing materialism applies not only to those of a modern consciousness, but also to those at previous levels of consciousness.

A disturbing example of this is the perverse doctrine of *prosperity theology* which is the belief that worshiping God and donating to the church will be rewarded with more *stuff*, i.e., health and wealth. Basically, this is a throw-back to the days of burnt offerings (tribal consciousness) in that individuals are giving in order to get.

Another criticism of modernist consciousness is another kind of *materialism*, also called *physicalism*, which is the belief that nothing exists other than the world of physical matter. Some people believe that nothing exists that is not matter/energy, i.e., that there is no immaterial soul, and consciousness is nothing more than neural activity and biochemistry. There is the tendency to reject any notion that cannot be investigated and proven by science. A related philosophical idea is *reductionism*, which is the idea that complex phenomena can be understood by breaking it down into its individual smallest parts. In the next chapter I will discuss a phenomenon known as *emergence* which would suggest that many phenomena are more than the sum of its parts.

Postmodern Consciousness

Some conceive of a further stage of spiritual development called *Postmodern*. An estimated 5 to 10 percent of the world's population is at this stage. In many respects it is reaction against some aspects of modernism, particularly to both types of materialism, i.e., the philosophy of physicalism and the shallowness of cultural materialism (the focus on acquisition of wealth). Postmodernism does not limit itself to scientific exploration to understand the world and life. Postmodernism is open to exploration of spiritual possibilities, even if they cannot be tested scientifically. Take for example the notion of a God. We should not dismiss the possibility that a God exists just because we cannot prove God's existence. We also cannot prove God's non-existence. Postmodernism stresses a return to the spiritual quest. Perhaps a good way to describe individuals at this stage of consciousness is "spiritual but not religious". Although it is not necessary to conceive of a God to explain the universe, that does not preclude the possibility that there is a God, although perhaps not bearing any similarity to the God of traditional religion.

Postmodernism emphasizes a worldcentric morality, i.e. compassion and concern for all of humanity and not just for the people of one's own country. It stresses inclusion and universal human rights. It opposes racism and sexism. It stresses social justice. It stresses taking care of our planet. Not only does it stress care of all humanity, but it emphasizes animal rights and care for all of life. A hymn that reflects aspects of a postmodernist viewpoint is *This is My Song* (which is sung to the tune of Finlandia):

This is my song, O God of all the nations, A song of peace for lands afar and mine. This is my home, the country where my heart is, Here are my hopes, my dreams, my holy shrine. But other hearts in other lands are beating, With hopes and dreams as true and high as mine.

My country's skies are bluer than the ocean, And sunlight beams on clover leaf and pine. But other lands have sunlight too, and clover, And skies are everywhere as blue as mine. O hear my song, thou God of all the nations, A song of peace for their land and for mine

It is at this stage that I would expect to find Kohlberg's post-conventional morality. At this stage individuals realize that what is moral and what is legal are two completely different things. Something can be illegal (for example smoking marijuana) but not immoral, and something can be considered immoral but not illegal. At this stage individuals will defy a law if they personally feel it is immoral. Conscientious objectors to war would be an example of this. At this stage people develop personal principles that guide their behavior, and these principles might be different than what predominates in the society in which they live. These principles typically reflect the principles of liberal democracy such as individual freedoms, the dignity of all human beings, justice, fairness, and commitment to truth. These principles are reflected in the Universal Declaration of Human Rights, a resolution of the United Nations made in 1948.

At this stage people try to live their lives consistent with their principles rather than loyalty to tradition, a person, an ethnic group, country, a political party, or even family. Individuals act because "it is the right thing to do," not because it is of personal benefit, or that it gets one out of trouble, or that it is expected by society, family, political party, or country. Ends do not justify the means.

There is a term called *wokeness* that has entered our political lexicon. It reflects this postmodern world view and emphasizes awareness of social and racial injustice. The term reflects the political left's push for societal awareness of such issues as institutional racism, global warming and environmentalism, LGBTQ rights, and gender equality. For the political right the term *woke* has been viewed pejoratively and associated with political correctness and left-wing radicalism. I would view the political right's disdain, however, as resistance to progress. One way of defining the term "conservative" is to be cautious and to be leery and even fearful of change. One way of defining "progressive" is to be at the forefront of societal progress. Spiritual/moral consciousness has evolved in human's history. Most people no longer think genocide is okay, as they once did. Most people no longer think it is fine to torture and kill people because they have "wrong" beliefs. Most no longer think that owning other humans is good. There has been evolution in consciousness leading to human rights and democracy. There have been individuals at the forefront of these changes, and other individuals who have fought these changes to the end.

I personally like the concept of "wokeness." It resonates with my experience. I have *awakened* to a wider and more accurate worldview due to ongoing education and contemplation. I have awakened to esoteric knowledge that is beyond the exoteric. An example is the apostle Paul's "Damascus experience" in which it is said "scales fell from his eyes." Saul, as he initially was called, was a persecutor of the early Christians until he had a conversion experience. He heard the voice of God and became blind for three days until Ananias laid hands on him. He was filled with the Holy Spirit and regained his sight because the "scales fell from his eyes." He became a follower of the Christ. The important meaning is that Paul finally awakened to the truth of Jesus. I have had experiences through study and contemplation in which I have had "aha" experiences. It felt like scales fell from my eyes- I awoke to new realizations. To quote the old hymn *Amazing Grace*: "I once was blind but now I see."

There are also weaknesses frequently associated with postmodernism. One weakness is some tendencies to embrace new *ageism*, a movement which gained popularity in the 1970s and 1980s. The movement included diverse and many unscientific beliefs and practices including the ancient practice of astrology, reincarnation, channeling and other psychic phenomena, crystals, angels, alternative medicines and medical treatments, the occult, and the coming of an age of Aquarius from where the term "new age" comes from. The movement represented a growing interest in spirituality, but unfortunately it also was associated with some regression in terms of magical beliefs.

Another weakness is an emphasis on *relativism*. There is often more emphasis on feelings than logic. The Oxford dictionary defines relativism as the doctrine that knowledge, truth, and morality exist in relation to culture, society, or historical context, and are not absolute. You might hear a premodernist say that such and such is "my truth" rather than stressing the importance of finding *the* truth. The following quote from Ralph Waldo Emerson reflects this position:

> *The soul is the perceiver and revealer of truth. We know truth when we see it, let skeptic and scoffer say what they choose. Foolish people ask you, when you have spoken what they do not wish to hear, 'How do you know it is truth, and not an error of your own?' We know truth when we see it, from opinion, as we know when we are awake that we are awake.*

A criticism of this view is provided by philosopher Daniel Dennett:

> *Postmodernism, the school of "thought" that proclaimed "There are no truths, only interpretations" has largely played itself out in absurdity, but it has left behind a generation of academics in the humanities disabled by their distrust of the very idea of truth and their disrespect for evidence, settling for "conversations" in which nobody is wrong and nothing can be confirmed*

Integral Consciousness

The final stage of consciousness I will discuss is *Integral*. By the term "integral" I am referring to a few types of integration. First, I mean multi-disciplinary. Let us learn from the knowledge gained from all academic disciplines including history, philosophy, psychology, and all the branches of science. Let us also integrate all of the wisdom from various cultures and spiritual traditions. Ken Wilber in *The Integral Vision* (2007) writes about his integral vision:

> *What if we took literally everything that all the various cultures have to tell us about human potential- about spiritual growth, psychological growth, social growth- and put it all on the table? What if we attempted to find the critically essential keys to human growth, based on the sum total of human knowledge now open to us? What if we attempted based on extensive cross-cultural study, to use all of the world's great traditions to create a composite map, a comprehensive map, an all-inclusive or integral map that included the best elements from all of them?*

This integral vision has been Wilber's life work. Wilber stresses the evolutionary nature of these stages of consciousness. He said that rather than perceiving opposing worldviews, we should recognize that one stage builds upon another. Each higher stage transcends but includes the positive aspects of the previous stages. Steve McIntosh in his book *Integral Consciousness and the Future of Evolution* (2007) gives a nice summary of this:

> *An enduring contribution of tribal culture can be seen in the necessity of family loyalty- and this same sense of primal loyalty can be magnified by the values of the higher levels to include not just loyalty to our blood kin, but loyalty to the entire family of humanity. Similarly, the fierce sense of individual autonomy that arises with warrior consciousness can be carried forward to preserve personal freedom and individual liberties even within complex, interdependent societies.*
>
> *Traditional consciousness provides an increased ability to see the difference between right and wrong. Modernist consciousness provides new insight into the material nature of the external universe and the natural "rights of man." Postmodern consciousness provides the ability to recognize the excesses of modernism, as well as*

the many alternatives to the modernist way of seeing things. And now, through the emerging values of integral consciousness we are given fresh insight into how consciousness and culture develop and evolve, and this shows us how we can become agents of evolution by participating more directly in its unfolding.

More important than what religious tradition one comes from or belongs to is the stage of spiritual development one is at within each religious tradition. This is the most important takeaway from this chapter. Let me say it again: your "religion" is not important. Your level of spiritual development is. Let me use my own religious tradition of Christianity as an example. Being a "Christian" is more than a binary choice. Many Christians would disagree with this statement. They might say that "Jack asked Jesus to be his Lord and Savior, and so now he is a Christian." Many believe that *conversion* is a one-time event. I disagree. Conversion should be an ongoing *process*. Let me compare it to marriage. Getting married might be a one-time event, but that does not mean the work of marriage is over. The critical essence of a marriage is having relationship, and relationships take work. Being a Christian is about having relationship with God, and this takes work. Being a Hindu, Buddhist, or Muslim is about having a relationship with God, and this takes work. This involves growing up and also "waking up." More about this later in the book.

Spiritual Development in the Bible

One can see these stages of spiritual development played out in the Hebrew scriptures. The stage of development of the earliest peoples in the Old Testament were tribal. Religion consisted only of making sacrifices to God in order to please God and to gain favor. The first instance of sacrifice in the book of Genesis is of the sons of Adam and Eve giving a sacrifice to God; Cain brought "an offering of the fruit of the ground" and Abel gave "the firstlings of his flock."

After the great flood Noah "built an altar to the Lord and took of every clean animal and of every clean bird, and offered burnt offerings on the altar." In chapter 12 of Genesis Abram is said to have built altars to God.

Up until the time of Moses religious practice entailed only creating altars to God and making offerings to please God, with one exception. In chapter 17 of Genesis Abram is told by God to be circumcised and to also have all male offspring circumcised at eight days old. This distinguished the descents of Abram from the other peoples of Mesopotamia.

Warrior Consciousness sees its beginnings in the Hebrew scriptures with Moses, although Tribal Consciousness also continued for many centuries. Remember that this stage of consciousness is characterized by absolute allegiance to authority and a legalistic adherence to laws and rules. Of course, the most well-known of Moses' laws are the "Ten Commandments," but there are hundreds of others which are enumerated in the Old Testament books of Exodus, Leviticus, Numbers and Deuteronomy. These writings along with the book of Genesis together are known as the *Torah*, the books of Mosaic law. There are laws about how to properly make sacrifices and offerings, moral laws (e.g., not to kill or steal), cleanliness laws (e.g., what are clean and "unclean" foods), purity laws (e.g., how to deal with lepers, menstruation and seminal cmissions), social laws (e.g. in regards to slavery, marriage and divorce, property inheritance), and laws about how to commemorate and celebrate the Jewish feasts (holidays) such as Passover.

The reader is also reminded that Warrior Consciousness entails a desire for domination and a rigid "us versus them" mentality. The good people were the followers of YAWEH, and the bad people were those who followed the other gods. This was a religion of extermination and genocide of one's "enemies."

When the Lord your God brings you into the land that you are about to enter and occupy, and he clears away many nations before you- the Hittites, the Girgashites, the Amorites, the Canaanites, the Perizzites, the Hivites, and the Jebusites, seven nations mightier and more numerous than you- and when the Lord your God gives them over to you and you defeat them, then you must utterly destroy them.

*Make no covenant with them and show them no mercy.
Deut. 7:1-2*

*For you are a people holy to the Lord your God; the Lord
your God has chosen you out of all the peoples on earth to
be his people, his treasured possession. Deut. 7:6*

Traditional Consciousness makes its advent with the Hebrew
prophets hundreds of years later. Morality now becomes central to
the Hebrew's religion. Take the prophet Micah for example:

*With what shall I come before the Lord and bow myself
before God on high? Shall I come before him with burnt
offerings, with calves a year old? Will the Lord be pleased
with thousands of rams, with ten thousands of rivers of oil?
Shall I give my firstborn for my transgression, the fruit of my
body for the sin of my soul? He has told you, O mortal,
what is good; and what does the Lord require of you but to
do justice, and to love kindness, and to walk humbly with
your God? Micah 6:6-8*

And the prophet Amos:

*I hate, I despise your festivals, and I take no delight in your
solemn assemblies. Even though you offer me your burnt
offerings and grain offerings, I will not accept them; and the
offerings of well being of your fatted animals I will not look
upon. Take away from me the noise of your songs; I will not
listen to the melody of your harps. But let justice roll down
like waters, and righteousness like an ever flowing stream.
Amos 5:21-24*

These Hebrew prophets are saying it is not offerings and
sacrifices that matter. Nor are the festivals and holidays of prime
importance. What matters is love and justice. This traditional
consciousness continues in the Christian New Testament with the
writings of Paul and the writings about the words of Jesus.

Modern consciousness is not reflected in the Hebrew or Christian scriptures as it is the result of the Enlightenment of the 17th and 18th centuries CE.

The Culture Wars

When one understands these stages of consciousness and spiritual development one can make more sense of the present "culture wars" in the United States and elsewhere. In our country Traditional, Modern, and Postmodern worldviews predominate. Let us see how these often-conflicting world views impact the hot button issue of homosexuality, as an example.

The traditionalist world view of Christianity holds that homosexuality is sinful because it says so in the Bible, which is the ultimate source of authority. The Bible is believed to be the literal word of God, and so if God says it, it of course must be believed and followed. It is the duty of Christians to help homosexuals by witnessing to them about the error of their ways. Homosexuality is clearly unnatural; God created Adam and Eve, not Adam and Steve.

The traditionalists long for a return to "traditional" gender roles and patriarchal authority. Evangelical Christian churches and the Roman Catholic Church have long been opposed to women holding positions of authority and are attracted to alpha males. The traditionalists like strong leadership from men who are confident, independent, assertive (maybe even a little aggressive), charismatic, strong, and bold. These are characteristics traditionalists do not like, however, in their women.

Those with a warrior world view might believe that homosexuals should be punished- even put to death. It was not uncommon for gay people to have been executed in the past, and even in recent times executions have happened in countries that have sharia law, including Iran, Somalia, Afghanistan, and Saudi Arabia.

The modernist argues that science has shown that homosexuality is an immutable trait that cannot be changed. It would make no sense for God to punish people for being who they were made to be. Homosexuality is natural; research has shown that bisexuality and homosexuality are common throughout the animal kingdom. The writers of the Bible had no knowledge about homosexuality as an orientation. People at that historical time period and throughout most of the history would have found it inconceivable that two people of the same sex would marry, as marriage existed not for love, companionship, or sex but for procreation, political reasons, and subsistence. Women had no way of surviving without a man to take care of them until only recently. Stephanie Coontz in her book *Marriage, a History (2005)* said:

> *In the eighteenth century, people began to adopt the radical new idea that love should be the most fundamental reason for marriage and that young people should be free to choose their marriage partners on the basis of love. This sentimentalization of the love-based marriage in the nineteenth century and its sexualization in the twentieth each represented a logical step in the evolution of this new approach to marriage.*

> *Until the late eighteenth century, most societies around the world saw marriage as far too vital an economic and political institution to be left entirely to the free choice of the two individuals involved, especially if they were going to base their decision on something as unreasoning and transitory as love. The more I learned about the ancient history of marriage, the more I realized what a gigantic marital revolution had occurred in Western Europe and North American during the Enlightenment.*

The modernists would also argue that *biological sex* is not such a clear-cut concept as the traditionalists would like to believe. Most commonly males are those who are genetically XY which is expressed physiologically (phenotype) with a penis and scrotum. Females are those who typically are genetically XX which is expressed physiologically with a vagina and breast development. However, there are exceptions. There are XY individuals born with a vagina and breast development (and no penis/scrotum); this is called Androgen Insensitivity Syndrome.   There are also XX individuals born with a scrotum and penis (and no vagina or breast development); this is called Congenital Adrenal Hyperplasia. There are males with an additional X (female) chromosome making them XXY; this is called Klinefelter's Syndrome. Determining one's sex is not always as simple as some would think.

While the term *sex* refers to biology, the term *gender* refers to psychological traits. Traditionalists generally prescribe rather rigid roles and traits to males and females. Males should be *masculine*, and females should be *feminine*. The modernists would argue that gender is more the result of culture than biology. Traditionalists have believed that certain types of work are meant for men (e.g., science, engineering, construction) and other jobs are meant for women (e.g., nursing). The modernists would point out that the evidence certainly suggests otherwise. There are very successful women generals and admirals in the military, accomplished women scientists and mathematicians, and well-respected women police officers and construction workers. There are also successful male teachers, nurses, and caregivers.

The postmodernists would add that we need to let people have the freedom to be who they are and to do the work that they wish to pursue. All of humanity should be respected and cherished. Nobody should be denigrated or minimized. They also might question how love can ever be wrong. How can it be wrong to find a person who you really connect with and want to share your life with? How can it be wrong to care so much about a person that their life becomes as important to you as your own?

Perhaps nothing personifies the current cultural war more than Donald Trump. Modernists and postmodernists have been confounded and stunned by Trump's rise to power. For one thing, modernists value objective truth and an accurate view of reality. As a result of Trump, disinformation has become epidemic. The term *alternative facts*, otherwise known as lies, have entered our lexicon. Trump has demonstrated that the strategy (used previously with success by autocratic tyrants) of being able to convince the populace of a falsehood will be successful if you say it enough times and with enough confidence. The Washington Post reported that Trump made 30, 573 false or misleading claims during his four years in office.

Another value of modernism is democracy. In another Washington Post article (Oct. 29, 2020) titled *Trump's most worrying attacks on democracy, in one giant chart* it was reported that "President Trump has done more to undermine American democracy than any chief executive in the modern era, according to data compiled by the Varieties of Democracy project" which is an international organization that monitors the state of democracy around the world. Trump has had relentless attacks on all the American democratic institutions that are checks on executive power, namely the press, the judiciary, the department of justice, and members of congress. This move toward autocracy culminated in Trump's refusal to accept the results of a free and fair election and then attempting to lead a coup. This has affected America's standing and reputation in the world:

> *Konstantin Kosachyov, chairmen of the international affairs committee of the Russian upper house was reported to have said "The celebration of democracy is over. This is, alas, actually the bottom, I say this without a hint of gloating. America is no longer charting the course, and therefore has lost all its rights to set it. And especially to impose it on others."*

> *President Hassan Rouhani of Iran said in a televised speech "What happened in America showed what a failure Western democracy is...A populist man damaged the reputation of his country."*

> *President Emmerson Mnangagwa of Zimbabwe tweeted: "Last year, President Trump extended painful economic sanctions placed on Zimbabwe, citing concerns about Zimbabwe's democracy. Yesterday's events showed that the U.S. has no moral right to punish another nation under the guise of upholding democracy."*

Another key tenet of modernism is reliance on science. There are numerous examples of rejection of science in the administration, but of note is the Trump administration's rejection of climate science and numerous instances of not following scientific recommendations in regards to the Covid 19 pandemic. The New England Journal of Medicine, one of the most prestigious medical journals in the world had an October 8, 2020 editorial about the U.S. response to the pandemic:

Covid-19 has created a crisis throughout the world. This crisis has produced a test of leadership. With no good options to combat a novel pathogen, countries were forced to make hard choices about how to respond. Here in the United States, our leaders have failed that test. They have taken a crisis and turned it into a tragedy.

The magnitude of this failure is astonishing. According to the Johns Hopkins Center for Systems Science and Engineering, the United States leads the world in Covid-19 cases and in deaths due to the disease, far exceeding the numbers in much larger countries, such as China. The death rate in this country is more than double that of Canada, exceeds that of Japan, a country with a vulnerable and elderly population, by a factor of almost 50, and even dwarfs the rates in lower-middle-income countries, such as Vietnam, by a factor of almost 2000. Covid-19 is an overwhelming challenge, and many factors contribute to its severity. But the one we can control is how we behave. And in the United States we have consistently behaved poorly.

Also important to modernist and postmodernist consciousness are human rights and rejection of racism, homophobia, xenophobia, Islamophobia, and sexism. Not only does Trump not show concern about these issues, but he plays upon people's hatred to his advantage. The predominant stage of consciousness here is warrior consciousness. Modernist consciousness stresses morality and increased care for others. It stresses the tenets of the golden rule, to do unto others as you would have them do unto you. The actions by Trump leading up to January 6, 2020 and by his adherents on that date reflect a warrior consciousness, i.e., allegiance to an authoritarian and desire to dominate/vanquish the "other side".

Many wonder how Christian evangelicals could have overwhelmingly supported this president. After all, evangelicals primarily espouse a traditional stage of consciousness which emphasizes the importance of morality. For them character greatly mattered during the Clinton administration. Why is it that the allegations of sexual misconduct by twenty-six women against Trump and a conviction for sexual abuse (essentially rape) are unimportant? Many psychiatrists and psychologists (myself included) have used such diagnostic terms as *psychopath*, *sociopath*, and *malignant narcissist* to diagnose this president. What this means is that this is an individual who lacks empathy, cares for nobody but himself, and would do anything to maintain power and money. Those are attributes that one would least want in a leader, and yet such individuals do gain power (e.g., Mussolini, Hitler, Stalin, Putin). Why in particular would Christians be drawn to this man, as he is the antithesis of Jesus.

Kristin Kobes Du Mez PhD is a professor of history at religiously conservative Calvin University in Grand Rapids and has shared some insights about Trump and his followers in her book *Jesus and John Wayne: How White Evangelicals Corrupted a Faith and Fractured a Nation* (2020):

> But evangelical support for Trump was no aberration, nor was it merely a pragmatic choice. It was, rather, the culmination of evangelicals' embrace of militant masculinity, an ideology that enshrines patriarchal authority and condones the callous display of power, at home and abroad. By the time Trump arrived proclaiming himself their savior, conservative white evangelicals had already traded a faith that privileges humility and elevates "the least

of these" for one that derides gentleness as the province of wusses. Rather than turning the other cheek, they'd resolved to defend their faith and their nation, secure in the knowledge that the ends justify the means. Having replaced the Jesus of the Gospels with a vengeful warrior Christ, it's no wonder many came to think of Trump in the same way. In 2016, many observers were stunned at evangelicals' apparent betrayal of their own values. In reality, evangelicals did not cast their vote despite their beliefs, but because of them.

The present cultural "wars" in the United States and other western countries are said to be between "conservatives" and "progressives." I would say the conflict is due to warrior and traditional stages of consciousness conflicting with modern and postmodern stages of consciousness.

The split in the current Supreme Court between "conservatives" and "liberals" is also really a split between a traditional consciousness and a modern/postmodern consciousness, even though the conflict is often framed currently as an argument between *originalism* and other methods of interpreting the constitution of the United States. It is the job of the legislature to create laws, and it is the job of the Supreme Court to interpret laws and to determine the constitutionality of laws.

Since the 1980s the idea of originalism has gained some popularity. Its most well-known proponents had been Antonin Scalia (who was approved for the Supreme Court in 1986) and Robert Bork (who was rejected for the Supreme Court in 1987). Originalists maintain the principle that the court cannot make constitutional decisions unless the issue at hand is specifically addressed in the constitution. For example, Kurt Andersen (2020) notes "Bork ruled as a federal judge that the navy could fire a sailor for being gay because there was no explicit "constitutional right to engage in homosexual conduct"". Of course, most things are not specifically addressed in the constitution. If in the future there was a rise in antisemitism in the country and the congress made a law outlawing Jews from procreating, originalism would suggest that it could be constitutional because the rights of Jews to procreate is not explicitly granted in the constitution.

The conservatives on the court have not been consistent in applying this principle of originalism. For example, in the court ruling of Citizens United the court in a 5-4 decision determined that corporations could donate unlimited money in election spending. Yet corporations are not mentioned anywhere in the constitution. In fact, American corporations were not developed until the 1790s (after the ratification of the constitution in 1788). Many legal scholars opine that conservatives' ideology really is about a traditional, fundamentalist worldview.

Senator Sheldon Whitehouse wrote a book titled *The Scheme* (2022) which details a concerted effort by big business and American moneyed elites to put individuals on the Supreme Court that protect and promote their interests for power and money and to promote a fundamentalist worldview. I will discuss this further in chapter six of this book. Whitehouse points out that the perpetrators of this "scheme" need legal theories to "give the movement intellectual cover and allows its adherents to shield themselves with 'theories' or 'doctrines,' without confessing the extreme outcomes they seek or the special interests they serve."

> *The biggest canard of them all is "originalism," the legal theory that launched the Federalist Society and the conservative right-wing legal movement. "Originalism" started as the notion that courts had strayed from the original text and meaning of the Constitution and should return to a mythical "original" interpretation, But originally, voting was limited to people who were white, male, and owned property. Originally, Black slaves were quantified as "three-fifths" of a person. Originally, women had virtually no economic role or property rights. Originally, Blacks and whites could not marry, and gays could be prosecuted and imprisoned. And originally, an agrarian society needed little consumer protection; without massive industries, it needed no protections from abuse by massive industries. For an arch-conservative, you can see the charm of "originalism." But most normal people don't*

*think that what everyone needs is a bit more 1788 in their
lives.*

Jesus chastised the Jewish pharisees for their legalism and
picayune adherence to Jewish laws and missing the most important
religious principles which were the basis for Jewish law: to love God
and to love our neighbors. Similarly, the conservatives on the court
seem to be missing the values that I believe our founding fathers
primarily pursued, namely democracy, humanism, increased
individual freedoms, and other enlightenment principles. These
values are reflected in the Declaration of Independence and the U.S.
Constitution.

To clarify many rights based on these principles the founders
wrote the bill of rights and other amendments to the constitution
including the equal protection clause of the 14th amendment.
Supreme court justice Robert Jackson put it well in the majority
opinion of *West Virginia State Board of Education v. Barnette* in
1943: "The very purpose of a Bill of Rights was to withdraw certain
subjects from the vicissitudes of political controversy, to place them
beyond the reach of majorities and officials and to establish them as
legal principles to be applied by the courts. One's right to life,
liberty, and property, to free speech, a free press, freedom of worship
and assembly, and other fundamental rights may not be submitted to
vote; they depend on the outcome of no elections."

What does it require to develop spiritually? How do we
expand our consciousness. How do we develop a more accurate and
comprehensive world view? First, it takes education. If we profess
dedication to a sacred scripture, we should be knowledgeable about
that which we venerate, particularly being able to explain why it
should be venerated.

I would advocate what has been referred to as a *liberal arts*
education. Unfortunately, many believe the only reason for an
education is to establish a vocation and to make money. A broad
education is also important to be developed as a human being and to
answer for ourselves the purpose and meaning of life and to develop
an accurate world view. Most importantly, a liberal education strives

to teach students how to think. Princeton University has a nice explanation of a liberal arts education on their website:

> *A liberal arts education offers an expansive intellectual grounding in all kinds of humanistic inquiry. By exploring issues, ideas and methods across the humanities and the arts, and the natural and social sciences, you will learn to read critically, write cogently and think broadly. These skills will elevate your conversations in the classroom and strengthen your social and cultural analysis; they will cultivate the tools necessary to allow you to navigate the world's most complex issues.*
>
> *A liberal arts education challenges you to consider not only how to solve problems, but also trains you to ask which problems to solve and why, preparing you for positions of leadership and a life of service to the nation and all of humanity. We provide a liberal arts education to all of our undergraduates, including those who major in engineering.*
>
> *As President Christopher Eisgruber, class of 1983, stated in his 2013 installation address: "[A] liberal arts education is a vital foundation for both individual flourishing and the well-being of our society."*

What I am really talking about in this book is human development which entails spiritual development, emotional development, cognitive development, and moral development. These things all correlate with each other, and to truly develop as a human being it takes not only education and the ability to think critically but also the ability to reflect and introspect. It requires us to come to terms with parts of ourselves which are suppressed or repressed. In Jungian terms this is called the shadow.

Psychotherapy

Human development comes not only from learning about the external world but also examining our internal world. To grow emotionally we must get to know ourselves. For me the biggest psychological hurdle of my life was coming to terms with being gay. Other people have various other issues to come to grips with, such as dealing with childhood abuse/neglect or other life traumas, coming to terms with an addiction, struggles with existential questions, or just learning how to love and accept oneself. While there are many ways to get to know oneself and to resolve issues, counseling and psychotherapy are probably the most direct and expedient way.

There is much about ourselves that is unconscious and out of awareness. The unconscious is often compared to an iceberg, where what we are aware of is only "the tip of the iceberg" of our mind. Our unconscious minds contain a vast reservoir of information. Much of what is in the unconscious is scary and threatening. We guard against threatening information about ourselves with defense mechanisms. For example, an alcoholic might rationalize his drinking; "I drink because I have chronic pain." "I got arrested for drunk driving because my license plate was expired." The alcoholic might minimize: "I don't drink every day." "I can quit any time I want."

If we were the victim of child sexual abuse, we might suppress this trauma (i.e. consciously pushing memories out of awareness), or we might repress these memories (which is the unconscious suppression of memories).

Another common defense mechanism is projection in which difficult or unacceptable unconscious thoughts or feelings about oneself are not owned but are instead attributed to others.

Buried unresolved issues have great effects on our lives despite being unconscious. Let me give you an example: homophobia and anti-gay bullying. Research has suggested that those individuals with the strongest hostility to LGBTQ people are more likely to have repressed homosexual attraction themselves. Think about it. Other than individuals who might have suffered trauma from a gay person in the past (and thus project this hatred onto other gay people), why would people have such intense hatred and go out of their way to bully or even assault gay people if these people have nothing to do with their lives?

The purpose of insight-oriented psychotherapies is to discover things about ourselves which in turn will help us to be more productive, loving, honest, thoughtful, and insightful. It can improve our self-esteem.

Cognitive behavioral therapy can help us eliminate self-defeating behaviors and to change thoughts that are irrational and self-defeating. It is our thoughts that affect our feelings, and so by changing irrational thoughts we can change unpleasant feelings and conditions such as depression and anxiety. Psychoanalytic therapies go even deeper and help us discover conflicts and traumas that are unconscious.

Many people regularly operate by letting their emotions rule over intellect. There are many times that we do need to pay attention to intuition and our instincts. If I meet a stranger, and my intuition tells me to not trust that person, I should pay attention to that, even though I consciously might not know why. If I give it some thought I might be able to figure out my feelings though. Perhaps there is good basis for my distrust, but maybe the stranger only reminds me of someone else from my past who was malicious. In this case I need to remind myself that my feelings have to do with the person from the past and not this new person (the technical terms for this are projection and transference).

Psychotherapy and counseling give us the opportunity to "wrestle with our demons," or what Jungians refer to as "the shadow", i.e., those parts of the self that are undesirable and often instinctual and irrational. Carl Jung said "Everyone carries a shadow, and the less it is embodied in the individual's conscious life, the blacker and denser it is."

I have found it not at all uncommon for evangelical Christians to look for a "Christian counselor" to do therapy with. Implicit in this request is the desire to find someone who thinks the same way and has the same values. Such people, I find, are really looking for someone to be an authority and to tell them what to do. At its extreme this type of counseling is known as *nouthetic* counseling which discourages introspection and questioning and emphasizes "right" behavior as defined by a literal reading of the Bible. This is completely the opposite of professional counseling whose goal is to help the client find their own answers by introspecting and processing. It is unprofessional for licensed therapists to tell clients how to live their lives. I believe a very good model for what should happen in counseling or psychotherapy is the *Johari Window* shown in the following table:

Open (Things you are aware of about yourself, and others are as well)	Blind (Things about ourselves that we aren't aware of, but others can see)
Secret (Things that we are aware of about ourselves, but we keep hidden from others)	Unknown (Things that are in our unconscious. Neither we nor others are aware of these things)

This model reflects four windows of our personhood that each of us have. The upper left window reflects the part of us that is completely open. There are things that I know about myself that most people who know me also know about me (such as that I am a psychologist and my spouse's name is Mark).

The bottom left window reflects the things we keep hidden and secret from others. For a long time before "coming out" I kept my feelings about my sexual orientation a secret from everybody.

The top right window reflects things about ourselves that others can see but we have a difficult time seeing in ourselves. This is because of defense mechanisms. For example, many people, because of denial, have a hard time accepting an addiction such as alcoholism. It is usually readily apparent to others long before it is to the one afflicted.

The bottom right window reflects the unconscious. There are things that neither us nor significant others are aware of about ourselves. The goal of therapy then is to find a safe place to share secrets, to get feedback from a therapist or others about our blind spots (group therapy can be especially helpful for this) and perhaps even to become aware of unconscious material.

There is an old saying: "We are only as sick as the secrets we keep." We need caring and trustworthy people with whom to share our secrets. The things that are most difficult to share are the things that most need to be expressed. The Catholic Church knows this; it is part of the reason for confession.

When we can expose our fears, insecurities, and wrongdoings to the light of day, we can begin to see them more clearly. We can utilize feedback from others. When we share what we are afraid to share with others, we learn that we are not alone. Other people struggle with the same things!

The model below reflects the changes I would hope people make as the result of therapy; there are less defense mechanisms, more of myself is shared with others, and perhaps issues that I was unconscious of have become conscious. I should know myself better and love and accept myself more.

Open	Blind
Secret	Unknown

Psychotherapy historically has existed to treat psycho-pathology. The first major therapeutic approach that emerged was psychodynamic therapies such as the therapies developed by Freud, Jung, and Adler. Primarily these approaches were used with what has been called *neuroses*, including such issues as depression, anxiety, mood instability and lack of emotional resilience. These therapies were not helpful for *psychoses* such as Schizophrenia.

Psychoses really were not successfully treated until the advent of pharmacological agents in the 1950s.

A completely different psychotherapy developed in the 1920s based on classical and operant conditioning. B.F. Skinner and other *behaviorists* focused on changing behaviors only and devalued the importance of insight. Behaviorists are not interested in thoughts and feelings- only problematic behaviors. Philosophically some behaviorists do not accept that people have free will. They say we operate by the laws of physics; it is all stimulus and response. Behavioral therapies are sometimes referred to as *Second Force* therapies, whereas psychodynamic therapies are referred to as *First Force*.

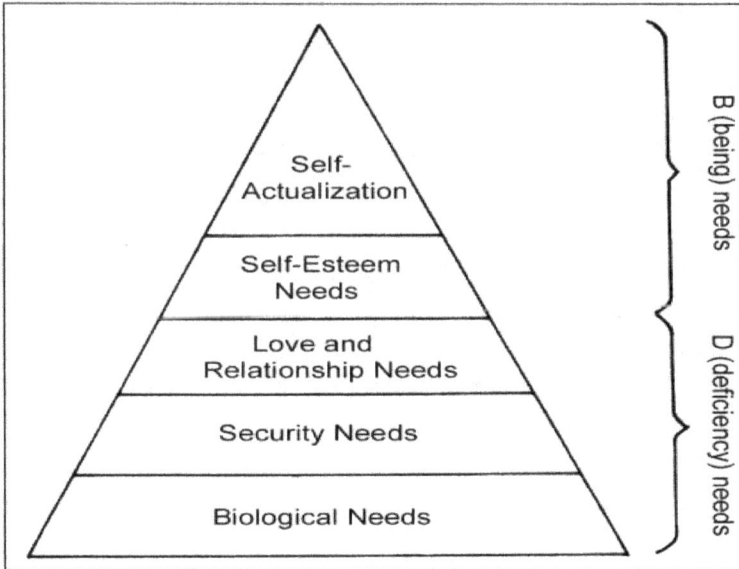

Third Force therapies are rooted in humanistic and existential theories. The focus is on identifying and addressing inner needs and finding fulfillment. Two important therapists from this tradition are Carl Rogers and Abraham Maslow. Many readers likely are familiar with Maslow's Hierarchy of Needs as depicted above.

The most basic needs on Maslow's hierarchy are physiological needs, i.e., the need for food, water, and oxygen. Once these needs are met, the next level of needs become most important. These are safety needs, i.e., the need for security, order, and stability. The next level up is belongingness needs, i.e., the need for love and connection with others. The next level up is self-esteem needs. This is the need to accomplish things and be recognized for it. Fame and fortune can be included in this. At the top of Maslow's well-known pyramid are self-actualization needs. The bottom three levels are "deficit needs," meaning that if you feel you do not have enough of these needs at a certain level, you are motivated to rectify this. The top two levels deal with "being needs" rather than "deficit needs." At this level we deal with self-fulfillment, i.e., the desire to be all that we can be. It is the need for personal growth and evolution.

Abraham Maslow is an important figure for yet another evolution in psychotherapy which are so-called *Fourth Force* therapies, which are based on transpersonal philosophy. Maslow later in life came to believe in a still higher need on his hierarchy which was the need for self-transcendence. All the first five levels of need focus on satisfying oneself. Maslow believed that there was a still higher level need in which the focus is on the care of others. It is an altruistic drive. It is the need for selflessness rather than self-centeredness. Transpersonal therapy seeks "fundamental trans-formation of normal egoic existence to some ultimately more satisfying or valuable condition" (Daniels, 2013)

Michael Dowd in his book *Thank God for Evolution* (2007) outlined "fundamental questions of existence" that people struggle with.

> *Who are we? - the question of identity*
> *Where did we come from? - the question of origin*
> *Where are we going? - the question of destiny*
> *Why are we here? - the question of purpose*
> *What ultimately matters? - the question of meaning*
> *How are we to live? - the question of morality/right action*
> *What happens when we die? - the question of finality and continuity*

These are questions I have pondered for my entire life. As a child I was given answers to these questions by various "authority figures," but they were answers meant for a child. For the most part that was probably okay, as I was a child. Unfortunately, many people never develop further than this and get stuck in tribal, warrior, and traditional stages of consciousness. St. Paul comments on this:

> *When I was a child, I spoke like a child, I thought like a child, I reasoned like a child; when I became an adult, I put an end to childish ways.*

Paul also says:

> *Do not be conformed to this world, but be transformed by the renewing of your minds, so that you may discern what is the will of God- what is good and acceptable and perfect.*

In a November 5, 2019 interview, integral philosopher Ken Wilber was questioned about his perspectives on spirituality now that he had entered his 70s. Wilber said he feels increased urgency in sharing/teaching what he has learned to be most important in life.

> *As the wisdom holders, we need to help people find what's important — to Grow Up by moving through the early stages of emotional maturing, Clean Up by doing shadow-up, Wake Up by doing spiritual practice, and Show Up by serving humanity in the world.*

Growing Up: is what I talked about in this chapter.

Cleaning Up: is what I talked about in the last section of this chapter.

Waking Up: is what I will be talking about in Chapter 5.

Showing Up: is what I will be talking about in Chapter 6.

Questions for Contemplation or Discussion

Chapter Three. Human Development

Michael Dowd said that the following are "fundamental questions of existence." How would you answer these questions? As important as knowing *what* one believes is knowing *why* one believes it.

1. Who are we? - the question of identity

2. Where did we come from? - the question of origin

3. Where are we going? - the question of destiny

4. Why are we here? - the question of purpose

5. What ultimately matters? - the question of meaning

6. How are we to live? - the question of morality/right action

7. What happens when we die? - the question of finality and continuity

Chapter Four

God Part 1:

What Science Can Teach Us

I believe in God, but it is not the God I believed in as a child. I do not believe in a guy in the sky, and one, by the way, that closely resembles Santa Claus (an old white guy with a long white beard who judges whether I am good or bad and who rewards me with presents for good behavior). The nature of reality described in chapter two suggests to me that the *almighty* needs to be greater and grander than a humanoid. The Bible in the book of Genesis opines that god created man in his image. More accurate would be that man has created God in *man's* image. The Greek philosopher Xenophanes of the late sixth and early fifth centuries BCE commented on this tendency:

The Ethiops say that their gods are flat-nosed and black, while the Thracians say that theirs have blue eyes and red hair. Yet if cattle or horses or lions had hands and could draw, and could sculpt like men, then the horses would draw their gods like horses, and cattle like cattle; and each they would shape bodies of gods in the likeness, each kind, of their own.

My conception of God would have some similarities to that of philosopher/theologian Paul Tillich who described God as the ground of being.

> *God is being-itself, not a being. As the power of being, God transcends every being and also the totality of beings - the world. Being-itself is beyond finitude and infinity; otherwise it would be conditioned by something other than itself, and the real power of being would lie beyond both it and that which conditioned it. Being-itself infinitely transcends every finite being.*

I also resonate with the conception of God of Dutch philosopher Baruch Spinoza of the 17th century. Contemporary philosopher Steven Nadler in the Stanford Encyclopedia of Philosophy writes that for Spinoza "God is the infinite, necessarily existing (that is, self-caused), unique substance of the universe. There is only one substance in the universe; it is God; and everything else that is, is in God."

My own definition of God is the following:

> *God is the incomprehensible source of all in our universe and beyond, whose essence is love, truth and beauty, and who becomes increasingly manifest in the unfolding evolution of the cosmos. God encompasses the totality of all existence.*

Much of religion today is based upon writings written thousands of years ago by men who had no knowledge about science. They had no knowledge about the causes of destructive natural phenomena such as earthquakes, volcanoes, floods, lightning, etc. Their belief was that divine beings exerted control over natural phenomena and the fortunes of human beings. These early gods were very human-like; they walked and talked with humans, they loved the smell of roasted meat, they had strong emotions, and they were often petty and flawed. Gradually the portrayal of gods became more transcendent, and gradually monotheism developed. For some reason religions and religious people grant authority to the beliefs of these very primitive people. They believe, without any evidence, that these ancient prophets had a direct connection with God that people no longer can have.

What if religion was now based upon empirical evidence? What if we stopped believing things just because we were taught it as a child? If our beliefs were to become based on empirical evidence, how would this change our world view? Would the world be a better place if humanity was better educated and if decisions were based on objective truth rather than unfounded beliefs? This chapter examines ramifications of the information presented in chapter two. When using our best evidence for determining reality, what can be learned about ultimate truth? How would this affect how we live our lives?

Anthropocentrism

Galileo was born in Pisa in 1564 and raised in Florence. He initially studied medicine but discovered a passion for mathematics and decided to make this his occupation, much to the dismay of his father. He eventually became the chair of mathematics at the University of Pisa in 1589, and in 1592 he became chair of mathematics at the University of Padua. Galileo made several important contributions to science including disputing Aristotelian notions about the physics of falling bodies and refining and improving the telescope. With his telescope he discovered that the surface of the moon was not smooth, discovered four moons around the planet Jupiter, discovered the planet Saturn, and discovered many additional stars that could not be seen with the naked eye.

What Galileo is perhaps best known for, however, was his belief in the Copernican view of the solar system- that the earth is a planet that revolves around the sun. This was a big deal because the Roman Catholic Church made it a big deal. The church deemed the Copernican theory heretical because the belief seemed to contradict scripture. Galileo was placed under house arrest in 1633 until his death in 1642. The Copernican theory was so threatening to the church and to the public because not only did it threaten a literal interpretation of scripture, but it also threatened the belief that mankind here on earth was the center of the universe.

Charles Darwin was born in 1809. He was the fifth of six children, and his father was a physician. His mother died when he was eight years old, and so he was then raised primarily by his elder sisters. Although both parents' families were primarily Unitarian, Charles attended an Anglican school. Like Galileo he was encouraged to attend medical school and began studies at the Edinburgh Medical School. Also, like Galileo he disliked the study of medicine, and so his father sent him to Christ's College in Cambridge to become an Anglican parson, i.e., a religious cleric. Darwin found his passion though in natural history which would become his lifelong preoccupation.

Darwin spent five years (1831-1836) studying fossils and nature while circumnavigating the globe on the HMS Beagle. He particularly gained new insights while visiting the Galapagos Islands. He developed and adopted a theory called *transmutation*, which is now known as *evolution*. He theorized that animals and plants mutated in response to environmental factors over very long periods of time, and that all species of life have descended from common ancestors. For a long time, he kept publicly quiet about his views, knowing that the theory would be highly offensive to many, particularly in the church. Darwin did finally present his research and conclusions in *On the Origin of Species* in 1859. The evidence for biological evolution was indeed highly distressing to many people after the book's publication, and it continues to be very distressing to many to this day. Just as Copernicus' and Galileo's findings supporting a heliocentric model (planets revolving around the sun) over a geocentric model (the earth as the center of all) distressed the public in the 1600s, so did Darwin's evolutionary findings upset many people's worldview because it also made humans seem less important.

Anthropocentrism can be defined as the belief that human beings are the most important entity in the universe. This is an extremely cherished belief for, I dare say, most people at least in the United States. I, however, do not think that this is a conclusion that we are able to make when looking at the evidence presented in chapter two of this book.

The history of the earth is 4.5 billion years, and homo sapiens have been around for only two hundred thousand years. Converting these 4.5 billion years to a calendar year as I did in an earlier chapter, homo sapiens did not make their appearance on the planet until December 31 at 9:25 pm. That is the equivalent to a character making her first appearance in the last paragraph of a novel and believing that she is the main character of the book.

The point is also made when considering the immensity of space. Believing that the entire purpose for the universe is to accommodate mankind is like a speck of dust on a grain of sand thinking that the earth's entire purpose was to support the existence of that speck of dust.

Modern genetic science also throws hot water on the idea of the uniqueness of homo sapiens. Genetic scientists have been able to decipher the genetic code for humans and for other species. All of life, whether birds, reptiles, insects, bacteria, mammals, or vegetables have descended from the same common life form. What is more, the human DNA sequence and the chimp DNA sequence is almost 99 percent identical. It would probably be disconcerting to many to also find out that researchers believe that chimpanzees are more similar genetically to humans than they are to gorillas.

Human beings do have some specialness, though, in that they are currently the most advanced life form on the planet (although it is possible that even more advanced life forms exist elsewhere in the universe). There are many who would disagree with the premise that humans are more progressed than other life forms or that there is a direction to evolution. I disagree with that belief. There is overwhelming evidence, I believe, for cosmic evolution, which I will elaborate.

Considering the immensity of the universe, I think it unlikely that the only life to be found in the universe is on our planet. I also think it unlikely that the only conscious life is to be found here. In a 2017 article in Forbes magazine entitled *The Number Of Earth-Like Planets In The Universe Is Staggering - Here's The Math* the author reports "there are up to 76,000,000,000,000,000,000,000 stars similar to ours and almost all of them have some form of planets. Based on the Kepler observations, it is now estimated that a quarter of those stars have at least one rocky planet similar in size to the Earth and in the habitable zone. That means there are up to 19,000,000,000,000,000,000,000 stars like ours with at least one planet like Earth."

I also think it a mistake to think of human beings as being the culmination of creation. I am hopeful that God's creation will continue to evolve. I hope that current human nature is not the climax of god's creation! I think most of us could conceive and hope for a more evolved humanity. The television and movie franchise Star Trek is a good example of such imaginings.

The word *evolve* means to gradually change over time, especially from simple to more complex forms. Some, however, do not perceive biological evolution as being progressive, including Charles Darwin. Darwin's theory of evolution is based on *natural selection*; organisms change and diversify in response to their environment in order to better survive and thrive. Darwin did not promote a theory that there was a general direction to evolution, i.e., that biology was progressing from simpler to more complex organisms. I will present evidence for my belief that evolution is indeed progressive.

There have been five major extinction events in the history of the earth, and each extinction eventually ushered in a new dominant life form that was more advanced than the previous dominant life form. The last major extinction was the Cretaceous-Tertiary extinction 60 million years ago which was responsible for the extinction of the dinosaurs and the rise of mammals, eventually leading to ourselves, homo sapiens. Our anthropocentric world view (which also might be called "human narcissism") tends to make us believe that the "end of the world" and the extinction of human beings would be one and the same. Not so. Due to a host of possibilities (e.g., meteor strike, nuclear holocaust) our species certainly could go extinct, leading to the evolution of a new dominant life form on earth. The current global warming crisis could be one such precipitant to eventually lead to human extinction.

Another aspect of our anthropocentrism is the belief that mankind is separate from the rest of creation. I was brought up with the belief that everything in the physical cosmos was created by God for the benefit of humankind. I was taught that mankind had *dominion* over the earth. This is based on Genesis 1:26-28:

> *Then God said, "Let us make humankind in our image, according to our likeness; and let them have dominion over the fish of the sea, and over the birds of the air, and over the cattle, and over all the wild animals of the earth, and over every creeping thing that creeps upon the earth."*
>
> *So God created humankind in his image, in the image of God he created them, male and female he created them.*
>
> *God blessed them, and God said to them, "Be fruitful and multiply, and fill the earth and subdue it; and have dominion over the fish of the sea and over the birds of the air and over every living thing that moves upon the earth."*

This belief was the view of prehistoric people who had no benefit of science to understand the world. We now know that all living things descended from a single common ancestor and are related, and that all living things are comprised of matter (atoms). Everything on this earth, including people, are comprised of atoms, and these atoms originated in stars. When we die our bodies decompose, and the atoms from our bodies become something else. In fact, the atoms that were originally in our bodies are not the same atoms that make up our bodies at the end of our lives. 98 percent of the atoms in our bodies change every year. The pattern of who we are remains the same, but the atoms change. So human beings are not separate from nature; we are a part of nature in every possible sense.

Beyond Biology: Cosmic Evolution

Although Charles Darwin did not espouse the belief that evolution is progressive, others have, including myself. When examining the history of the universe one can plainly see ever increasing complexity- evolution. At first the universe contained nothing but pure energy. Then matter quickly developed: first quarks and gluons, then protons and neutrons, then electrons and neutrinos. Electromagnetism was responsible for subatomic particles becoming atoms. Because of gravity, atoms (matter) began clustering into stars and galaxies.

At first there were only hydrogen and helium atoms, but then later with the death of stars, all the other chemical elements came into being. This was the birth of *chemistry*. Eventually life developed; the birth of *biology*. The first life forms were microscopic and single-celled. Then some organisms developed the ability to capture energy from the sun (photosynthesis). Eventually animals developed that thrived on oxygen rather than carbon dioxide. Multi-celled organisms evolved. Sexual reproduction evolved. Central nervous systems evolved. Brains evolved to include limbic systems and cerebral cortices. Sentience evolved. Consciousness evolved. Culture evolved. Technology evolved.

When looking at the history of the universe in its entirety one can see, I think, that the cosmos is a single entity that has evolved. Absolutely everything in existence is related to each other. Astrophysicist Eric Chaisson uses the term *cosmic evolution* to describe the big history of the universe. Why is the universe evolving? Why is there ever-increasing complexity? Why is there a directionality to the life of the cosmos? This cosmic evolutionary process is the most convincing evidence to me for the existence of God. God is the force responsible for this evolutionary process.

My conception of cosmic evolution is similar, I believe, to the conception of the *Logos* by Philo of Alexandria. Philo was a Jewish philosopher who lived during the same time period as Jesus of Nazareth. Robert Wright in *The Evolution of God* (2009) writes:

Philo believed the Logos had existed before humans or the earth, or, for that matter, matter. Prior to creating the universe, God formulated the Logos the way an architect might conceive a blueprint or the way a computer programmer might design an algorithm. Long before modern science started clashing with the six-day creation scenario in Genesis, Philo had preempted the conflict by calling those six days allegorical: they actually referred not to God's creation of the earth and animals and people, but to his creation of the Logos, the divine algorithm, which would bring earth and animals and people into existence once it was unleashed in the material world- that is, once the material world was created to serve as its medium. Then God's plan could tangibly unfold. The Logos, writes the scholar David Runia, is "God's instrument both during creation and in the cosmos's providential administration." As Philo himself put it, "The Logos was conceived in God's mind before all things and is manifest in connection with all things."

Wright also wrote that the Logos has given history a direction- "in fact, a moral direction: history moved toward the good." That is also my belief about cosmic evolution. I believe the universe is evolving in terms of increasing complexity but also to increasing goodness. In addition, I also believe conversely that it is goodness that evolves the cosmos. I will be writing more about that later in this book.

Classical Physics

I ask for the reader's forbearance now as I broach the subject of physics. I promise I will try to avoid being too technical and using jargon. My plan is to briefly summarize the history of the field stopping at topics which I think have something to say about God. Most people's familiarity with physics revolves around the practical innovations the field has contributed to our lives: electricity, light bulbs, radio, television, refrigeration, automobiles, airplanes, computers, and the internet, for example. What most people do not think of, however, is the implications of how physics can affect our world views and what the field might have to say about God.

Physics is a scientific discipline concerned with the study of matter and energy. Physics seeks to understand the structure and workings of the universe. The beginnings of physics go back at least to ancient Greece. Thales of Miletus (7th and 6th centuries BCE) was an early advocate for the belief that there were naturalistic causes for phenomena of nature (such as the rising and setting of the sun, earthquakes, and volcanic eruptions) rather than the supernatural causes which were prevalent at that time. In the 5th century BCE, the idea arose in Greece that matter was composed of indestructible elements that they called "atoms". As a result of observations and data collection, Aristotle founded a system of physics in the 4th century BCE. Although he was wrong about many things, his ideas continued to be influential for two millennia.

One of the things that Aristotle got wrong was his geocentric model of the cosmos, i.e., that the earth was the center of the universe. During the Renaissance, Copernicus, Galileo, and Kepler presented evidence for a heliocentric model of the solar system (that the planets revolved around the sun) which eventually gained acceptance. Also, during the Renaissance, Rene Descartes made important advances in mathematics and geometry.

It was during the Enlightenment that the field of physics really matured thanks primarily to the work of Isaac Newton. Newton made several important contributions to physics including inventing calculus, formulating his three laws of motion, and especially formulating the theory of gravity. What Newton was able to establish was that the solar system operates systematically and reliably, much like a clock. It is not affected by capricious supernatural entities. The workings of the cosmos could be explained mathematically with such equations as $F=ma$ (which means force equals mass times acceleration). Newton is most famous for his discovery of gravity which is a force that operates both in our everyday lives here on the earth as well as throughout the universe with celestial bodies. Newton noted that the stronger the mass is of objects, the stronger the amount of gravity, and the farther away objects are from each other, the weaker is the strength of gravity. He was able to express this mathematically. Although Newton described how gravity works, he did not describe or know what gravity really was.

Newton's work had a profound effect on science and on the worldview of educated people. It also had significant effects on religion. An intellectual movement known as *deism* arose out of the Enlightenment that asserts that knowledge of God comes only from reason and not from special revelations. Many of America's founding fathers were deists, including Thomas Jefferson, Benjamin Franklin, and George Washington. Deists assert that the knowledge obtained from physics reveals that the solar system is like a complex piece of machinery, and like all complex instruments (such as a watch) it could not have come into being without there being a maker. In other words, if you found a pocket watch on the beach you would realize immediately that it was created by someone and could not have just evolved on its own.

Deists reasoned that there must be a God, an intelligent designer, who created this complex solar system, although the belief also was that God then did not interfere in his creation. Newton, on the other hand, believed that like a watchmaker, the creator had to tinker with the universe from time to time to keep it working correctly. Raised an Anglican, Newton was a religious man, although his views would not have been considered orthodox. The splendor of the universe was evidence to him and the deists of a creationist God.

The idea of an interventionist deity began to decrease among the educated. This was a huge paradigm shift in world view. No longer did most people believe that God could be cajoled through prayer to affect nature. The laws of nature are set and are unchangeable. We know when the sun will rise and set each day. We know that earthquakes occur along fault lines. We have some abilities to predict weather.

Biblical scholar Marcus Borg in *Jesus: The Life, Teachings, and Relevance of a Religious Revolutionary* (2006) wrote about other changes that affected people's conception of God as a result of the Enlightenment. Borg wrote that prior to the Enlightenment people thought of God as both *immanent* and *transcendent*. The former term refers to the notion that God's presence is everywhere and in everything. The apostle Paul said that God is the one "in whom we live and move and have our being" (Acts 17:28). The idea of God's immanence became less prevalent with the Enlightenment. "Transcendent" refers to God's beyondness, i.e., "our father who art in heaven." Borg writes that prior to the Enlightenment

> *Most Christians thought of God not only as more than the world, but also as present in the world. The world was shot through with the presence of God. But the Enlightenment led to a new way of thinking of the universe, as a closed-system of matter and energy operating in accord with natural laws. In effect, the Enlightenment removed God from the universe; nature became disenchanted, the world became desacralized. The notion that God is "everywhere," God's immanence, was eclipsed.*

Certain philosophical ideologies began to pervade science including reductionism, determinism, and materialism. The universe is seen as orderly and mechanical. *Materialism* refers to the belief that nothing exists but physical matter, and even if there are non-physical realities, they should not be the concern of science, since it would be out of the realm of scientific investigation. *Reductionism* refers to the belief that complex phenomena can be best understood by breaking it down to its most fundamental parts. In other words, a complex object is nothing more than the sum of its parts. *Determinism* is the belief that everything is cause and effect, and this belief can even be extended to people (i.e., no belief in free will).

Many people believe that scientists are not religious or spiritual, and that there is a "war" between religion and science, but neither belief is correct. Many scientists are open to the possibility of some conception of God, and there is not necessarily a contradiction between a commitment to scientific thinking and spirituality. Isaac Newton was religious, and so was the next great pioneer of physics: James Clerk Maxwell.

Maxwell lived from 1831 until 1879 and was an active Presbyterian. His major accomplishment was to unify two forces of nature: electricity, and magnetism (and then later to unify electromagnetism with light). People had long been aware of the phenomenon of static electricity. In dry weather when we touch metal, we might get a "shock." When we take our clothes out of the dryer our socks may cling together. Benjamin Franklin in addition to his other accomplishments as one of the founding fathers of America determined that lightning also was an electrical phenomenon. He also determined that there were two types of electricity which he named *positive* and *negative,* denotations that we still use today. Opposite charges attract each other, and like charges repel.

Like electricity, there was some awareness of the phenomenon of magnetism for thousands of years. There is a mineral magnetite called *lodestone* which consists of iron oxide which is a natural magnet. It attracts other pieces of the same material and iron. Also, like electricity, magnetism is a force that either attracts or repels. Instead of being labeled as positive and negative, though, they are called either north or south poles. Although electricity and magnetism were considered two separate forces of nature, it was known that they had effects on each other. Moving electrical charges make magnetic fields, and moving magnets make electric fields. James Clerk Maxwell was able to unify electricity and magnetism with four equations, and we now think of electromagnetism as one unified force.

Electromagnetism is an important force for several reasons. It is the force that keeps electrons bound to the nucleus of an atom. (By the way, there is another force that keeps the protons and neutrons bound in the nucleus of the atom. This is called the *strong force.*) Electromagnetism is also the force that keeps gravity from pulling us through the chair we are sitting on and keeps our atoms together in our bodies instead of their combining with other objects we encounter. An atom contains mostly empty space. If the nucleus of the atom, which contains over 99 percent of the atom's mass, was increased to the size of a marble, the entire atom would be the size of a football field. Gravity does not pull me through the floor because the negative charge of the electrons on my feet repels against the negative charge of the electrons on the floor.

Maxwell determined that electromagnetism travels by *waves*, and the speed of these waves is 186,000 miles per second which happens to be the speed of light. Maxwell concluded then that light is also a wave. Maxwell had thus unified three out of four known forces of nature at that time: electricity, magnetism, and light (but not the fourth, gravity). By the way, gravity is a force only of attraction and cannot repel like electricity and magnetism.

There is a popular t-shirt that pays homage to Maxwell's 4 equations as shown below. In the book of Genesis of the Bible God said "Let there be light" and the laws of physics came into being causing there to be light.

And God said

$$\nabla \cdot \mathbf{D} = \rho$$

$$\nabla \cdot \mathbf{B} = 0$$

$$\nabla \times \mathbf{E} = -\frac{\partial \mathbf{B}}{\partial t}$$

$$\nabla \times \mathbf{H} = \mathbf{J} + \frac{\partial \mathbf{D}}{\partial t}$$

**and then
there was light.**

A *wave* is an unusual phenomenon in that matter is not traveling but electromagnetic energy is. Take the classic example of a wave on a lake; the energy of the wave is moving across the lake, but the water molecules are not themselves moving. At a sporting event in a stadium when the crowd does "the wave," it is energy that is moving around the arena, not the people themselves. Particles have mass and exist independently of other material objects; waves have neither of these characteristics.

Electromagnetic waves have varying wavelengths which correlates with the amount of energy that is in the waves. Higher frequency wavelengths (expressed in units of measurement called hertz) have more energy than lower frequency waves. In the chart below we see a band in the middle labeled "visible light." These are the electromagnet waves that our eyes can detect. To the left of this band are higher frequency wavelengths that our eyes are unable to detect (ultraviolet light, x-rays, and gamma rays), and to the right of the band are lower frequency wavelengths that we also are unable to detect with our eyes (infrared radiation, microwaves, and radio waves). Although our eyes cannot detect these waves, we have developed specialized equipment that can.

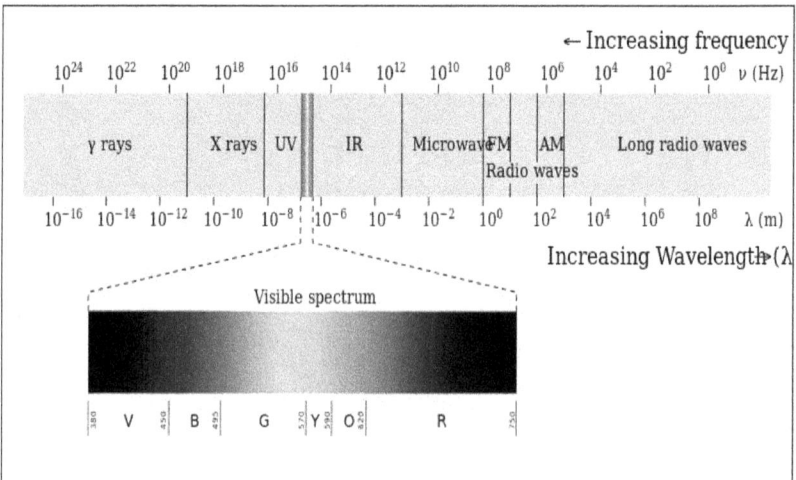

Sound also presents in waves, although there are differences between light waves and sound waves. The medium for sound waves is air. When we clap our hands, we are compressing air which causes a vibration that disturbs surrounding air molecules and travels out in a wavelike pattern. Light waves, on the other hand, can travel through empty space. If we were in outer space and my fellow astronaut clapped his hands next to me, I would hear nothing because there is no air to act as a medium for sound waves to travel. Light on the other hand, will travel through space until it comes upon an object to interfere with it.

Human beings can detect sound waves from a frequency of 20 Hz to 20,000 Hz. Sounds that have a frequency that are too high for us to hear (i.e., above 20,000 Hz) are referred to as ultrasound, and sounds that are too low are referred to as infrasound. Some animals can detect higher frequencies than humans. For example, dogs can detect frequencies as high as 45,000 Hz. Bats can detect frequencies as high as 120,000 Hz. Dolphins can detect frequencies as high as 200,000 Hz. Elephants can detect very *low* sound frequencies, i.e., 5 Hz.

I have been spending quite some time talking about waves, and you are likely wondering what all of this has to do with God. I am going to leave you in suspense here, but I promise that I will be getting back to this later in this chapter.

Now let me move on to another giant of physics: Albert Einstein. He is the most well-known physicist to have ever lived, and deservedly so, for he made several very important contributions to the field. Let us start with the world's most famous mathematical equation:

$$e = mc^2$$

What this equation says is that energy and matter are the same thing. The universe is believed to have begun with a "big bang" of energy followed immediately by the formation of hydrogen and helium atoms. Eventually over billions of years we have had the creation of more and more matter (things). Humans have learned how to convert mass to energy, i.e., nuclear energy plants and atomic bombs, but for the most part do not know how to turn energy into matter, which would require tremendous amounts of energy. Interestingly, the book of Genesis in the Hebrew scriptures suggests the formation of matter (things) from nothing, which science is also suggesting, i.e., matter from energy.

In 1905 Einstein published his *theory of special relativity* which suggests that time and space are not two separate entities but are two aspects of one unified entity called *space-time*. Einstein presented evidence that nothing can go faster than the speed of light, and that the speed at which one is traveling affects the passage of time. A real-world example are GPS satellites. Because of their high speed across the sky their clocks run slower and need to be regularly adjusted for the satellites to work properly.

Einstein's theory has some startling ramifications. If a person is stationary in space, then they are moving through time at the speed of light. If a person was able to move through space at the speed of light, time would completely stand still for them. If a person is moving at a velocity through space that is less than the speed of light, that person would be experiencing both changes in space and time. All objects travel at one and only one speed in space-time. One person might experience more space and less time, while another might experience more time and less space, but the combination adds up to the same for everyone. Mind bending, right?

Ten years later in 1915 Einstein published his *theory of general relativity* which explains just what the force of gravity is. You may remember that Newton explained the laws of gravity (i.e., how it worked), but really did not know what caused gravity. Einstein was able to explain that gravity is the force created by a disturbance of space-time. Picture a king-sized mattress to represent space. Then picture a bowling ball being placed in the middle of the mattress and the indentation it makes in the mattress. This indentation is like the effects of a large celestial body such as the sun or a planet on space-time. If you were to place a marble on the edge of your mattress away from the indentation there may be no effects on the marble, but as you move the marble closer the bowling ball's effects on the mattress will cause the marble to move to the bowling ball. The size of celestial bodies and the distance between celestial objects affects how strong the force of gravity is.

Einstein's body of work shows us that the universe is much more complex than Newton's model would suggest. Reality is not so simple, neat, and tidy. Einstein's theories of relativity suggest that reality is relative. The Oxford dictionary gives a physics definition of relativity as "the dependence of various physical phenomena on relative motion of the observer and the observed objects, especially regarding the nature and behavior of light, space, time, and gravity." Einstein also was a very spiritual person, and he wrote about his conception of God as well as his thoughts about several other social and philosophical issues. Below are a few examples:

> *You will hardly find one among the profounder sort of scientific minds without a peculiar religious feeling of his own. But it is different from the religion of the naive man.*
>
> *For the latter God is a being from whose care one hopes to benefit and whose punishment one fears; a sublimation of a feeling similar to that of a child for its father, a being to whom one stands to some extent in a personal relation, however deeply it may be tinged with awe.*
>
> *But the scientist is possessed by the sense of universal causation. The future, to him, is every whit as necessary and determined as the past. There is nothing divine about morality; it is a purely human affair. His religious feeling takes the form of a rapturous amazement at the harmony of natural law, which reveals an intelligence of such superiority that, compared with it, all the systematic thinking and acting of human beings is an utterly insignificant reflection. This feeling is the guiding principle of his life and work, in so far as he succeeds in keeping himself from the shackles of selfish desire. It is beyond question closely akin to that which has possessed the religious geniuses of all ages.* (Einstein, 2014)

In a 1936 letter Einstein wrote:

Everyone who is seriously involved in the pursuit of science becomes convinced that a spirit is manifest in the laws of the Universe- a spirit vastly superior to that of man, and one in the face of which we with our modest powers must feel humble. (Macalister, 2008)

Historian Walter Isaacson (2007) related the following story in his biography of Einstein:

One evening in Berlin, Einstein and his wife were at a dinner party when a guest expressed a belief in astrology. Einstein ridiculed the notion as pure superstition. Another guest stepped in and similarly disparaged religion. Belief in God, he insisted, was likewise a superstition.

At this point the host tried to silence him by invoking the fact that even Einstein harbored religious beliefs.

"It isn't possible!" the skeptical guest said, turning to Einstein to ask if he was, in fact, religious.

"Yes, you can call it that," Einstein replied calmly. "Try and penetrate with our limited means the secrets of nature and you will find that, behind all the discernible concatenations, there remains something subtle, intangible, and inexplicable. Veneration for this force beyond anything that we can comprehend is my religion. To that extent I am, in fact, religious."

Quantum Physics

Thus far I have not really talked much about particle physics. The idea of there being an indivisible unit of matter known as an atom originated with the Greek philosopher, Democritus (460-370 BCE). Particle physics as a field of study really began at the turn of the 20th century though. English physicist J.J. Thomson is credited with discovering the electron. Thomson's conception of the atom was improved upon by New Zealand physicist Ernest Rutherford who described the structure of the atom as resembling our solar system with the center core containing a positive charge and negatively charged electrons orbiting around this nucleus. About two years later in 1913 Danish physicist Niels Bohr further improved upon Rutherford's model by describing how electrons fly around the nucleus in fixed orbits.

There are around 100 naturally occurring elements (i.e., types of atoms) with a few dozen more that were created by scientists. The nucleus of atoms contains protons (which are positively charged) and neutrons (which are electrically neutral). Electrons which are negatively charged orbit the nucleus. The nucleus is held together by a force known as the *strong force*. We now know that the atom is not the smallest indivisible unit of matter, and things are much more complicated than we once thought. Protons and neutrons are made up of quarks. There are also other elemental particles known as leptons (electrons, meuons, taus, and neutrinos), gluons, photons, and bosons.

I had talked previously about light being a wave. Well, it turns out that light also has qualities of particles. It was Einstein that argued that light could be regarded not only as a wave but also as a stream of tiny particles he called *quanta*. These would later be called *photons*. Einstein won the Nobel prize for his work on the *photoelectric effect* in which he described light's qualities as a particle. French physicist Louis de Broglie later determined that other particles of matter (electrons and protons as well as photons) could also be regarded as waves.

It was discovered that the physics of the microscopic world is much different than that of the macroscopic. Einstein's general theory of relativity is very important in describing the universe at the cosmic level, but when dealing with matter at the atomic level gravity has little effect. The forces that are important at the subatomic level are electromagnetism, the strong force, and the weak force.

At the cosmic level the universe appears to be very predictable and mechanistic. Not so at the subatomic level. *Quantum mechanics* is the branch of physics that describes nature at the level of atoms and subatomic particles. It explains the structure of atoms, their combination into molecules, the interaction of light with matter, and many other phenomena.

German physicist, Werner Heisenberg, is one of the main trailblazers of quantum physics. He is known primarily for the *uncertainty principle* which asserts that we cannot know the precise position and velocity of a particle simultaneously. If we know a particle's position, we cannot know precisely its velocity. If we know its velocity, we cannot know precisely its position.

Actually, it is not that we do not know the particle's position or velocity, it is that the particle in fact does not *have* an exact position or velocity. There is a range of possibilities, and most amazing of all is that our observation of the particle affects what choice the particle makes out of the range of possibilities. A quantum system exists only as a set of probabilities. It is only at the moment of observation that particles snap into existence. This completely contradicts the mechanistic and deterministic conception of the universe that scientists previously held.

"Observation" requires consciousness. So what I am saying is that consciousness participates in the creation of reality!

Although Einstein's work on photons significantly contributed to quantum theory, he was quite disturbed about the ramifications of his own work. The idea was distressing to him that the universe could be "probabilistic" rather than certain. To the idea that observation affects particles he once remarked "Does the moon not exist until a mouse sees it?" Einstein had frequent correspondence with Danish physicist Niels Bohr (Nobel prize winner) about quantum mechanics and opined that "God does not play dice with the world," to which Bohr replied to him with "Stop telling God what to do."

Another perplexing discovery in quantum physics is the phenomenon of *entangled particles*. Subatomic particles, such as photons, that interact with each other can become inextricably linked, so that no matter how great the distance is between them they behave as one. So, if one photon is observed which affects that photon's position or velocity, its twin will also be affected in the same way even if it is on the other side of the universe. This too disturbed Einstein who called it "spooky action at a distance".

174

Einstein was a realist who held the belief as he put it that "a real factual situation" exists "independent of our observations." However, over the years there has been mounting evidence in support of quantum entanglement.

So, let me stop here to summarize the effects that classical physics and quantum physics have had on religious beliefs and world views. For millennia the workings of the universe were thought to be the result of ongoing actions by God or gods. Gods could be implored to affect the natural world. This viewpoint was forever changed with Newton and classical physics which demonstrated that the universe was orderly and operates by *laws* of nature, not by the whims of God. God was seen as the creator of this reality which is apart from us as spiritual human beings. It suggested *determinism* which is the belief that all events are predetermined by previous causes.

Quantum mechanics again would cause us to re-think our worldview as it demonstrates that reality is not so neat and tidy as we once thought. Gone was the deterministic and mechanistic paradigm of Newton. Most of us grew up to perceive the world as being *out there*. As observers we felt independent from the world. But we are active participants in the world we are observing, and by observing the world we are affecting the world. Everything is part of the one reality. Everything is connected to everything else.

Philosopher Ken Wilber authored a book titled *Quantum Questions* (2001) which "centered on the remarkable fact that virtually every one of the great pioneers of modern physics- men like Einstein and Schrodinger and Heisenberg- were spiritual mystics of one sort or another". "The essence of mysticism is that in the deepest part of your own being, in the very center of your own pure awareness, you are fundamentally one with Spirit, one with Godhead, one with the All, in a timeless and eternal and unchanging fashion." (Wilber, 1998).

Erwin Schroedinger who was awarded the 1933 Nobel prize in physics for his work on quantum mechanics said:

The scientific picture of the real world around me is very deficient. It gives a lot of factual information, puts all our experience in a magnificently consistent order, but is ghastly silent about all and sundry that is really near to our heart, that really matters to us. It cannot tell us a word about red and blue, bitter and sweet, physical pain and physical delight; it knows nothing of beautiful and ugly, good or bad, God and eternity. Science sometimes pretends to answer questions in these domains, but the answers are very often so silly that we are not inclined to take them seriously.

Walter Heisenberg who was awarded the 1932 Nobel prize in physics for the creation of quantum mechanics said:

The first gulp from the glass of natural sciences will turn you into an atheist, but at the bottom of the glass God is waiting for you.

Max Planck, a founder of quantum physics said:

Both religion and science require a belief in God. For believers, God is in the beginning, and for physicists He is at the end of all considerations...To the former He is the foundation, to the latter, the crown of the edifice of every generalized world view.

Max Born, Nobel prize winning physicist who was instrumental in the development of quantum mechanics said:

Those who say that the study of science makes a man an atheist must be rather silly.

Thermodynamics and Entropy

Let me return now to classical physics, although a subfield not yet discussed, thermodynamics. The focus will still be on atoms, however. Thermodynamics is the study of heat, temperature, and energy. Again, you may be wondering what this possibly could have to do with the concept of God. Hang in there. I will explain why I believe it does, although this will require a short lesson in physics once again.

What exactly is temperature? Temperature is the measure of average kinetic energy of atoms in a system. Atoms that are moving very rapidly have a higher temperature than atoms that are moving slowly. *Heat* can be defined as the transfer of thermal energy from one object to another. When I am heating a pan of water on my gas stove, I am transferring energy from the gas flame to the atoms in the water. As more and more energy is transferred, the water molecules vibrate faster and faster causing increasing temperature.

Energy can be stored in various forms. In addition to thermal energy which we just discussed, there is chemical energy (for example the energy that is stored in coal, gasoline, and sugar), radiant energy such as the light coming from the sun, nuclear energy (the energy that is released when atoms are split), mechanical energy (such as the movement of a car), etc. Energy can be in two states: potential energy or kinetic energy. The gasoline in your car has potential energy. The running of your car has kinetic energy. Spinning my car tires on the pavement can cause thermal energy.

This brings us to the *four laws of thermodynamics.* The first law is called the "zeroth law" because the other three laws had already been formulated and numbered. It was felt that the zeroth law really should come before the other three, and so it was called "zeroth" so that the other laws did not need to be renumbered. The laws of thermodynamics are unquestioned by scientists. Einstein said "thermodynamics is the only physical theory of universal content which, within the framework of the applicability of its basic concepts, I am convinced will never be overthrown." English physicist Sir Arthur Eddington said:

The second law of thermodynamics holds, I think, the supreme position among the laws of physics. If someone points out to you that your pet theory of the universe is in disagreement with Maxwell's equations- then so much the worse for Maxwell's equations. If it is found to be contradicted by observation- well, these experimentalists do bungle things from time to time. But if your theory is found to be against the Second Law of Thermodynamics, I can give you no hope; there is nothing for it but to collapse in deepest humiliation.

I will now discuss the first three of the four laws before then getting to what all of this has to do with God. I am only going to discuss the first three because they are the ones pertinent to our discussion about God.

0th Law
Basically this law says that if system A is in thermal equilibrium with system C, and system B is also in thermal equilibrium with system C, systems A and B are in equilibrium with each other. This law achieves practical applicability with the use of thermometers among other things.

1st Law
This law states that energy can be converted from one form to another but that total energy cannot be created or destroyed in a closed system. Therefore, within the universe, presumably a closed system, there is a finite amount of energy/matter. We cannot create new energy, and the energy that exists can never be destroyed. Energy can only be converted to other forms of energy.

2nd Law
The second law says that in closed systems randomness and disorder always increases. This is called *entropy*. Whenever an energy transaction occurs (for example using energy from gasoline in my car) there is a degradation of overall energy, although the total amount of energy never decreases (as stated by the 1st law). Energy

becomes degraded in energy transactions so that it is rendered more unavailable for *work*. Gasoline is a high-grade energy source. The internal combustion engine in my car converts the energy from the gasoline into power that moves my vehicle down the street. However, car engines are only 30 percent efficient; 35 percent of the energy is expelled as exhaust heat, 30 percent goes into coolant heat, and 5 percent goes into friction. The high-grade energy from gasoline is converted into lesser quality energies.

Nature does not like gradient differences. Matter and energy want to disperse. If I set down a hot cup of coffee on my kitchen table and get called away for a half hour, the heat from that coffee will disperse into the room until it gets down to the room temperature. Likewise, a star like our sun is extremely hot and that thermal energy also disperses throughout our solar system, fortunately sending solar energy to earth. Eventually our sun will lose all its thermal energy, although it will take billions of years, not the half hour it takes for my coffee to cool. Physicist and astronomer, Eric Chaisson (2001) gives a couple examples to demonstrate the dispersal of energy, i.e., entropy.

> *Geologists have estimated that if a single thimbleful of water were poured into a river, after only a few years the circulation on a global scale would be so complete that a similar thimbleful of water taken from anywhere on Earth would contain some molecules from the original thimbleful. Others have expressed much the same idea regarding atmospheric circulation by estimating that every breath of air we inhale contains molecules that were once breathed by Galileo, Aristotle, and the dinosaurs.*
>
> *That's mixing; that's entropy- the propensity to equalize, to achieve the lowest energy state, to spread things around evenly, in short to reestablish equilibrium at any and every opportunity.*

Entropy applies to "closed systems." Human beings are open systems. This means that our bodies do not contain a finite amount of energy. Rather energy constantly comes into us through food, and leaves us through "work." If we stop the flow of energy into our bodies we die and all the remaining energy/matter decays.

There was an interesting television show on the History Channel several years ago titled "Life After People." The premise of the show was that all the human beings on earth suddenly disappeared (the show does not explain why, and nor was this important to the show's purpose which was to show the urban decay that would result over years, decades, centuries, and millennia). This show strikingly demonstrated the effects of entropy. With no care being given to buildings and other infrastructure (i.e., energy inputs), everything quite quickly decayed.

Presumably our universe is a closed system. So, if the second law of thermodynamics (which scientists believe is almost unquestionably true) says that closed systems always decay- always devolve to increased disorder and randomness- then why do we actually see increased complexity! The universe began as pure energy. Then elementary particles came into existence. They evolved into atoms. Atoms became galaxies and stars. Destruction of stars created heavy elements. Planets developed. Molecules turned into life. Intelligent life evolved. Consciousness evolved. Complex civilizations developed. How can we reconcile this with the second law of thermodynamics?

I think that most of us can intuitively see that the universe has become more and more complex. The increased complexity here on earth is reflected in the greatly increased energy consumption in the last couple hundred years due to industrial/technological/cultural evolution. Christian et al (2014) report:

> *Human energy consumption is measured in exajoules. A joule is the power required to produce one watt for one second; an exajoule is a million million million joules.*
>
> *In 1850, most of the energy used by humans still came from traditional sources; human and animal labor, water power, wind power, and the energy locked up in wood. By the year 2000, total human energy use had multiplied by many times and overwhelmingly that energy*

came from the three major forms of fossil fuels: coal, oil, and natural gas.

David Christian's book indicates that energy consumption in 1850 was 25 exajoules, and in 2000 it grew to 450 exajoules. The greatly increased complexity in societies due to cultural evolution has required greater and greater consumption of high-quality energy, and unfortunately a byproduct of this transfer of energy has also caused significant society problems in the form of pollution and climate change.

Cities are dynamic steady-states, like any open system. They acquire and consume resources, produce and discard wastes, all the while processing energy for all manner of services: transportation, communications, construction, health, comfort, and entertainment, among a whole host of maintenance tasks. Modern cities are as much a product of an evolutionary process as any galaxy or organism, and many are still developing, seeking to establish dynamically stable communities within our planet's larger, vibrant ecological system. Their populations are dense, their structures and functions highly complex; cities are voracious users of energy... (Chaisson, 2001)

The universe is supposed to devolve, level off, decay, and become more disordered. I do accept that the second law is valid and that overall, entropy is happening in the universe. However, there are pockets of the universe that are increasingly ordered and complex. What would be causing this? Why are there areas in the universe that are actually evolving? Likely some of the reason for this was gradient differences early in the history of the universe. The energy/matter of the early universe likely was not evenly spread out. Gravity was the force that would clump matter together, eventually forming the galaxies and stars. However, there is more to the increased complexity that has developed in the universe than what can be explained by gravity or the other known forces of nature. We may someday have naturalistic explanations for this, but regardless it is this evolution of complexity that I believe is God.

Top scientists in the field of thermodynamics, as in other areas of physics, are open to some type of belief in God. Lord William Kelvin was known for his work in thermodynamics. The Kelvin temperature scale was named in his honor:

> *If you study science deep enough and long enough, it will force you to believe in God.*

James Joule was an important contributor to thermodynamics. The unit of heat known as the "joule" was named after him.

> *It is evident that an acquaintance with natural laws means no less than an acquaintance with the mind of God therein expressed.*

It is commonly believed that scientists and those who are committed to the fields of science are atheistic. However, as I have shown you, many of the greatest scientists to have ever lived have expressed a belief in God, although not an anthropomorphic God that resembles Santa Claus or Superman, but rather agreement with Albert Einstein who said "I believe in Spinoza's God, who reveals himself in the lawful harmony of all that exists."

Emergence

Many scientists have advocated a belief in reductionism which is the belief that we can understand complex phenomena by breaking it down to its smallest constituent parts. Particle physics is concerned with breaking down matter to its fundamental components. It was once believed that the atom was the fundamental particle of matter. Then we learned that atoms were made up of neutrons and protons in the atom's nucleus with electrons orbiting this nucleus. Then we learned that there were even more fundamental particles than the neutrons, protons, and electrons.

These fundamental particles are divided into two classes: fermions and bosons. Fermions are the matter particles that make up atoms and structures. They come in two subsets: quarks and leptons. Bosons also come in two classes. Most bosons are "gauge" bosons. These are the particles that carry the four forces of nature: gravity, electromagnetism, and the weak and strong nuclear forces. The other type of boson is the *Higgs boson*. The Higgs boson was hypothesized to exist for many years. It finally was discovered on July 4, 2012. It explains how elementary particles have mass. It is such an important elementary particle that it has sometimes been referred to as the *God particle*.

I and others do not believe that simply reducing matter to its smallest constituents really explains our universe and the nature of reality. There is a phenomenon called *emergence*. Robert Laughlin is a professor of physics at Stanford University. He shared the Nobel prize in physics for his work on the "fractional quantum Hall effect." In his book *A Different Universe: Reinventing Physics from the Bottom Down* (2005) he wrote "Much as I dislike the idea of ages, I think a good case can be made that science has now moved from an Age of Reductionism to an Age of Emergence, a time when the search for ultimate causes of things shifts from the behavior of parts to the behavior of the collective."

The concept of *emergent evolution* suggests that as the cosmos evolves, entirely new phenomena arise that are completely unexpected. With emergence we see that the whole is greater than the sum of its parts. In many ways it is a concept that is in direct opposition to reductionism. What I would like to do is lead you on a thought experiment. Just like the poet Dante was led on a tour of heaven, hell, and purgatory in *The Divine Comedy*, I would like to lead you on a tour of our universe from its very beginnings. Pretend that we are bystanders able to witness all of history, but with no knowledge of what will happen. I think that we will see that the universe has evolved in extraordinarily unexpected ways.

It is presumed that before the birth of our universe there was nothing but empty space. Suddenly from a tiny, microscopic speck came an unimaginable explosion which created all the energy and matter that there is in the universe. This explosion propelled all this energy at the speed of light in all directions, and the energy continues its travels to this day. The universe is continuing to expand. Before the Big Bang there was no heat. A split second after the Big Bang the universe had a temperature of 1000 trillion degrees Celsius. Not only was this the beginning of energy and matter, it also was the beginning of space, time, and the laws of physics. This is the first great emergent event. Out of nothing came the beginnings of everything.

At the very beginning of the universe there existed no matter at all- just pure energy. However, within a split second the most fundamental particles formed; quarks and photons. As the universe expanded, the energy from the Big Bang began to diffuse through space and the universe began to cool. Neutrons, protons, and electrons were able to form, but they were unable to cluster into more complex structures, i.e., atoms. For the first few hundred centuries of the universe radiation reigned over matter.

"Sometime between the first few millennia and a million years after the bang" according to Eric Chaisson, "the charged elementary particles of matter began clustering into atoms." The forces responsible for the creation of atoms we now know as the electromagnetic force and the nuclear forces. The creation of atoms became widespread. This was the beginning of the age of matter, another emergent event. Who could have anticipated that energy would turn into matter? Initially the matter of the universe consisted only of hydrogen and helium atoms.

The next emergent event was the clustering of matter into galaxies. The hydrogen and helium atoms clumped themselves together into what we now know as galaxies. It is likely that most galaxies formed first, according to Chaisson, and that the formation of stars occurred later. Later, planets formed in the various star systems. The force responsible for all this is *gravity*. Gravity was a new emergent phenomenon that organized all the matter in the universe. Think about it; what an amazing phenomenon that the universe self-organized. Most of the universe now contains no matter other than what is found in galaxies, and most of space is devoid of galaxies.

Stars have lifespans. Some stars burn out only after a few million years. Some stars can live for many billions of years. Our sun, an average sized star, is estimated to have a lifespan of 10 billion years (we are half-way through that lifespan). It is through the destruction of stars that most atomic elements were created. This brought in the era of *chemistry*, and the universe became much more interesting. I consider this another emergent event. Just about everything, including us, are made up of atoms that were created in exploding stars. Life on earth could not exist without carbon. Animals could not have evolved without oxygen. Many planets, such as the outer planets of our own solar system, are composed only of gases, but solid planets, such as the Earth, are made possible due to rocks (often composed of silicon and oxygen) and metals such as iron.

In addition, atomic elements combined with each other to create compounds which made possible other essential substances such as water and salt. Who could have imagined that combining the gases of oxygen and hydrogen could produce the substance water that has this unusual new property of *wetness*? Who could have dreamed that combining sodium (an alkali metal) with chlorine (a poisonous gas) would create salt? The universe would be nothing but energy and gases were it not for the creation of all the other elements which in turn made possible all the stuff we have in existence.

Then another great emergent event occurred: life. Most of us intuitively perceive a qualitative difference between the living and the non-living, for example between a plant and a rock or between a butterfly and a chair. Still, both scientists and philosophers have a difficult time giving an easy definition of just what life is. Scientists believe that life arose as the result of chemical processes, and likely the earth is not the only place where some type of life exists.

All life on earth arose from a common ancestor and therefore every living thing is related to every other living thing on the planet. The evolution of life here on the earth radically and fundamentally changed the planet.

Photosynthetic bacteria were responsible for oxygenating earth's atmosphere. These bacteria were able to obtain energy from carbon dioxide and give off oxygen. The oxygenated atmosphere allowed for the evolution of other bacteria that were able to ingest oxygen and give off carbon dioxide. The living organisms of the earth had devised a system to keep the biosphere of the planet in balance.

The creation of life allowed for a new scientific discipline: biology. The laws of physics originated with the big bang. Chemistry began with the explosion/deaths of stars which created most elements in the universe. Biology began with the creation of life.

I would submit that the development of sense organs also was an important emergent event. Eyes, ears, tongue, nose, and skin allow animals to see, hear, taste, smell, and touch. Think about it; for over ten billion years the universe was unable to see or hear itself. Most people have heard the following philosophical question: "If a tree falls in a forest and no one is around to hear it, does it make a sound?" Many of us may respond to this question similarly to Einstein's response to the quantum enigma: "Does the moon not exist until a mouse sees it?" In other words, is not the sound still there despite no one being there to hear it?

Well, that brings us to the question of just what exactly is *sound*. Sound is something that is heard, so if there is no sense organ like an ear to hear it, there is no sound. There are, however, acoustic waves. If a hammer hits a nail, a violin string is plucked, or a baby cries, there is a vibration created that can travel through a medium. That medium is most frequently air. Sound is the *reception* of these waves by our ears and the *perception* by our brains. Not only is it necessary to have the sense organ such as our ears, it is also necessary to have a brain that makes sense of the sound waves. The vibrations in our ears cause an electrical signal to go to our brain which causes us to have the perception of sound. It is the brain that is responsible for all perception. If we could detach our brain from the rest of our body, we would be unable to see, feel, taste, smell or hear anything.

When the spectacular explosions of stars going supernova occurred in the universe there was no sound. First, there were no ears to receive the vibrations and no brains to perceive the sound.

Second there is no air in space. If I am with a fellow astronaut doing a space walk outside my rocket ship and my companion crashes a cymbal, I would hear nothing in space.

While sound waves require a medium (such as air, liquids or a solid), light does not. With powerful modern telescopes we can see light from stars that originated billions of years ago.

Sound waves are different than light waves. The latter are electromagnetic waves, and as previously described it is only a small band of waves (i.e., a frequency of 400 nm to 700 nm) that our eyes can detect. When light waves have a frequency of 400 nanometers we perceive the color violet, at 550 nanometers green, and at 700 nanometers red. It was with the evolution of eyesight that the universe for the first time was able to see itself and to perceive colors.

Most of us have some knowledge about the *biology* of sense organs, but I would venture to guess that few have thought about the *physics* of sense organs. When we see colors or we hear sounds, what really is happening? All that is happening is that our sense organs are detecting waves (mechanical waves in regards to sound and electromagnetic waves in regards to light). The magic happens when our brains produce a qualitative experience to the perception. Philosophers use the term *qualia* to refer to this phenomenon.

At its most sublime, these sights and sounds can be considered *beauty*. Why can the colors of a sunset produce a moving experience when the experience is really nothing more than the detection of electromagnetic waves at certain frequencies? Why am I moved to tears or get chills up my back by a piece of music when the experience is really nothing more than the perception of various sound waves? Why are the combination of certain sound waves pleasant or moving, while other combinations are irritating?

There is a famous thought experiment about a brilliant color scientist named Mary. Mary is said to be locked up as a prisoner in a black and white room. She sees absolutely nothing that is not black and white. Mary is convinced to become an expert on a phenomenon known as "color." From black and white books, she reads everything that is available on the topic. She becomes the world's foremost expert on the topic, although she wonders what it is like to *experience* color.

One day her captors release her, and she is free to roam the town. She sees grass. "So that is what it's like to experience green." She sees a garden full of flowers. "So that is what it's like to experience red." Despite knowing all the pertinent facts about color, she discovered there was more to learn by *experiencing* color. The experience of red is very different than the experience of green. The experience of orange is much closer to the experience of red than it is to the experience of green because their electromagnetic frequencies are closer.

Qualia is an important topic when discussing the concept of *consciousness*, which is another emergent event- perhaps the most important and consequential emergent event thus far. This important topic will be covered in the next chapter of this book. Before concluding this chapter, I would like to discuss another interesting and pertinent topic: holons.

Holons

The term *holon* has been attributed to author Arthur Koestler who developed this idea in his book *The Ghost in the Machine*. The concept also was written about in the books of Ken Wilber, particularly *Sex, Ecology, Spirituality: The Spirit of Evolution* (1995). A holon is something that is both a complete whole as well as a part of something else. The concept is that everything in nature is a holon and that the universe consists of a hierarchy of holons. As the universe evolves what is a whole at one stage of evolution becomes a *part* also at a later stage. Early in the evolution of the universe there were various subatomic particles. They in turn became parts of neutrons and protons. They in turn along with electrons became part of atoms. Atoms became parts of molecules. Molecules became parts of cells, and so on. Wilber explains:

> *All developmental and evolutionary sequences that we are aware of proceed by hierarchization, or by orders of increasing holism- molecules to cells to organs to organ*

systems to organisms to societies of organisms, for example. In cognitive development, we find awareness expanding from simple images, which represent only one thing or event, to symbols and concepts which represent whole groups or classes of things and events, to rules which organize and integrate numerous classes and groups into entire networks. In moral development (male and female), we find a reasoning that moves from the isolated subject to a group or tribe of related subjects, to an entire network of groups beyond any isolated element. And so on...

These hierarchical networks necessarily unfold in a sequential or stagelike fashion, because you first have to have molecules, then cells, then organs, then complex organisms- they don't all burst on the scene simultaneously. In other words, growth occurs in stages, and stages, of course, are ranked in both a logical and chronological order. The more holistic patterns appear later in development because they have to await the emergence of the parts that they will then integrate or unify, just as whole sentences emerge only after whole words. (Wilber, 1995).

The notion of holons is a further suggestion that the universe continues to evolve and get increasingly complex.

Conclusions

I believe that science has much to teach us about God, and unfortunately our culture has considered science and religion to be two separate realms that should not inform each other. We are used to learning about God from philosophers and prophets, and indeed there is much to learn from them. I will share some of this wisdom in the next chapter. However, there is also much to learn from historians and scientists. Let me share a little of what I believe science and history can tell us about God and reality.

First, I believe God must be much bigger and grander than the God I believed in as a young person. God must be beyond comprehension and understanding. Conceivably God is as much beyond our understanding as New York City is beyond the understanding of a mouse. The universe is believed to contain more stars than there are grains of sand on the earth. Our galaxy the Milky Way is only one of 100 billion galaxies in the universe and covers over 100,000 light years across. Our universe keeps expanding. What is it expanding in? Likely empty space, and so it is conceivable that there are other universes that could exist, what scientists call the *multiverse*. The immensity of what we know about the universe and possibly the multiverse is extraordinary, mind-blowing, almost beyond belief!

Considering the vastness of space and the length of time that the universe and earth have existed, I must conclude that all of reality was not created specifically for homo sapiens and that our species is but one point on the long evolutionary timeline.

I believe that probably the most convincing argument for the existence of God is cosmic evolution. There is a direction to evolution. The universe has evolved from pure energy, to simple matter, to complex matter. The universe has evolved from lack of complexity to increasing degrees of order and complexity. Why? The second law of thermodynamics, which scientists argue is almost certainly correct, states that energy wants to disperse. The law states that entropy, the natural tendency to disorder, always increases. So, although throughout the universe overall entropy does increase, why in certain places is there increased order and complexity? What is responsible for this phenomenon? My answer would be God, although by this I am *not* suggesting a supernatural explanation. I believe it is fully possible (and probably likely) that more naturalistic explanations will eventually be found. Nevertheless, it is this force of cosmic evolution, whether we call it *God, spirit, Élan vital,* or something else that I would conclude is the purpose and meaning for all existence.

The concept of holons is consistent with the idea of increasing complexity and has something to say, I believe, about God. Early Christians have noted that God is the "alpha and omega," i.e., the beginning and the ending. Put into "holon" terms, God is the *all*. God preceded the Big Bang, and God is the totality of what the universe (or perhaps multiverse) will evolve to be. As parts evolve into wholes, and those wholes become parts of other wholes, and those wholes become parts of still grander wholes, the climax might be what Pierre Teilhard de Chardin termed the *omega point*, what the universe or multiverse eventually evolves to become.

Not only is the universe becoming more complex quantitatively, it also is evolving qualitatively. Emergence is the phenomenon in which completely novel and unexpected evolutionary events occur. Perhaps the most incredible emergent event to have occurred thus far in cosmic evolution has been the emergence of consciousness, which will be the primary focus of the next chapter of this book.

Scientists have been in search of a "theory of everything" which would explain how the different forces of nature are unified. The explanation for the unification of these forces would go a long way in informing me further about God, for I see God as being this unifying force. Sir Isaac Newton informed us that the force that causes an apple to fall from a tree to the ground and the force that causes the moon to revolve around the earth is the same force: *gravity*. James Clerk Maxwell informed us that two known forces, electricity and magnetism, were really a single force that became known as *electromagnetism*. With the discovery of radiation scientists discovered the *strong nuclear force* which holds together the nuclei of atoms and the *weak nuclear force* which is responsible for some forms of radioactivity. In the 1960s scientists were able to explain the unification of the electromagnetic and weak forces, the electroweak force.

Scientists still have a long way to go to provide a unified "theory of everything" though. We do not yet know how gravity can be unified with the other forces described above. Why is the physics of subatomic particles (quantum physics) different from classical physics (the physics of large objects)? *Quantum gravity* is being researched to explain this. Just what are these new forces that we now know as dark matter and dark energy?

The Center for Astrophysics (a collaboration of Harvard and Smithsonian) on their website explains:

Dark matter makes up most of the mass of galaxies and galaxy clusters, and is responsible for the way galaxies are organized on grand scales. Dark energy, meanwhile, is the name we give the mysterious influence driving the accelerated expansion of the universe. What these substances are and how they work are some of the major challenges facing modern astronomers.

God, for me, is the entity that unifies all these forces and explains the evolution of the universe. I believe there is more to existence than just matter/energy- the physical world. That is what I will be talking about in the next chapter. I believe that God is the whole of all- the supreme holon.

Questions for Contemplation or Discussion

Chapter Four. God Part 1

1. Who is God to you?

2. What is it that informs your beliefs? Why do you believe what you believe?

Chapter Five

God Part 2:

From Parts to The Whole

Consciousness

The term *consciousness* can have several meanings. A football player can be knocked out and have a "loss of consciousness." It can mean awareness, as in "he was not conscious of what he was doing." My use of the term is focused on it being a subjective experience. I believe it was an emergent event for organisms to be able to *experience* life. It involves a sense of self. When I think thoughts, feel pain, or experience emotions there is a sense of a *me* that is experiencing all of this.

Philosopher Thomas Nagel put it this way: "An organism is conscious if there is something that it is like to be that organism." Nagel wrote an influential article that was published in the Philosophical Review in 1974 titled *What is it like to be a bat?* Bats are very different from other mammals in that they have limited vision and primarily find food by echolocation which involves bouncing sound waves off objects to navigate and find food. They basically see with sound. What is it like to be a bat and to "see" this way? The question suggests that there is an inner subjectivity that is likely different for bats than other animals. What is it like to be a bat, a cow, a person, me?

There are many philosophers and neuroscientists who are materialists and/or reductionists who think that consciousness really is nothing more than biological processes, and that the experience of consciousness is nothing more than an illusion. Philosopher Daniel Dennett is one of the more well-known proponents of this view.

The idea of mind as distinct in this way from the brain, composed not of ordinary matter but of some other, special kind of stuff, is dualism, and it is deservedly in disrepute today.... The prevailing wisdom, variously expressed and argued for, is materialism: there is only one sort of stuff, namely matter- the physical stuff of physics, chemistry, and physiology- and the mind is somehow nothing but a physical phenomenon. In short, the mind is the brain." (Dennett, 1999).

Philosopher David Chalmers is one of the most well-known proponents of an opposing view that physics and biology do not fully explain consciousness. Chalmers agrees with Dennett that physics and biology do explain (or are on the road to explaining) many aspects of consciousness such as alertness, memory, perception, thinking and judgment (what Chalmers calls the *psychological* concept of mind). We know that artificial intelligence can surpass the human brain in many cognitive domains such as memory and processing speed. In 2011 a computer called "Watson" beat two champions on the Jeopardy game show. In 1997 a computer called "Deep Blue" beat champion Gary Kasparov at chess. Artificial intelligence is becoming more and more integral to American life including such innovations as self-driving cars, internet search engines such as Google, and home devices such as "Alexa" or "Siri."

The psychological concept of mind is what neuropsychologists are very familiar with. The practice of clinical neuropsychology involves evaluating various cognitive domains which are associated with various regions of the brain. The hippocampus is involved with recent memory. The occipital lobe is involved with the processing of visual information. The auditory cortex is involved with hearing. The limbic system is involved with emotions. The frontal lobe is involved with planning, attention, and judgment. The temporal lobe is important for storing memories. We know that cognition is the result of physical processes in the brain.

We also know that psychological mind and the brain affect behavior and perception in many ways that are *unconscious*. For example, when driving people frequently get lost in their own thoughts about something. Their consciousness is focused on one issue or another that consumes their attention rather than their driving. Yet they can satisfactorily drive and they safely arrive home perhaps remembering nothing at all about the drive. Driving is a task that requires significant cognitive resources, and yet we can manage it "unconsciously," or on autopilot if you will. There is much that our brains do on an unconscious level.

Nobel prize winning psychologist and economist Daniel Kahneman suggests that there are two different modes of thinking which he labels System 1 (which is thinking which happens automatically and quickly) and System 2 (which requires conscious effort and attention). "The capabilities of System 1 include innate skills that we share with other animals. We are born prepared to perceive the world around us, recognize objects, orient attention, avoid losses, and fear spiders" (Kahneman, 2011). To be able to read and understand what I wrote here in this book requires system 2. Both modes of thinking are aspects of psychological mind.

Chalmers says that these represent what really are the *easy* problems of consciousness. He said that Dennett and others do not explain, however, the *hard* problem of consciousness, which is *subjectivity* or what Chalmers calls the *phenomenal* concept of mind. The domain of the psychological mind is what the mind *does*, while the domain of the phenomenal mind is what it *feels*.

> *Consciousness, however, is as perplexing as it ever was. It still seems utterly mysterious that the causation of behavior should be accompanied by a subjective inner life. We have good reason to believe that consciousness arises from physical systems such as brains, but we have little idea how it arises, or why it exists at all. How could a physical system such as a brain also be an experiencer? Why should there*

196

be "something it is like" to be such a system? Present-day scientific theories hardly touch the really difficult questions about consciousness. We do not just lack a detailed theory; we are entirely in the dark about how consciousness fits into the natural order. (Chalmers, 1996)

The hypothesis that consciousness is an illusion really is an unsatisfying explanation to me. There must be something special about an organism to be able to *experience* an illusion. To have an illusion is to experience. Computers cannot have an illusion. It seems the phenomenon of illusion requires having consciousness.

I wrote previously about the phenomenon of *qualia* in regards to music and color. The term really is synonymous with consciousness or having subjective experience. In addition to auditory experiences such as music and visual experiences such as seeing colors, qualia include olfactory experiences such as smelling a rose or freshly baked bread, taste experiences such as a tart cherry or cinnamon, tactile experiences such as the feel of water or sandpaper, experiences of hot and cold, experience of pain, itches and tickles, the experience of mental imagery such as a sexual image, and the experience of emotions. It also includes the sense of having a self. Chalmers puts it this way:

One sometimes feels that there is something to conscious experience that transcends all these specific elements: a kind of background hum, for instance, that is somehow fundamental to consciousness and that is there even when the other components are not. (Chalmers, 1996)

There is a sense that there is a *me* that is inhabiting my body and brain. Why do we have this sense? What is the evolutionary purpose for being an *experiencer*? Philosophers have struggled with this question for a long time, and many philosophers have utilized a thought experiment about zombies. The zombies I am talking about are not like the zombies you will find in horror films that are the walking dead, beings that are severely cognitively deficient. The zombies I am talking about are those who are just like you and me except they are not conscious. If I were to have a hypothetical zombie twin, he would look like me, talk like me, walk like me, think like me, and have the same memories as me. Our *psychological minds* would be the same. My twin, however, would be missing *phenomenal mind*, i.e., consciousness. Most of us have the imagination to see that this could be conceptually conceivable. If then an organism is perfectly capable of living and thriving without phenomenal mind, what is its purpose, and what is it? Why would organisms need *experiences*?

There are differing theories about what consciousness is. As already mentioned, many conceive of consciousness only as biochemical processes. Many scientists and philosophers are physicalists. Either they believe that nothing exists outside of the material world of matter or that they just do not concern themselves with the possibility that there is non-material existence since they as scientists can only employ scientific methodology to the physical.

Most of the general public in the United States, however, hold a dualistic belief that in addition to the physical universe there is a spiritual realm. Most believe that people have a *soul* that is separate from their physical bodies. The concept of a soul really is synonymous with the concept of consciousness, i.e., what Chalmers calls both the psychological and phenomenal mind. This includes reason, feelings, personality, perception, and qualia. I grew up with the belief that the essence of people is their soul, and that the body is just a container for the real person. The very first prayer I was taught as a child was:

> Now I lay me down to sleep,
> I pray the Lord my soul to keep.
> If I should die before I wake,
> I pray the Lord my soul to take.

Religion has a long history of advocating a dualism between that which is physical and that which is spiritual. One of the earliest religious ideas was *animism*, the belief that everything possesses a spiritual essence, especially animals and humans, but also inanimate objects. Throughout history, particularly in the west, the idea of a soul has predominated. The religions of the earliest civilizations such as the Egyptians, Mesopotamians, Canaanites, Persians, Hebrews, Greeks, and Romans all had a belief in a soul or spirit. All the current western religions place great emphasis on the soul.

Religious people are not the only ones who are dualists. There have been secular philosophers that also have been dualists. Plato believed in the immortality of the soul and that the intellect was immaterial. The influential and famous philosopher, Renee Descartes of the 17th century is probably best known for his dualistic ideas of mind and body, now known as *Cartesian dualism.* He was famous for the dictum "Cognito ergo sum" which means "I think, therefore I am." Descartes believed that because of his subjective experience (the "hard" problem of consciousness) he must be real, although he reasoned his physical body and the entire physical world *could* possibly be an illusion. Plato and Descartes were both philosophers who were also theistic.

There are also non-theistic philosophers who argue for a *naturalistic dualism.* David Chalmers (1996) makes the argument against materialism (that there is nothing in existence outside of the physical universe) by citing the above discussed zombie thought experiment:

1. *In our world, there are conscious experiences.*
2. *There is a logically possible world physically identical to ours, in which the positive facts about consciousness in our world do not hold.*
3. *Therefore, facts about consciousness are further facts about our world, over and above the physical facts.*
4. *So materialism is false.*

Chalmers goes on to say "consciousness is a feature of the world over and above the physical features of the world." So just what is consciousness, and where does it come from? Is consciousness a single construct? Does the construct of consciousness gradually evolve? Is consciousness a dichotomous construct, i.e., is an organism either conscious or not?

The Evolution of Consciousness through Biology

My own current belief, based upon available evidence, is that there is more to existence than the physical, material world. Phenomenal consciousness and qualia cannot be explained, I do not believe, with our current understanding of physics, biology, and chemistry. Certainly, we continue to learn more and more in the physical sciences and much remains unknown, including the properties of dark matter and dark energy. We may eventually come to a naturalistic explanation for phenomenal consciousness.

I do not conceive of a strict dualism, however. It seems to me that consciousness is something that gradually evolves concurrently with the material world. The first prerequisite for consciousness seems to be life. As far as anyone knows there is no evidence for consciousness in anything that is not alive. There is no evidence that a rock, a computer, or a robot are conscious. Living organisms can sense and interact with their environments. Living things have some degree of awareness. Even plants and trees can respond to sunlight, temperature, water, and gravity, so in a sense they have the beginnings perhaps of consciousness.

Another important step in biological evolution was the development of nervous systems and the emergence of *sentience*. The term *sentience* has been defined in various ways. What I mean by the term is "the ability to *experience* sensations." An important development in biological evolution was the birth of vertebrates around 500 million years ago. The vertebrates include fish, amphibians, reptiles, birds, and mammals. With the advent of vertebrates, we have complex and specialized nervous systems which contain a brain, spinal cord, and peripheral sensory and motor nerves. Invertebrates are not believed to be capable of feeling pain, with a possible exception: octopuses.

Vertebrates do experience pain as well as many other sensations. As vertebrates we have developed complex sense organs allowing us to see, hear, feel, smell and taste. The input from these sense organs travel to our brains where the information is processed. Without brains our eyes, ears, taste buds and peripheral sensory nerves would be useless. Without brains we would have no senses. Without brains, we would not be capable of experiencing pain.

However, our brains can produce sensory experiences even if our sense organs such as eyes and ears are not working. People who develop blindness can see in their dreams (although those who are born blind and thus have never experienced sight cannot). There is a syndrome called Charles Bonnet Syndrome in which blind people experience visual hallucinations. Deaf people also can experience auditory hallucinations (although these people also cannot experience sound if they were born deaf).

During my employment at pain clinics, I have met with many patients who have chronic debilitating pain that is the result of dysfunction to their central nervous system (i.e., brain, brainstem, and spinal cord). For example, a patient may have had a stroke and as a result has chronic pain to a foot. There is no problem with the foot. The pain is coming from the brain. A relatively common phenomenon of people who had a limb amputated is *phantom limb pain*. Although a limb, such as a foot, has been amputated, the person can still feel pain or other sensations in the foot that is no longer there. The pain is *real*; it is just originating from the brain or spinal cord and not from the foot.

Our sense organs are very important for giving us information about the world and increasing our level of consciousness. Animals vary in terms of the acuity of their senses which affects their perceptions of the world. I already mentioned the oft cited article by Thomas Nagel titled *"What is it like to be a bat?"* Presumably the world view of a bat is different than it is for us given that they do not primarily see objects but navigate instead by echolocation. Psychologist Susan Blackmore (2017) discusses further these differences in animals.

> *Snakes, for example, have an acute sense of smell and some have special sensors that detect infrared to catch their prey. Birds have little or no sense of smell, but they can see ultraviolet light that humans cannot. In fact, many birds have a four-colour visual system, which gives them a much richer ability to see colour than we have with our*

human three-colour system. What is it like to see a colour that humans cannot see? We cannot even imagine this because we have to use our visual brain to imagine with and it lacks any representation of ultraviolet colours.

Insects, meanwhile, have compound eyes with thousands of separate lenses rather than a single eye like birds and mammals. They too can see in the ultraviolet. Lots of insects have an acute sense of smell, using trails to lead others to food; or communicating with each other using pheromones that they can detect through their antennae. What is their experience like? What is it like to smell a rotting mouse corpse using a sensitive antenna? For a fly that lays her eggs in such a corpse, it presumably smells delightful. From learning about the senses of other animals we must conclude that, in this forest, every creature would be having a completely different experience. They would each inhabit an entirely different world, or Umwelt.

The term *umvelt* refers to the *perceptual experience* of animals. Presumably the perceptual world is different for various animals, particularly if they depend on sense organs that are very different than the sense organs we humans depend on, such as echolocation for bats, electrical fields for sharks, magnetic fields for sea turtles, etc. We tend to think that our senses give us a clear representation of reality, when in actuality our brains create our experience of reality. Our senses detect stimuli which are converted to electrical signals which travel to our brains. The photoreceptors in visual systems of animals detect electromagnetic waves, the chemoreceptors in olfactory systems of animals detect molecules, the mechanoreceptors detect vibrations, pressure, and touch, etc. Our brains then convert these various stimuli to perceptions and experiences.

Principals of biological evolution would suggest that the purpose of all this is for animals to better survive, not for animals (including humans) to get a clearer perception of reality. The understanding of reality requires reason. Our human perceptual experience gives us the impression that the world is made up of individual things, when actually the entire cosmos is a single entity. More about this later in the chapter.

Another important development in the evolution of consciousness came with the development of the limbic system in the brains of mammals. This neural structure advance is important for emotion, empathy, and altruism. It is the reason that people generally desire mammals as pets instead of reptiles or amphibians.

Homo sapiens are not the only species that have emotions. Most of us pet owners believe that our pets have emotions. I have witnessed in my dogs what appears to be happiness, excitement, jealousy, irritability, anger, and fear. We can only make assumptions about our pets' feelings as they cannot express in words how they feel. We do have to be careful about anthropomorphism, i.e., the inappropriate attribution of human traits to animals, but we also must be careful to avoid anthropocentrism, i.e., tendencies to elevate our own species above and apart from the rest of nature. The brain structures responsible for emotions, empathy and altruism also exist in other mammals, and so why wouldn't other animals have these qualities? Why in the world would one assume that only humans feel when we know that there is evolutionary continuity among the various species.

Biologist Marc Bekoff, professor emeritus of Ecology and Evolutionary Biology at the University of Colorado, has researched extensively the emotional lives of animals. In his book *The Emotional Lives of Animals* (2008) he writes:

> *It's bad biology to argue against the existence of animal emotions. Scientific research in evolutionary biology, cognitive ethology, and social neuroscience supports the view that numerous and diverse animals have rich and deep emotional lives. Emotions have evolved as adaptations in numerous species, and they serve as a social glue to bond animals with one another.*

Not only does Bekoff maintain that non-human animals have emotions, but that many also have a sense of morality. "Animals not only have a sense of justice, but also a sense of empathy, forgiveness, trust, reciprocity, and much more as well" (2009). Zoologist and ethologist Frans De Waal also has written extensively about the capacity of many mammals for empathy, sympathy, altruism, and morality.

Another milestone in the evolution of consciousness is the development of self-consciousness. It is the awareness of oneself as a distinct individual. It requires one to be able to think about one's own mental state. Researchers have utilized the *mirror test* to try to determine when in evolutionary development animals develop self-awareness. The crucial question is whether animals can recognize themselves in mirrors. Human children typically develop this ability between 18 and 30 months. Chimpanzees, bonobos, and orangutans consistently pass the test. There also has been evidence for the ability in elephants, magpies (a type of crow), and dolphins.

Human beings have had increasingly larger brains evolve over several million years. Humans and chimpanzees converged from a common ancestor about seven million years ago. Many people have difficulty believing the notion of humans evolving from an ancestor of the chimpanzee. This is due mostly, I think, to people having difficulty grasping the length of time that seven million years is. It is approximately 280,000 human generations!

One of our earliest ancestors, Australopithecus afarensis from 3 to 3.7 million years ago had a brain mass relative to the whole body of 1.2%. This increased to 1.46% in homo erectus (1.8 to 0.03 MYA) and increased to 2.75% in homo sapiens. The development of our large neocortex has enabled modern humans to think conceptually, to reason, and to systematically problem solve. Historian Yuval Noah Harari in his bestselling book *Sapiens* called this the *Cognitive Revolution*.

This brings us to another incredibly important milestone in the evolution of consciousness: the development of symbolic language. Many animals can communicate on some level. Various vocalizations by animals can be used to warn others of danger or to woo mates, but only humans have evolved the brain power to develop symbolic language.

Rather than using sounds or gestures to refer to one particular thing, we can use sounds as conceptual parcels that refer to whole categories of ideas and things. Furthermore, through syntax, or the careful arrangement of words according to grammatical rules, we can convey multiple possible relationships between different people, things, and ideas. (We can tell the difference between "I kicked you" and "I was kicked by you.") The result is that we share so much information that the amount of shared information in each community begins to accumulate from generation to generation. That sustained increase in shared knowledge is the foundation of human history because it ensures that, as a general rule, later generations will have more knowledge than earlier generations so that their behaviors will slowly change over time (Christian et al., 2014).

Not only is symbolic language important for the accumulation of knowledge, it also is important, I believe, for the evolution of consciousness. When we *think* we are mostly utilizing language. We have a running dialogue in our heads pretty much all the time which is very difficult to turn off. The ability to shut our minds off and to just *experience* rather than think is one of the first skills to learn in order to meditate. Consider the answer to a question like "What is it that makes life meaningful and why?" .... Now try to answer it in your mind without the use of words in your mind. We really cannot think without symbolic language. We cannot introspect or conceptualize without symbolic language. We cannot create a narrative without symbolic language.

Thus far in this discussion about the evolution of consciousness I have not yet gotten to the "hard problem" of consciousness, i.e., phenomenal consciousness. When does the subjectivity of "being me" develop. I personally do not believe it evolved in humans until after the development of symbolic language. We become aware of ourselves as individuals, I think, largely through ongoing internal narratives. Because symbolic language is an ability that only humans have, they are the only species, I believe, who are phenomenally conscious.

Psychologist, Julian Jaynes, whose life work was to research and write about consciousness agreed with this assessment. He is most known for his book *The Origin of Consciousness in the Breakdown of the Bicameral Mind* (1976). Jaynes presented several interesting hypotheses in this book including his belief that symbolic language has been around for less than twelve thousand years (rather than over a million years which is the prevailing thought by historians), and that consciousness, as he defines it, did not develop until around the end of the second millennium BCE in Mesopotamia and Greece.

Regardless of when symbolic language first evolved, I cannot imagine having a rich, inner life without language. I would have no narrative of my life. I would not be able to contextualize my life. I would not be able to plan for a future. I would have no sense of a *me* making decisions.

So, in summary, I believe consciousness is a phenomenon that evolves, and the first emergent event that is a prerequisite for consciousness is life. As living organisms develop, they acquire the ability to sense in some way their environment and to interact with it.

The next important step in the evolution of consciousness came with the vertebrates who have a nervous system and the ability to experience sensory stimuli.

The next important step came with mammals who evolved the limbic system in the brain enabling the ability to experience emotions.

The next important step was the ability for self-awareness and developing a theory of mind, i.e., realizing that I am an individual who is separate from other individuals. Primarily only the more advanced mammals seem to have evolved this ability. This has enabled us to develop greater empathy and sympathy which has led to the development of morality.

Homo sapiens are unique in that our brains greatly evolved and as a result we are capable of complex thinking. We can reason and think abstractly. We were able to develop symbolic language which allowed us to think in narratives. It allowed us to develop phenomenal consciousness.

The concept of levels of consciousness can have practical implications for such controversial issues as abortion and animal rights. Many people tout the belief that life begins with conception. Actually, life begins earlier than this. One must have a *living* egg and *living* sperm to create a living embryo. Embryos and fetuses are alive, but the important question for me is at what point do "the lights come on"? When does it become sufficiently conscious? When does brain activity begin?

The key milestone for me is when the fetus becomes sentient, i.e., sense organs are functional, and the brain can perceive sensory input. Although electrical brain activity can be first detected when the fetus is forty to forty-three days old, this is very primitive and disorganized neural activity. Sensory systems seem to come online around week 24. A particularly important sensory event, I believe, is the ability to experience pain. This has been addressed by the American College of Obstetricians and Gynecologists:

> *A human fetus does not have the capacity to experience pain until after viability. Rigorous scientific studies have found that the connections necessary to transmit signals from peripheral sensory nerves to the brain, as well as the brain structures necessary to process those signals, do not develop until at least 24 weeks of gestation. Because it lacks these connections and structures, the fetus does not even have the physiological capacity to perceive pain until at least 24 weeks of gestation.*
>
> *In fact, the perception of pain requires more than just the mechanical transmission and reception of signals. Pain is "an emotional and psychological experience that requires conscious recognition of a noxious stimulus." This capacity does not develop until the third trimester at the earliest, well past the period between 20 weeks and viability. The evidence shows that the neural circuitry necessary to distinguish touch from painful touch does not, in fact, develop until late in the third trimester. The occurrence of*

intrauterine fetal movement is not an indication that a fetus can feel pain.

A common argument from opponents of abortion is that a fetus (and even an embryo) is not just living but that they have the potential for human life. The reverence is not for life itself but for human life. The argument is that it is wrong to kill anything that has the potential to become a human being. However, with the technology that now exists with cloning, somatic cells such as blood cells, muscle cells and nerve cells also can be used to create a human being. Is it then wrong to destroy any cell of the human body?

The development of sentience is also a key development, I think, in considering animal rights, particularly the capacity to feel pain and to suffer. We know that vertebrates experience pain. This was a conclusion of a 2009 consensus study of the National Research Council on the "Recognition and Alleviation of Pain in Laboratory Animals". It used to be widely believed that humans and other animals were qualitatively different. We now know conclusively that this is not true, particularly with recent research in genetics. All of life is related and is on the same continuum.

There was a time in humanity's history when infanticide was acceptable, slavery was okay, and genocide of other ethnic groups was fine. These practices are now widely condemned and abhorred. Humanity has evolved. I believe there will come a time when our treatment of animals will join the list of practices that are viewed as cruel and barbaric.

I look forward to the day when all sentient beings are treated with the compassion and respect they deserve. I might also add that I look forward to decreased incidences of unwanted pregnancies, decreased abortions, and if abortions are required that they happen as early in fetal development as possible. I also look forward to the day when all children are born into homes where they are wanted, loved, and have adequate resources to thrive.

What I have described is a conception of consciousness as being a construct that is emergent and has evolved along with biological evolution. A differing view of consciousness or mind is *panpsychism* which is the conception that consciousness is a fundamental property of the universe that has always existed just like mass (of matter) or the various forces of nature such electromagnetism. Panpsychist views and emergent views are usually seen as being in opposition to each other, although I do not think they need to be. I believe that life has evolved with emergent events that have allowed us to access in ever increasing degrees this mysterious and ubiquitous force that for me could be called God. In other words, I believe in a pre-existent God who has become increasingly manifest to us as we have developed the abilities to perceive and understand, with the most recent emergent and significant event being the emergence of consciousness, an essential aspect of God.

I have previously talked about *qualia* as being an aspect of consciousness. Qualia are the subjective experiences of sensory stimulation. Let us take the example of color. Color occurs because of light, and light consists of electromagnetic waves. A particular color, for example teal, occurs because it has a particular electromagnetic wave length. Electromagnetism is a force of nature that has existed since the beginnings of the universe, but it took evolution billions of years before there was life forms that were able to see light and even longer to *experience* light.

Acoustic waves have existed on earth since the appearance of an atmosphere. The air is a medium over which acoustic waves can travel. However, it took millions of years for life forms to develop sense organs to hear sound, and likely millions of years even longer for organisms to appreciate the beauty of a melody or a harmonious chord.

Beauty is something that took billions of years to emerge. Like sound (and pain), it is something that requires a conscious being to perceive and experience it before it can exist.

The qualities of truth, beauty, and goodness (known as the *Transcendentals*) are said to describe God. They also are the qualities, I believe, that we should most aspire to. By striving toward these ideals, we are drawn closer to God. God is the epitome of these attributes. It has been only through the process of the evolution of consciousness that we humans have been able reach these ideals to the extent that we have.

Let me review these critical biological milestones in the evolution of consciousness:

1. Life
2. Nervous System (Vertebrates)
3. Limbic System (Mammals)
4. Self-Awareness (Higher mammals)
5. Cognitive Revolution and Symbolic Language (Sapiens)

Evolution of Consciousness through Culture

At this point there has been little biological change in Homo sapiens from our hunter-gatherer ancestors. When our ancestors left Africa 50,000 to 80,000 years ago, they would have looked like us, behaved like us, and had brains the same size as us. They would have had our cognitive abilities and possessed symbolic language. There has been little change in our biology as humans since then. However, the evolution of consciousness has continued due to cultural evolution. This is what I discussed in chapter three on human development. Further significant progress in stages of consciousness occurred particularly due to:

1. The Axial Age
2. The Enlightenment
3. Human Rights Movement

The Axial Age was the period between 800 and 200 BCE. It was one of the most significant periods of time in the history of the world because morality began to take center stage in the world's religions. Religion made the third great step in its evolution: from pleasing the gods for selfish reasons, to a code of detailed and strict laws and regulations, to an elevated consciousness about the importance of love and caring of one's neighbors. It was during this time that the "golden rule" appeared in its various iterations.

The Enlightenment of the 18th century was a time when another stage in the evolution of consciousness occurred. There was new emphasis on the discovery of truth which can be found only through reason. New procedures were developed to discover truths (the scientific method). New value was placed on ideals such as liberty, freedom, tolerance, and progress.

Although Thomas Jefferson expressed high ideals in the Declaration of Independence, we had a long way to go as a country to realize a "more perfect union." Slavery continued. Women had no rights. We have made progress with a more perfect world with the advent of the civil rights movement. A very important milestone occurred in 1948 when the United Nations General Assembly made a "Universal Declaration of Human Rights" which affirmed the "recognition of the inherent dignity and of the equal and inalienable rights of all members of the human family". Whereas during the Axial Age there was new emphasis on loving our neighbors this really meant those in our *tribes*. Now there was movement for love and justice for all including those of other races, ethnicities, genders, sexual orientations, and cultures. So, in other words, religion went from being *egocentric* (only concerned with self) to *ethnocentric* (being concerned about only one's tribe, clan, or nation), to being *worldcentric* (care and concern for all peoples).

It has been proposed by numerous mystics, philosophers, psychologists, and researchers that there is another level of consciousness known as *transpersonal*. At the heart of this perspective is the realization that the cosmos is not made up of separate entities, and that this perception is an illusion. The entire cosmos is one whole. Sometimes difficult concepts are best understood with metaphors, and a favorite of mine is a story related by Mitch Albom in his book *Tuesdays with Morrie* (1997).

> *"I heard a nice little story the other day," Morrie says. He closes his eyes for a moment and I wait.*
> *"Okay. The story is about a little wave, bobbing along in the ocean, having a grand old time. He's enjoying the wind and the fresh air- until he notices the other waves in front of him, crashing against the shore.*

'My God, this is terrible,' the wave says. 'Look what's going to happen to me!'

Then along comes another wave. It sees the first wave, looking grim, and it says to him, 'Why do you look so sad?'

The first wave says, 'You don't understand! We're all going to crash! All of us waves are going to be nothing! Isn't it terrible?'

The second wave says, 'No, you don't understand. You're not a wave, you're part of the ocean.''

Eastern religions have stressed the unity of all things more so than has western religions. Fritjof Capra in his book *The Tao of Physics* (1975) explains "The most important characteristic of the Eastern world view- one could almost say the essence of it- is the awareness of the unity and mutual interrelation of all things and events, the experience of all phenomena in the world as manifestations of a basic oneness. All things are seen as interdependent and inseparable parts of this cosmic whole; as different manifestations of the same ultimate reality. The Eastern traditions constantly refer to this ultimate, indivisible reality which manifests itself in all things, and of which all things are parts. It is called *Brahman* in Hinduism, *Dharmakaya* in Buddhism, *Tao* in Taoism. Because it transcends all concepts and categories, Buddhists also call it *Tathata*, or Suchness."

It is through meditation that people can learn to directly experience this oneness. "In ordinary life, we are not aware of this unity of all things, but divide the world into separate objects and events. This division is, of course, useful and necessary to cope with our everyday environment, but it is not a fundamental feature of reality. It is an abstraction devised by our discriminating and categorizing intellect. To believe that our abstract concepts of separate 'things' and 'events' are realities of nature is an illusion." (Capra, 1975).

Mysticism

Mysticism is the experience of becoming one with God. This is usually accomplished with meditation. Although mysticism is mostly associated with the eastern religions, there have been Christian mystics as well. Religious scholar Ursula King in her 2001 book *Christian Mystics: Their Lives and Legacies throughout the Ages* defines a mystic as "a person who is deeply aware of the powerful presence of the divine Spirit: someone who seeks, above all, the knowledge and love of God and who experiences to an extraordinary degree the profoundly personal encounter with the energy of divine life. Mystics often perceive the presence of God throughout the world of nature and in all that is alive, leading to a transfiguration of the ordinary all around them. However, the touch of God is most strongly felt deep within their own hearts."

Mystics are found in all religions including Christianity. This includes Jesus of Nazareth. Jesus scholar, Marcus Borg (2006), noted:

> *For Jesus, God was not simply an article of belief, but an experienced reality. In this, he was like the most central figures of the Jewish Bible and tradition; the stories of Israel present them as people who had experienced God...I suggest that, broadly understood, the term mystic designates the kind of person Jesus was- someone who experienced God vividly and whose way of seeing and life were changed as result. What most shaped Jesus was the Jewish tradition and his mystical experience of God. He was, I argue, a Jewish mystic.*

King said that "Christian mystics have experienced God in countless ways- as the ultimate Godhead or Ground of Being, as God who is Father but also Mother, or as God intimately present in the humanity of Jesus through his life, death, and resurrection, in the glory of the cosmic Christ or in the presence and gifts of the Spirit. Christian mystics share certain characteristics, but they are all very different as individuals who lived in different times and places."

"All mysticism is characterized by a passion for unity. To the mystic, true Being and Ultimate Reality are One. This can be experienced as both impersonal and personal, as Ground of Being, Ultimate Source, Perfect Goodness, Eternal Wisdom, Divine Love, God, or the Godhead. This Reality contains, yet transcends, everything there is. It is the One in whom all is lost and all is found." (King, 2001).

Mystics were among the earliest Christians, including Clement of Alexandria (c. 150-c. 215) who said that the goal for Christians are to become like God ("I say, the Logos of God became man so that you may learn from man how man may become God.") and Denys (Dionysius) (C. 500) who wrote *Mystical Theology*. "The writing focuses entirely on the utter unity of God, the undivided Ultimate Reality and Godhead that lives in complete darkness beyond all light. Dionysius writes that the 'unchangeable mysteries of heavenly Truth lie hidden in the dazzling obscurity of the secret Silence, outshining all brilliance with the intensity of their darkness.' God is totally beyond the power of the intellect; contemplation is the only way to 'divine darkness,' which can never be grasped by the human mind." (King, 2001).

Christian mysticism reached its apex in the Middle Ages. Medieval mystics include St. Francis of Assisi (1181-1226), St. Bonaventure (1221-1274), Hildegard (1098-1179), and St. Bernard of Clairvaux (1090-1153). Bernard "developed a doctrine of mystical love and struggled to combine mystical absorption in God with service to others and the institutional Church." (King, 2001). Bernard wrote:

> *To lose yourself, as if you no longer existed, to cease completely to experience yourself, to reduce yourself to nothing is not a human sentiment but a divine experience... It is deifying to go through such an experience. As a drop of water seems to disappear completely in a big quantity of wine, even assuming the wine's taste and color, just as red, molten iron becomes so much like fire it seems to lose its primary state; just as the air on a sunny day seems transformed into a sunshine instead of being lit up; so it is*

necessary for the saints that all human feelings melt in a mysterious way and flow into the will of God. Otherwise, how will God be all in all if something human survives in man.

Another important medieval mystic was Meister Eckhart (1260-1327). "In his mysticism the ground of God and the ground of the soul are the same ground." He had a "strong emphasis on the absorption of the self into God in unitive mystical experience." "He drew the famous distinction between God and the Godhead. God is revealed to us as a person, but behind this revelation, this manifestation, there is the unrevealed Godhead, the 'ground' of God, undifferentiated and above all distinction, an eternal unity of which nothing can be said, the 'Nameless Nothing,' the unoriginated purity of Being, the *puritas essendi,* the Eternal Now, which we can only meet in utter stillness and silence and which Eckhart celebrates in soaring thoughts and startling paradoxes. Meister Eckhart's metaphysics of the Godhead is sometimes compared with what Indian Vedanta teaches about Brahman without attributes, especially as found in the works of Shankara." (King, 2001).

Mysticism became more out of vogue with the Protestant Reformation, although there continued to be Christian mystics throughout the centuries, including among Protestants. I would like to yet mention two Christian mystics from the modern era: Thomas Merton (1915-1968) and Pierre Teilhard de Chardin (1881-1955). Merton was a convert to Catholicism and became a Trappist. He was influenced both by Catholic mystical theology and Eastern mysticism and has become an influential proponent of mysticism. He advocates self-emptying through meditation so that God can take full control:

In meditation we do not seek to know about God as though he were an object like other objects which submit to our scrutiny and can be expressed in clear scientific ideas. We seek to know God himself, beyond the level of all the objects which he has made...The infinite God has no boundaries and our minds cannot set limits to him or to his love.

Teilhard was a French Jesuit priest and a geologist and paleontologist. His philosophical and theological thoughts are of great interest to me in that his views about God are informed by his scientific knowledge, and because he places great emphasis on evolution as do I. He believed in the spiritual evolution of the universe, and he envisioned the eventual convergence of everything into a final unity that he called the *Omega Point*.

Teilhard wrote that he experienced a sense of oneness with nature even as a child, and he continued to have mystical experiences throughout his life. He experienced the presence of God in all things which he called the "divine milieu." "The presence of the Incarnate Word penetrates everything, as a universal element, it shines at the common heart of things, as a center that is infinitely intimate to them and at the same time...infinitely distant."

Teilhard saw matter and spirit as being two aspects of one and the same cosmic energy. "Matter is the Matrix of Spirit. Spirit is the higher state of Matter." He saw love as being the indispensable force that bonds humanity and humanity with God. "Someday, after mastering the winds, the waves, the tides and gravity, we shall harness for God the energies of love, and then, for a second time in the history of the world, humankind will have discovered fire."

Although most Christians, I think, do not give much thought to the immanence of God, many Biblical scholars such as John Shelby Spong (2018) opine that is the meaning of the Holy Spirit. "Christology arose in the late third and early fourth centuries with the suggestion that God had entered human life, which served to give human life a dignity it had not had before...Next, we began to entertain the story of the Holy Spirit, which served to universalize the Christ story. Now all people, not just Jesus, could be God-filled." There is a well-known Christian hymn that states:

We are One in The Spirit,
We are One in The Lord.
We are One in The Spirit,
We are One in The Lord.
And we pray that all unity may one day be restored

Next let me speak about the eastern religions. The beginnings of Hinduism can be traced to an early civilization of the Indus River Valley (present day Pakistan). The civilization's origins date to before 2500 BCE. Like the religions of the Middle East, the earliest religions of Asia focused on rituals to please gods in order to keep the world running smoothly and ensuring human prosperity. These rituals and hymns to the gods were preserved orally for centuries until they were written down between the 4th and 6th centuries CE. They are called the *Vedas*. The Vedic religion of that time was called *Brahmanism*.

It was during the Axial Age that Indian people began to evolve in their religious concerns, i.e., that there were more important things than ritual and material concern. Some people began to strive to understand ultimate reality. Between 900 and 500 BCE the teachings of Indian religious sages were written down. These teachings are known as the *Upanishads*. The essential teaching is that our individual spirits or souls (called *Atman*) is identical to the essence of everything else (called *Brahman*). Everything is part of the One. The experience of separateness is an illusion. The following are some excerpts from the Shvetashvatara Upanishad (translation by Eknath Easwaran, 2007):

In the depths of meditation, sages
Saw within themselves the Lord of Love,
Who dwells in the heart of every creature.
Deep in the hearts of all he dwells, hidden
Behind the gunas of law, energy,
And inertia. He is One. He it is
Who rules over time, space, and causality. [I,3]

On this ever-revolving wheel of life
The individual self goes round and round
Through life after life, believing itself
To be a separate creature, until
It sees its identity with the Lord of Love
And attains immortality in the indivisible whole [I,6]

The Lord of Love holds in his hand the world,
Composed of the changing and the changeless,
The manifest and the unmanifest.
The separate self, not yet aware of the Lord,
Goes after pleasure, only to become
Bound more and more. When it sees the Lord,
There comes an end to its bondage. [I,8]

All is change in the world of the senses,
But changeless is the supreme Lord of Love.
Meditate on him, be absorbed in him
Wake up from this dream of separateness. [I,10]

He has thousands of heads, thousands of eyes,
Thousands of feet; he surrounds the cosmos
On every side. This infinite being
Is ever present in the hearts of all.
He has become the cosmos. He is what was
And what will be. Yet he is unchanging.
The lord of immortality.
His hands and feet are everywhere, his heads
And mouths everywhere. He sees everything,
Hears everything, and pervades everything
* [III, 14-16]*

He is pure consciousness, omnipresent,
Omnipotent, omniscient, creator
Of time and master of the three gunas.
Evolution takes place at his command [VI,2]

India gave rise to other faiths other than Hinduism, including Buddhism. Siddhartha Gautama was born in what is now Nepal around the year 563 BCE. Born a prince, he gave up his life of luxury to live a life of asceticism. He spent most of his time involved in deeper and deeper states of meditation. He believed that all sentient beings were transient and that all of reality is a single whole. *Nirvana* is achieved by overcoming the illusion that there is a self.

In China a major philosophy known as *Daoism* developed by a person or persons known as Laozi. The philosophy is explained in the 4th century BCE book known as the *Daodejing*. The Daodejing consists of two parts: chapters 1-37 focus on the *dao* or *way*, while chapters 38-81 discuss *de* which means virtue or integrity. The concept of the *dao* is very similar to the Hindu concept of Brahman. "The Daodejing describes a mystical ideal in the sense that those who realize the Way lose a strong sense of themselves as distinct, autonomous agents and to some extents are thought to merge into the dao's underlying patterns and processes. In such a state, one does not conceive of oneself as apart from and independent of the rest of the world. While aware of herself and the things around her, such a person does not stand back to view and analyze the dao. Since she sees herself as inextricably intertwined with the overall harmony of the dao, she never assumes the perspective of a narrowly self-interested agent seeking to maximize her individual well-being. Any such higher-order perspective is alien to the Daoist ideal." (Ivanhoe, 2003)

The Perennial Philosophy

Aldous Huxley (1894-1963) was a British writer who authored over fifty books including *The Doors of Perception*, a nonfiction work which describes Huxley's experiences with mescaline and which influenced the rock band The Doors to take the band name that they did, and *Brave New World*, ranked as one of the greatest novels of all time. Huxley also wrote *The Perennial Philosophy*, a comparative study of religion and especially mysticism in western and eastern religions, a subject which fascinated Huxley.

The term "perennial philosophy" was used by the philosopher and mathematician Gottfried Leibniz who adopted it from the writings of Italian Catholic theologian Agostin Steuco. The essence of the term is that at the core of all religions is a common philosophy. Religions differ in *exoteric* teachings (i.e., stories, myths) but not in the core teachings of the great sages and prophets on which religions are based, such as Jesus, the Hebrew prophets, Buddha, Laozi, and the writers of the Upanishads.

To my mind there are two fundamental principles that unify religions. First is that there exists an ultimate source, a ground of being. This source goes by different names including God, Godhead, Brahman, Buddha-nature, Ayn Sof, Allah, Tao, Ati, Great Perfection, the One, Satchitananda, and the Supreme Identity. I will use the term most familiar to me: God. God is both transcendent (beyond and surpassing all) as well as immanent (inhabiting all). God's presence is everywhere and in everything. All religions have as a core teaching the importance of unifying with God, the ultimate source of reality. This is expressed in various ways including merging with God, becoming one with God, having a relationship with God, doing God's will, loving God, etc.

Ken Wilber (2017) wrote about the religious traditions: they "divided their teachings into two broad areas, often called 'exoteric' and 'esoteric.' The exoteric was the 'outer teaching,' meant for the masses and the ordinary, and consisted of a series of tales, usually in mythic form, and it was taught that those who believed them would live everlastingly in a heaven with that tradition's ultimate Being or God or Goddess. But the esoteric teachings were the 'inner teachings,' the 'secret teachings,' usually kept from the public and open only to individuals of exceptional quality and character. These teachings weren't merely mythic stories and beliefs; they were psychotechnologies of consciousness transformation. By performing the specific practices and exercises, an individual could reach an actual awakening to his or her own True Nature, gaining a Great Liberation and ultimate Freedom from the terror-inducing limitations of ordinary life and a direct introduction to ultimate Reality itself."

The other core principle I believe of religions is for the care, compassion, and love of others. It is the call for morality. As I have previously discussed, this was the great revolution of religion that occurred in the Axial Age. It is expressed in the various iterations of the Golden Rule.

In everything do to others as you would have them do to you; for this is the law and the prophets. Jesus (Matthew 7:12)

Do to others as you would have them do to you. Jesus (Luke 6:31)

For the whole law is summed up in a single commandment, "You shall love your neighbor as yourself." St. Paul (Galatians 5:14)

Hurt not others in ways that you yourself would find hurtful. Buddha (Udanavarga 5:18)

One should never do that to another which one regards as injurious to one's own self. This in brief, is the rule of dharma. Other behavior is due to selfish desires. Brihaspati, Mahabharata (Hinduism)

Killing a living being is killing one's own self; showing compassion to a living being is showing compassion to oneself. He who desires his own good, should avoid causing any harm to a living being. Suman Suttam, verse 151 (Jainism)

Never impose on others what you would not choose for yourself. Confucius (Analects XV.24)

Try your best to treat others as you would wish to be treated yourself and you will find that this is the shortest way to benevolence. Mencius (VII.A.4)

Love for your brother what you love for yourself.
Muhammad (Hadith 13).

Christian theologian Marcus Borg published a book (1997) comparing sayings attributed to both Jesus and Buddha demonstrating the similarities between these two enlightened religious leaders which "involve both particular teachings (for example, love of enemies) and general principles (the primacy of compassion)." "What Jesus and the Buddha said about 'the way' is remarkably similar...it involves a new way of seeing...Both Jesus and the Buddha sought to bring about in their hearers a radical perceptual shift- a new way of seeing life. The familiar line from a Christian hymn expresses an emphasis common to both. 'I once was blind, but now I see.'"

"Second, both paths or ways involve a similar psychological and spiritual process of transformation." The Buddha stressed the importance of "letting go." Suffering is the result of desire. Happiness comes from letting go of desire. Jesus too taught to relinquish worldly desires for material wealth and self-aggrandizement. Jesus said it is easier for a camel to go through the eye of a needle than for a rich man to enter the kingdom of God. "Those who empty themselves will be exalted, and those who exalt themselves will be emptied; those who make themselves last will be first, and the first last." (Matthew 23:12)

"Third, the ethical fruit of this internal transformation is the same for both: becoming a more compassionate being."

Physics and Oneness

Religious mystics of all the great religious traditions testify to the oneness of reality. Interestingly, the knowledge we have acquired in scientific disciplines also suggest this. Our universe began with an event 13.8 billion years ago that we now refer to as the Big Bang and also refer to as a *singularity*, a term which does imply a unity. We live in the *uni*-verse. The universe is a single evolving entity. Humans do not just live in this universe; we are part of the universe. Humans do not just live on the earth; we are part of the earth.

At the time of the Big Bang all the energy and matter that would ever exist came into being. That energy and matter also would never be destroyed but would change in form. As Einstein's formula of E=MC2 informs us, energy can become matter, and matter can become energy. The tremendous heat that occurs in dying stars is responsible for most of the matter that we have on earth including the matter that make up our bodies. We, and almost everything we see on this planet, are the result of atoms that came from elsewhere in the universe.

Let me now refer again to two laws of thermodynamics. The fact that science refers to these as "laws" rather than "hypotheses" or even "theories" reflects the certainty that scientists have in their correctness. The first law of thermodynamics states that in a closed system the amount of energy can never be created or destroyed. Presumably our universe is a closed system. That means that with the Big Bang all the energy/matter that would ever exist came into being. All that energy/matter still exists and will exist until the end of time. However, although energy cannot be destroyed, it can be degraded and less capable of doing "work." This is the second law of thermodynamics; our universe is in a constant process of *entropy*.

All the matter in existence is related. We like to think of ourselves as separate and fully distinct individuals. We Americans perhaps particularly value the concept of individualism, i.e., being totally self-reliant and independent. However, from the perspective of physics and chemistry we are all very interrelated. We constantly lose atoms that then become part of other things or people in the world. We constantly replenish atoms when we take in nourishment. When we die our bodies decompose, and eventually all the atoms from our bodies become part of other things. It is nature's recycling program. So, picture if you can the next millennium in fast motion; people and other animals dying, bodies and other objects decomposing, atoms reconstituting themselves into other people, animals and objects being born, more death, more decomposition, more reconstitution, etc. When we die, all our energy does not. It gets repurposed and continues to live on.

When we consider biology, we are even more related. Every single living entity on earth is related. Every single living organism has descended from one common ancestor. When we die our physical bodies are not immortal. Neither are our chromosomes. Our genes, on the other hand potentially almost are. Evolutionary biologist Richard Dawkins in his book *The Selfish Gene* makes the point that natural selection really is about the propagation of genes rather than the propagation of individuals or species. Dawkins characterizes genes as "selfish" because he said it is their *intent* to replicate, whereas organisms are just the vehicle for their propagation.

> *The genes are the immortals, or rather, they are defined as genetic entities that come close to deserving the title. We, the individual survival machines in the world, can expect to live a few more decades. But the genes in the world have an expectation of life that must be measured not in decades but in thousands and millions of years.*

The stories and myths that we grew up with suggest that the cosmos is made up of various individual things. A good example of this are the two creation stories in the book of Genesis of the Hebrew and Christian scriptures. In chapter one of Genesis God is said to have made first the earth, then light, then the sky and oceans, then land, then vegetation, then the sun and stars, then animals, and then humankind. We in the Western world are programmed to think of the cosmos as a collection of individual things, and in fact our everyday perceptions lend credence to this view. In contrast the Eastern worldview stresses the inter-relatedness of everything. Capra (1975) explains:

> *In contrast to the mechanistic Western view, the Eastern view of the world is 'organic.' For the Eastern mystic, all things and events perceived by the senses are interrelated, connected, and are but different aspects or manifestations of the same ultimate reality. Our tendency to divide the perceived world into individual and separate things and to*

experience ourselves as isolated egos in this world is seen as an illusion which comes from our measuring and categorizing mentality. It is called avidya, or ignorance, in Buddhist philosophy and is seen as the state of a disturbed mind which has to be overcome...Although the various schools of Eastern mysticism differ in many details, they all emphasize the basic unity of the universe which is the central feature of their teachings...the Eastern image of the Divine is not that of a ruler who directs the world from above, but of a principle that controls everything from within.

Many scientists perceive the cosmos mechanistically and as a collection of parts. Philosophically they are *physicalists* or *materialists*. For these scientists the universe is made up of nothing but energy/matter, and the best way to understand energy/matter is to dissect it down to its most fundamental and indivisible parts. This has been the work of particle physicists, and their work certainly has contributed to our knowledge about the workings of the universe. However, other scientists maintain that the universe is more than the sum of its individual physical parts. One such physicist is David Bohm who is quoted in Fritjof Capra's book (1975):

One is led to a new notion of unbroken wholeness which denies the classical idea of analyzability of the world into separately and independently existing parts. We have reversed the usual classical notion that the independent 'elementary parts' of the world are the fundamental reality, and that the various systems are merely particular contingent forms and arrangements of these parts. Rather, we say that inseparable quantum interconnectedness of the whole universe is the fundamental reality, and that relatively independently behaving parts are merely particular and contingent forms within this whole.

This brings me to another question: Is there more to existence than the material world? I believe there is. One example is an idea. An idea does in fact exist, and yet it is not matter or energy. Richard Dawkins in The Selfish Gene primarily talks about genes, but he also talks briefly about something he calls *memes*.

> *Examples of memes are tunes, ideas, catch-phrases, clothes fashions, ways of making pots or of building arches. Just as genes propagate themselves in the gene pool by leaping from body to body via sperms or eggs, so memes propagate themselves in the meme pool by leaping from brain to brain via a process which, in the broad sense, can be called imitation.*

Dawkins points out that for millions and millions of years the DNA in our genes was the only significant means of replication. But now with the advent of culture we have this new means of replication. There now exists not only biological evolution but cultural evolution.

I also believe that *life* is more than just energy/matter. The concept of life is rather difficult to define, and there is not always a clearcut demarcation between that which is living and that which is not (a virus would be an example of this). To most of us though there seems to be an obvious difference between the living and the dead or inanimate objects. Unfortunately, this came painfully into my awareness recently with the death one month apart of our two senior dogs. Our dog, Dora, had been declining in physical health for a few years. She was quite deaf, had poor eyesight, and had to be carried up and down steps. Her death was not unexpected. Her son, Dexter, however, did die unexpectedly. He was healthy and rambunctious but developed GI difficulties, i.e., frequent vomiting and dark stools. Blood tests and imaging could not find a cause. He stopped eating and soon died from a seizure. It was jarring how this vital being was simply gone, despite all his atoms, cells and organs being just as intact as they ever were. It seemed obvious to me that there was more to Dexter than just his physical atoms.

In addition to culture and life apparently being different than energy/matter and being emergent phenomenon, I see consciousness also as being a further emergent event and that is qualitatively different than energy/matter.

The Great Chain of Being was a concept of medieval Christianity which described the believed hierarchy of all matter. At the top of the chain is God, and below God are God's creations. At the top are angels, and below angels are humans, below humans are animals, below animals are plants, and below plants are minerals or inanimate objects. The paradigm suggests that everything created by God are separate beings or things. We now know that everything evolved from pure energy and that everything is related to everything else. This would suggest a concept that Ken Wilber calls *The Great Nest of Being* which is also a hierarchical paradigm. This hierarchy might be described as matter, body, mind, soul, and spirit, or in other words energy/matter, life, mind, consciousness, and God. It is called "nest" instead of "chain" because each level evolves from a previous level rather than being totally separate and unrelated things.

God or Spirit is present at both the beginning and the end; the alpha and the omega. In the beginning was pure energy followed immediately by the beginnings of matter. After billions of years life evolved from this. Eventually life became sentient- able to sense, feel and think. Eventually consciousness developed. One needs matter before life can evolve. One needs life before sentience and reason can evolve. One needs sentience and reason before consciousness can evolve. Consciousness leads us to God.

Spirit

Ken Wilber (1998) uses the term "spirit" instead of "God" and explains the Great Nest of Being this way:

> *We have seen that the wisdom traditions subscribe to the notion that reality manifests in levels or dimensions, with each higher dimension being more inclusive and therefore "closer" to the absolute totally of Godhead or Spirit. In this sense, Spirit is the summit of being, the highest rung on the ladder of evolution. But it is also true that Spirit is the wood out of which the entire ladder and all its rungs are made.*

Spirit is the suchness, the isness, the essence of each and every thing that exists.

Wilber's conception of God or Spirit is like the conception of God expressed by philosopher Baruch Spinoza, theologian Paul Tillich, several physicists including Albert Einstein, and the conception that I have come to accept as well. Let me give you my own definition of God once again:

God is the incomprehensible source of all in our universe and beyond, whose essence is love, truth and beauty, and who becomes increasingly manifest in the unfolding evolution of the cosmos. God is the totality of all existence.

I encourage you to give some consideration to your own conception of God and come up with your own definition. I also encourage you to attempt to formulate a philosophy about the meaning of life. My own ideas about this certainly have changed from my early life when I was taught to believe that this life was a mere test period in which we had to prove our acceptance of correct beliefs about the Almighty. We had to accept "Jesus as our Lord and Savior." That acceptance and belief would get us into Heaven after we die. I was taught that getting into Heaven and avoiding Hell after death was really the only truly important life goal.

I was warned while growing up not to question too much the "orthodox" theology that I was being taught and to rely on "faith" rather than reason. I was warned that there was a slippery slope; if I questioned some of the Old Testament myths such as a literal Adam and Eve or a 6,000-year-old earth I would then start to question other teachings as well. They were right. I did. However, I was also warned that this would lead to a loss of belief in God and that I would no longer be a Christian. There they were wrong. Instead of a loss of faith, I believe I developed a more mature faith. The apostle Paul in his letter to the Corinthians wrote that when he was a child he thought and understood things like a child but now as an adult he put away these childish thoughts for a more evolved perspective. Personal evolution, cultural evolution, biological evolution, and cosmic evolution are now key concepts in my philosophy about the meaning of life. This will be the main topic of the final chapter of this book: conscious evolution.

The author of *Thank God for Evolution* (2007) and former United Church of Christ pastor Michael Dowd shared an exchange he had with a visitor to a previous church he was pastoring. "While greeting parishioners on their way out of the sanctuary, a visitor, a young man, extended his hand and declared, 'Well, Reverend, I'm an atheist!' I shook his hand and responded, 'Praise God, brother, so am I!' His face registered confusion. I continued light-heartedly, 'tell me about this God you don't believe in. I'm quite sure I don't believe in that God either.'

Nancy Ellen Abrams in her book *A God That Could Be Real* (2015) shares a memory of being in the second grade and seeing a picture book that showed God as an "old bearded man sitting on a cloud and giving orders." "I thought, of course that couldn't be real!" She describes how this led her to atheism at the age of fifteen. Abrams was committed to science and married astrophysicist Joel Primack which she said gave her a "ringside seat" to the newest discoveries in cosmology.

Abrams came to a point where she had to rethink her atheism when she developed an eating disorder. She was unable to control her compulsive eating. She apparently went to meetings of Overeaters Anonymous, a 12-step program, and discovered people who were successfully controlling their food intake with the help of a higher power, i.e., God. "How could an atheist like me find a higher power believable enough to enable me to do what I had never been able to do on my own?" Just as 12-step programs themselves suggest, she had to find a God of "my own understanding".

> *If I wanted to find a God that is real, I had to start from what's real, what actually exists. I realized that the question that matters is this: Could anything actually exist in the universe, as science understands it, that is worthy of being called God?*
>
> *If the answer to my question is yes, then this is a huge discovery. It means that those of us who feel conflicted*

*or even intellectually dismissive about a traditional kind of
God, but who long for some spiritual connection, can enjoy
the benefits of a genuine higher power in our lives, open-
heartedly.*

*This shift in approach was like waking from a
dream. Suddenly coherence became possible, because from
a cosmic perspective the answer to my question became yes.
Yes, there is something that truly fulfills the need for God
and is also consistent with a cutting-edge scientific outlook.*

I think that Michael Dowd would agree. He wrote "who
could deny that there is such a thing as "Reality as a whole' and that
'God' is a legitimate, though not a required, proper name for this
ultimacy?" Dowd said that from his experience most people concur
with the idea of an ultimate reality (or an ultimate *holon*) whether
one considers themselves a theist, atheist, agnostic, religious
nontheist, pantheist, or panentheist. Dowd lists some descriptors for
this ultimate reality:

* Source of everything   * Transcends and includes all things
* End of everything   * Expresses all forms of powerful
* Knows all things   * Holds everything together
* Reveals all things   * Suffers all things
* Present everywhere   * Transforms all things

Transpersonal Psychology

Let me now turn back to psychotherapy and give you a short
review about its evolution. As I discussed in chapter three, modern
psychotherapy is understood by many as beginning with Sigmund
Freud with his "talking cure." Through psychoanalysis (and
introspection) patients learn to break down unconscious defense
mechanisms such as repression and projection in order to gain
insight about oneself. The purpose is to discover and confront truths
about oneself in order to live more honest and functional lives.
Psychoanalytic therapies have been referred to as *First Force*
therapies.

The second major therapeutic approach (*Second Force)* was behavioral therapies (e.g., B.F. Skinner) which focused on resolving problematic behaviors; these therapies were unconcerned about inner processes and insight. They were concerned with such issues as phobias, addictive behaviors, and childhood behavioral problems.

Humanist and existential psychotherapies have been termed the *"third force"* of psychological therapies. These therapies not only treated pathologies but also were concerned with human growth, for example becoming self-actualized. Like psychodynamic therapies they focused on increased awareness and insight.

There has been further evolution of psychotherapies into a *fourth force* which focuses on issues of spirituality. This includes a sub-discipline of psychology known as *transpersonal psychology.* "Transpersonal psychology studies the self, conceived not only as isolated individual bound to the here-and-now of the present, but capable of expanding to include others, nature, or all of space and time, or of embodying some larger aspect of the world. These shifted boundaries may be reflected as non-ordinary states of consciousness" (Hartelius et al, 2013). Whereas first, second, and third force therapies focus only on the individual and the individual's personal needs, a transpersonal orientation recognizes that the boundaries used to define an individual are somewhat arbitrary and that we are a part of a much larger whole.

Transpersonal psychology works from the same premise that religious mystics and physics come from- that our individuality is an illusion and that we are a transient part of the cosmos. Hartelius et al (2013) note that transpersonal psychology "is an ambitious effort to redefine ourselves as humans and the world as we know it. It is a project that sets out to understand the cosmos in ways that are not constrained by either the sometimes-heavy hand of religious tradition or the objectifying eye of science. Instead, the transpersonal approach seeks a new vision, one in which both human science and human spirituality can be honored."

Hartelius et al (2013) also note that transpersonal psychology is part of something broader called *transpersonal studies* which is "a holistic perspective that examines human life in the context of an interconnected world. If one attempts a whole-person psychology, it soon becomes clear that the psyche is not a discrete thing functioning in isolation from body, community, or environment, but a local aspect of an interconnected whole- a whole that must be engaged in order to understand any of its facets. Transpersonal is then necessarily more than a psychology; it must also be a multidisciplinary scholarly orientation- an orientation that has been called transpersonal studies."

One of the early researchers/theorists of transpersonal psychology was Ken Wilber, who integrated over one hundred well established theories in the fields of consciousness, psychology, meditative traditions, philosophy, and sociology into a metatheory that he later called integral theory. Two very important components of his theory are the concepts of stages of consciousness (or development) and states of consciousness. His model of the stages of consciousness was influenced by developmental psychology, and his model of states of consciousness was heavily influenced by meditative religions, particularly eastern religion as discussed previously. Stages of consciousness are about "growing up," and eastern meditative traditions are about "waking up."

Wilber uses a color scheme for the various stages of development which is very similar to the various stages of spirituality I described in chapter three. Wilber's work was heavily influenced by the work of Clare Graves and by the work of Jean Gebser.

* Magenta is the color of tribal consciousness.
* Red is the color of warrior consciousness.
* Amber is the color of traditional consciousness.
* Orange is the color of modern consciousness
* Green is the color of postmodern consciousness.

All the above are steps in the group labeled *1st Tier*. Clare Graves said that what characterizes 1st tier levels is that people at each of these levels think that their values and beliefs are the only values and beliefs that are valid. They believe that the beliefs of those at the other stages of consciousness are just wrong.

Graves said that there is a "momentous leap" for those who cross into *2nd tier* consciousness which Wilber calls "integral". According to Wilber (2017) "The leap is simply that the integral level- called '2nd tier' to emphasize its difference from all 1st-tier stages- finds some value and partial truth in all the preceding levels, and so it includes them in its overall worldview. It is the first stage to include all the other stages, while all the other stages include only themselves."

Wilber emphasizes that in his stage theory each stage transcends but also includes previous stages. There is a natural progression in the evolution of spiritual development. One must go through each of the stages in order. You cannot skip a stage, and it takes some time to progress through stages. Continuing with Wilber's color scheme for stages of consciousness, these are the colors for 2nd tier:

* Teal
* Turquoise
* Indigo

In Wilber's model there are colors for transpersonal consciousness:

* Violet
* Ultraviolet
* Clear Light

I will not get into the details of what each of these colors represent in terms of increasing consciousness as this is beyond the scope of this book. The interested reader is referred to Wilber's 2017 book *The Religion of Tomorrow* for a detailed exposition of Wilber's theories.

British transpersonal psychologist Michael Daniels (2013) wrote about his perception of "three vectors of transpersonal development": the ascending, the descending, and the extending vectors. He writes that the ascending pathway "advocates a spiritual path of transcendence (of the relative, manifest world) in the achievement of 'higher' (absolute) spiritual consciousness. As such it represents an other-worldly perspective in which the purpose of life is to disidentify with ordinary, sensory experience of the phenomenal world, and to identify with the transcendental, absolute reality of spiritual consciousness."

Daniels conceptualizes his descending vector as the "depth psychological perspective" that "essentially argues that transpersonal development involves the exploration and integration of unconscious material that may be characterized as spiritual." The "descent" is into the unconscious. It involves uncovering and integrating unconscious trauma and aspects of ourselves that we do not like. It involves facing fears and inadequacies. It involves breaking through defense mechanisms.

Daniels characterizes the extending factor as "the relational, participatory approach" which "argues that transpersonal development involves realizing and expressing a spiritual connection to others and the world. Fundamental to this approach is the importance of moving beyond an egocentric concern with one's own individuation or personal spiritual development toward full participation with, commitment to, and responsibility for, other people, other species, and the world at large." The figure below is a visualization of Daniel's "Three vectors of ego-transcendence".

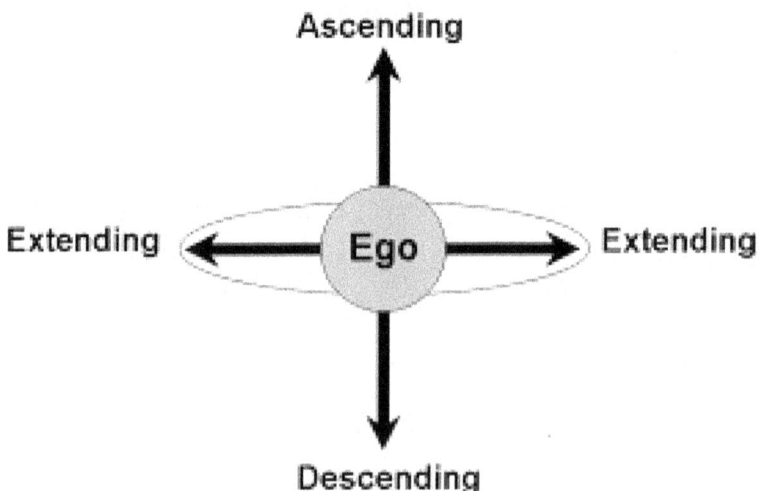

The result of spiritual development and growth is greater concern and compassion for an ever-expanding circle of care, i.e. a movement from caring only for myself, to caring for my immediate family, to caring for my "tribe" including friends and neighbors, to caring for my country, to caring for the world, to caring for the cosmos. Wilber's color scheme for the developmental stages of consciousness reflects this. It is important to keep in mind that these "stages" do not have rigid boundaries; it is more useful to conceive of a continuum such as the colors in a rainbow.

Wilber maintains that spiritual growth entails growing up, waking up, cleaning up and showing up. I could not agree more with Wilber who had a nice explanation on Facebook about "showing up."

> *The first three all have to do with our "inner work," the often-grueling personal work we do within our own consciousness and closest relationships. But the fourth — Showing Up — is where the fruits of our labor truly begin to ripen, where all of our accumulated knowledge, personal growth, spiritual practice, and shadow work become a limitless source of strength, presence, and wisdom, allowing us to engage the many dimensions and challenges of our world in a far more meaningful and impactful way, from becoming a better parent, to becoming a better leader, to becoming a better citizen of the world.*
>
> *After all, if our practice does not help us to show up more fully in the world, if it does not compel us to enact real change within each of our own spheres of influence, if it does not equip us to directly confront the many terrors and tragedies of our collective unfolding with fearless compassion and skillful action, then what's the point?*
>
> *If the sum total of our practice cannot benefit the world around us, exactly what (or whom) are we practicing for?*

I grew up being taught that after death there will be a final judgment of myself and others by God. Those who lived the right kind of life and believed the right things would be rewarded, and the others would be punished. I no longer believe this. What a self-centered philosophy that is! To think that the entire purpose for life was to save oneself. I no long believe my purpose is to strive for self-gain but rather that I contribute to the evolution of the cosmos. This will be my focus in the final chapter of this book.

Death

For many people the sole purpose for life is death- or more precisely the "after life." Many think the purpose of adherence to a religion is to gain eternal life in paradise. The belief is that the physical body dies, but the soul lives on forever (many believe either in Heaven or Hell).

Death really is the great unknown. None of us really know what happens after we die. It naturally does cause some anxiety, despite our deaths being the natural course of things and something we all universally experience. Religion supplies comfort to many for the anxieties and fears of death. Can those with a transpersonal worldview also find consolation about death? I believe so.

The traditional/orthodox viewpoint is that the body and the soul or spirit are two separate entities that combine during the short temporary existence on earth. A transpersonal viewpoint is that everything in existence including energy/matter and consciousness evolved together and emanated from God/Spirit. Consciousness or soul could not have evolved without other emergent events happening first.

The traditional/orthodox viewpoint also emphasizes the separateness of the individual and, I might add, the separateness of God. Certainly, in my own religious tradition of Christianity there is more emphasis on the transcendence of God rather than the immanence of God. Although in my childhood I remember being taught that God is everywhere (immanent) and that God is accompanying us all the time, the predominating theology was that God was separate and out there someplace.

Marcus Borg (2006) also addresses this. "The Bible also speaks of God's presence everywhere and in everything. This is most concisely expressed in words attributed to the apostle Paul: God is the one 'in whom we live and move and have our being' (Acts 17:28). Note what the language affirms: we live within God, we move within God, we have our existence within God. God is not somewhere else, but right here, all around us, the encompassing Spirit in whom everything that is, is." We dwell in God, and God dwells in us.

For many it is a very comforting thought to think about living on through eternity as the individual we are now retaining our personalities, knowledge, likes and dislikes, and perhaps even our bodies. Other individuals have the belief that after death there is nothing. We simply die, and that is that. I do not think that this need be the only two alternatives for a belief about death though. I will propose another idea that is perhaps somewhat provocative for many but still for me provides comfort.

One of the greatest needs we humans (and I would submit mammals and perhaps other animals as well) have is the need for relationships- closeness with others. We have a need to love and to be loved. This is perhaps most profoundly expressed in the type of love the Greeks called *eros,* which is the sex-linked experience of "falling in love." As infants we appear to begin our lives without ego boundaries, i.e., no sense of there being a "me." Eventually ego boundaries develop. We begin to experience the world as consisting of separate things including ourselves. The feeling of separateness is lonely. We crave closeness and intimacy. This feeling of separateness is most dramatically alleviated with sexuality and the experience of "falling in love" in which our ego boundaries collapse. We feel oneness with our beloved. This is often symbolized at wedding ceremonies in which two candles that symbolize the two individuals are substituted by a single candle.

But there is need for other types of closeness as well. Most of us desire friendships, children, pets. We join various communities to fulfill the need to be part of something bigger than ourselves. We desire other types of physical closeness besides sexual; we hug, we shake hands, we hold our children, we pet our dogs.

There is great strength when individuals join to form collectives. Alcoholics Anonymous and other 12-step groups as I have previously mentioned suggest finding a "power greater than oneself". For those who struggle with the concept of a God, they often suggest use of the group of A.A. itself as a higher power. Two heads are better than one. A group of twelve or fifteen is a power greater than oneself.

Many people are likely not aware that a single living heart cell beats. When combined with another heart cell they beat together in rhythm. When combined with a billion heart cells they beat together. A single heart cell really does not accomplish much, but when combined with other heart cells to form a human heart they keep a human alive for a lifetime. It is the same with neurons. Individually a living neuron really does not accomplish anything, but when a part of a group of eighty-six billion neurons they can form a human brain capable of calculus.

There is both strength and contentment in being part of a collective. I wonder if that is what death is like- the contentment and joy of feeling one with God. As humans on this earth, we have what mystics consider a misconception- that we are individuals and not connected to God and the cosmos. Death might be like a neuron discovering it is not alone and is part of a brain. I return to the story I previously related about the wave. A wave is really not essentially a wave, but rather it is a temporary condition and, in reality, is part of the ocean. A wave really does not die when it hits the shore; it continues as part of the ocean.

Kenneth Ring is a psychologist who spent his career studying near-death experiences (NDE) and has written several books on the subject including *Lessons From the Light: What We Can Learn from the Near-Death Experience* (2006). In this book he includes many case studies to demonstrate what typically happens in near-death experiences. Let me share one of these; the case of Craig. Craig was in his late 20s when he nearly drowned in a rafting accident. He became pinned underwater and with his air supply dwindling he experienced something that is common with NDEs; a life review.

Scenes from my life began to pass before my eyes at superhigh speeds. It seemed as if I was a passive observer in the process, and it was as if someone else was running the projector. I was looking at my life objectively for the first time ever. I saw the good as well as the bad. I realized that these images were sort of a final chapter in my life, and that when the images stopped, I would lose consciousness forever...I was amazed at how many scenes I was seeing but had long since been forgotten.

Craig then began to relax and to surrender to what he believed was inevitable. He no longer felt the need for air and no longer felt any discomfort. He then experienced another common occurrence in NDEs: he felt like he was in a tunnel and was speeding along toward a "huge mass of beautiful and brilliant white light" which eventually "engulfed me."

I felt as if I became one with the light. It seemed to have knowledge of everything there is to know, and it accepted me as part of it. I felt all-knowing for a few minutes. Suddenly, everything seemed to make perfect sense. The whole world seemed to be in total harmony. I remember thinking, "Ahhh, so that's it. Everything is so crystal clear and simple in so many ways." I had never been able to see it from this point of view... I felt better than I had ever felt in my life. It was as if I were bathing in total love and understanding, and basking in its radiance...It gives me a sense of traveling a long distance and finally making it home. I sensed that I had been here before, perhaps before being born into the physical world...I felt like I was an energy form that could never be destroyed.

Obviously, Craig was able to extricate himself from his predicament, as he was able to relate all of this. Kenneth Ring has spent his career interviewing survivors of NDEs and he notes that there are no commonalities in personality for those who experience NDEs. However, he notes interestingly that "the NDE tends to bring about lasting changes in personal values and beliefs- NDErs appreciate life more fully, experience increased feelings of self-worth, have a more compassionate regard for others and indeed for all life, develop a heightened ecological sensitivity, and report a decrease in purely materialistic and self-seeking values. Their religious orientation tends to change, too, and becomes more universalistic, inclusive, and spiritual in its expression. In most instances, moreover, the fear of death is completely extinguished and a deep-rooted conviction, based on their direct experience, that some form of life after death awaits us becomes unshakable and a source of enormous comfort."

Death continues to be one of the great mysteries. We do know that matter/energy never is destroyed and continues in various forms. Perhaps consciousness does as well. Perhaps our individual consciousness continues intact in some form, but perhaps we lose our individuality and instead experience upon death the joyous rapture of total and complete communion with God. I may no longer be an individual wave, but I am still a part of the ocean.

Questions for Contemplation or Discussion

Chapter Five. God Part 2

1. What resonates more with you: that the universe is made up of individual things and that it can be best understood by breaking things down to their smallest constituents, or that the universe is a single entity best understood in its entirety?

2. What are your beliefs regarding consciousness? What are your beliefs in regards to a soul?

3. What are your beliefs in regards to death?

Chapter Six

Conscious Evolution

I titled this book *Beyond Religion: Finding Meaning in Evolution*. Let me take the opportunity now to explain this title. When I suggest that we move beyond religion I am suggesting that we move beyond ancient myths, required adherence to traditions and rituals, dogmatic beliefs, rigid rules and laws, and magic.

What I suggest is replacing the above with something that can be affirmed by everyone whether one is a theist, deist, atheist, agnostic, pantheist, panentheist, or whatever. What I suggest is the adherence to one simple principle: striving to be less self-centered and increasing care and concern for all of life. This is the primary teaching of the greatest prophets and religious leaders. It involves increasing love, compassion, and caring.

I am also advocating that superstition be replaced by reason, ignorance be replaced by education, closed-mindedness be replaced by a thirst for new knowledge, and that xenophobia, homophobia, racism and all forms of hatred and fear be replaced by open minds and open hearts. I am advocating an emphasis on something that religions seem to have forgotten: ethics and morality. This is what I mean by moving beyond religion. I will discuss later the details of what I mean by "finding meaning in evolution."

Ethics and Morality

The terms "ethics" and "morality" are often used interchangeably, although there are some distinctions that can be made. I will not get into that here. For our purposes we can consider both terms as referencing the difference between right and wrong, or good and bad.

Just what is it that makes something immoral, wrong, or bad? I no longer believe that right and wrong is simply what an authoritarian deity at one time dictated. Are there moral absolutes, or is morality relative? There are those who not only think that morality is relative, but that truth is as well. I do not believe this. I certainly believe in the existence of objective truth and reality. I also believe, as did the philosopher Immanuel Kant, that a basis for morality can be established through reason. The next important question is whether morality should be judged based upon outcomes (i.e., the ends justify the means), or whether morality should be judged by ethical principles (even though we might not necessarily like the outcomes)?

Those who believe that ends justify means are often called *consequentialists*. Whatever provides the most benefit to the greatest amount of people is the most moral, they would say. Those who base morality on principles regardless of consequences are sometimes called *nonconsequentialists* who follow teleological theories of morality. Teleology is a philosophy that stresses the importance of the final purpose.

My view in regards to this dispute is that these two philosophies can be resolved. The principle that I believe is at the heart of immorality is self-centeredness. The increase of love and compassion in the universe leads to a cosmic evolution- further evolution of the entire universe, perhaps leading to something akin to Teilhard's conception of an Omega Point. So, what I am saying is that living by the principal of love for all life is good in and of itself, but that it also is the thing that inevitably leads to the best outcomes.

I believe that there is a continuum of morality. I wrote about this in a previous book, *Evolution of Morality and Psychopathology of Evil* (2019). From an evolutionary standpoint, morality is something that is relatively recent. It was not until the advent of mammals (and brain development that included the limbic system) that animals developed emotions and the capacity for empathy and sympathy, and some would say even the beginnings of morality.

I believe that individual humans today are on a continuum in regards to morality. If we plotted the entire human population's scores on this quality the result would be a bell curve which would visually show that most of us are in the average range on this quality, and that there are a relatively small number of individuals who score on the low end of this attribute and a relatively small number of individuals who score on the high end of the attribute. Some people are exceptionally selfish, some are exceptionally self-less and altruistic, but most of us are somewhere in the middle. This is shown in figure 6A.

At the far-left end of the bell curve is psychopathology. It is here that we find the people we consider to be *evil*. These are not people possessed or influenced by a malevolent being such as Satan. These are people with severe psychopathology. There are a few diagnostic labels that are used for these individuals including primarily *psychopath, sociopath,* and *malignant narcissist.* Psychologist Erich Fromm described malignant narcissism as "quintessential evil." Although these terms often are used interchangeably, to my mind there are a few differences between these three groups. Sociopathy has less to do with individual psychopathology and more to do with antisocial behaviors and values common to certain subcultures, for example a street gang or the mafia. Think sociology rather than psychology.

Psychopathy and malignant narcissism both involve severe pathology of individuals that is primarily characterized by a lack of conscience, lack of empathy, and extreme self-centeredness. The difference between these two categories is that malignant narcissists are also sadistic- they enjoy hurting people. Psychopaths, to my understanding, do not intentionally want to hurt people, but they do not really mind if others are hurt as collateral damage. The drive for them is money and power, and there is a callous disregard for others in this pursuit.

Psychopathy is a rare disorder. Even among criminals the prevalence rate is estimated to be only fifteen to twenty percent. And not all psychopaths are criminals. Many are successful. They are attracted to pursuits that bring power and money. Unfortunately, psychopaths have achieved positions of great power over history with disastrous results, e.g., Hitler and Stalin. Who could be worse as the leader of a nation than a person with no conscience, who cares only for him/herself, that has no scruples, and will do anything to achieve power? And yet it is this lack of guilt and conscience that allows them to do the things necessary to achieve power. Psychopaths are often masters of manipulation. They are skilled at reading people and then manipulating them to their advantage.

Figure 6A

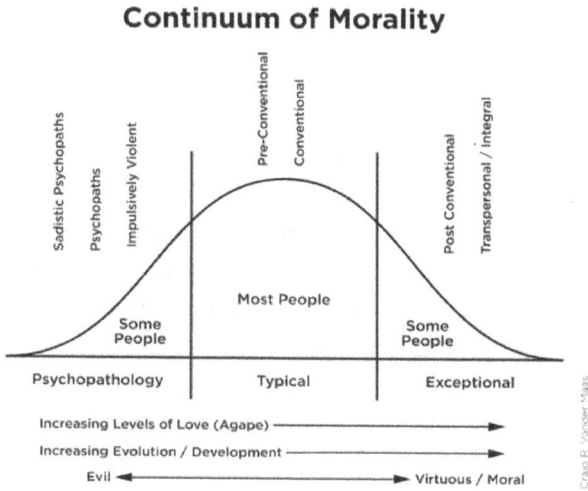

Continuum of Morality

Research suggests that genetics plays a role in psychopathy. There is evidence of differences in the brains of psychopaths from that of normal controls. Brain structures implicated include the frontal lobes, amygdala, the autonomic nervous system, hippocampus, corpus callosum and striatum.

To the right of this group of people on the continuum of morality is a group who still suffer from pathology but would not likely be considered evil. These are individuals who have done horrible things as the result of impulsive violence. They may have damage or deficits to their brains as the result of genetics or acquired brain dysfunction from such things as prenatal insults (e.g., toxic drug/alcohol/poison exposure), repeated childhood traumas, mental illness, and brain injuries. This would include some individuals who may need to be locked up to protect society.

In the center of my model of morality are most of us; those of us that are considered typical. Developmental psychologists concern themselves with various streams of development, such as cognitive development (Jean Piaget), faith development (James Fowler), and moral development (Lawrence Kohlberg). Kohlberg's research suggests that around the age of seven or eight children begin the process of moral reasoning. Individuals at this stage of development, which is called *pre-conventional* morality, are very self-centered. Good is what benefits me and bad is what causes pain. At this stage there is not empathy or concern about others. Some individuals never leave this stage, even as adults. In this stage as an adult, it is okay to steal something if one can get away with it. The phrase "might makes right" applies here as well.

Usually around the end of middle childhood and the early teens children develop *conventional* moral reasoning. At this level individuals incorporate societal norms and values. There is the desire to be *good*. One tries to live up to the expectations of significant others such as families and teachers. There is a subservience to authority. Again, many adults never move past this level of moral reasoning. There is a legalism at this level and a lack of ability to reason. There is still a good deal of self-centeredness at this stage in that by following the rules and norms of society one does not get into trouble and one receives desired approval from external sources.

It is at this level of moral development that tribalism becomes prevalent. Rather than determining what is right or wrong and good or bad by thoughtful reasoning, one's moral compass is dictated by one's *tribe*, which can be one's church, political party, or social support group. Tribalism requires loyalty to the group.

When one moves into *post-conventional* morality, there is a requirement for more abstract thinking and critical reasoning. Increased moral development requires increased cognitive development. There is a realization that there are universal moral principles, and it is more important to follow these principles than it is to follow specific laws and rules, as these laws may be in contradiction to the more important principles. These would be individuals who subscribe to the slogan of "question authority." These would be individuals who subscribe to civil disobedience when required. Unjust laws that discriminate should be fought against. Love and justice are principles that should be adhered to rather than hateful and unjust laws.

This post-conventional morality is reflected in the activities of Martin Luther King Jr. and Mahatma Gandhi who led nonviolent protests against injustice. Both were jailed for their activities. As I am writing this, Russia has invaded Ukraine and countless Russian soldiers have disregarded military orders to avoid killing Ukrainian citizens, and countless Russian citizens have been arrested for protesting their own government's aggression, thereby risking years of imprisonment.

What are you willing to die for? What is worth the death of you and your immediate family? What is so important that you would risk your freedom and life? Would you die for your country? If so, what do you mean by this? Would you blindly follow dictates from your country, or is it more important for you to follow certain principles? For me those principles are truth, justice and fairness, individual freedoms, and democracy. If it comes down to a choice between allegiance to my country and allegiance to these principles, I choose the principles. Are there any values that are more important to you than truth, justice, freedom, and democracy? If so, what are they? For what would you be willing to put aside these values and principles?

Many developmental theorists describe an even more advanced level of moral thinking. This level involves a universalizing love- compassion and care for all of life. There is a realization of the oneness of the cosmos. There is ever increasing selflessness. Kohlberg wrote about a stage seven morality which reflects a sense of oneness with the cosmos. There is a desire to be moral because of the knowledge that we are part of the whole, and that to take care of the whole is really to care for ourselves. Other theorists who have written about such a stage include James Fowler, Abraham Maslow, and Ken Wilber.

Conscious Evolution

The concept of "evolution" has often been perceived by many to be an ideology that is in opposition to the idea of "God" and spirituality, but there is now a growing movement that sees evolution as being the cutting-edge new paradigm of spirituality. Evolutionist thinker Carter Phipps in his book *Evolutionaries: Unlocking the Spiritual and Cultural Potential of Science's Greatest Idea* (2012 says:

> *The idea of evolution, the basic notion of process, change, and development over time, is affecting much more than biology. It is affecting everything, from our perceptions of politics, economics, psychology, and ecology to our understanding of the most basic constituents of reality. It is helping to give birth to new philosophies and, I will argue, is the source of a new kind of spiritual revelation.*

Human beings have evolved to become a conscious and intelligent species who now have the ability to become active participants in the process of cosmic evolution. In addition, there have been tremendous technological advances in the last few hundred years which gives humanity unprecedented power to effect changes. Humanity's power is predicted to increase tremendously in the next few years with the development of technology that harnesses the power of atomic fusion.

We already have the power and ability to either destroy ourselves or to hasten our evolution. Our choice will depend, I believe, on morality- whether we continue to be motivated mostly by selfishness and greed, or whether we evolve to be more compassionate, just, and loving.

So why do I consider selflessness to be the basis for morality? For one thing, this has been the primary principle taught by all the great religious and spiritual teachers since the Axial Age. It is the basis for the "golden rule" which is taught in some form by all the great religions of the world- to treat others with the same love and care that we would want to be treated. Jesus said that the two most important commandments are to love God and to love one's neighbor as oneself. Jesus said this is the basis for all of God's commandments. Philosophers have also used this criterion to determine morality, perhaps most notably Immanuel Kant. Kant sought to establish moral absolutes based on reason. He said that morality results from "good will." "A good will is not good because of what it effects or accomplishes, because of its fitness to attain some proposed end, but only because of its volition, that is, it is good in itself."

One of the controversies in the philosophical field of ethics is the question of whether morality is relative or if there are moral absolutes that exist. Many religious people feel that there are moral absolutes and that they come from God. Some of these moral absolutes are thought to be embedded in the famous Ten Commandments such as "thou shalt not steal" or "thou shalt not kill." And yet, shortly after Moses is said to have been given these commandments, Moses' protege, Joshua, is said to have been told by God to commit genocide on the people of Jericho. Relativists, as opposed to absolutists, see morality as dependent upon outcomes. For example, although stealing is wrong, it might be considered justified if it saves the life of a starving child. In this instance there is a "greater good."

I would consider myself an "absolutist" although perhaps not in the traditional sense. I believe that a behavior is moral if it is done out of love, compassion and caring, and that behaviors are immoral if done out of selfishness. So, in the above example, saving the starving child would be the right answer. Not only do I believe that love and caring are good intrinsically, but also that it leads to the best outcomes. I believe love leads to cosmic evolution, and selfishness and self-centeredness lead to regression.

It bears keeping in mind that the entire cosmos is one. This realization could lead to a new paradigm for interacting with the world. Instead of seeing the world as a competition where I as an individual am trying to best all the other individuals, I might recognize that everything is interrelated and that it is nonsensical to try to hurt others to benefit myself. It would be nonsensical for my right arm to try to defeat my left arm. It would be nonsensical for some of the neurons in my brain to try to defeat all the other neurons to achieve supremacy. What matters is the whole of my brain. The more healthier functioning neurons one has the better one's brain operates. The healthier the functioning of people are in our country, the healthier is our country. The same goes for the world.

Governments of countries have begun learning this lesson. Countries do better cooperating with each other rather than trying to defeat them. Shared commerce between countries has been effective in preventing wars, as has various alliances and organizations such as NATO and the United Nations. We have become accustomed to thinking that life is made up of *zero-sum* games. There are either winners or there are losers. Sports are generally like that: there are winners, there are losers, and sometimes there are ties. However, in many areas of life there can be situations where everyone is a winner and situations where everyone loses. International commerce is a situation where there can be benefit to all parties. War is a situation where usually most everyone are losers.

Let me return to the metaphorical story about the wave that is afraid of crashing into the shore and dying. That wave is overly concerned about the immediate and the transient and not seeing the big picture, as is the case for most of us. The focus tends to be on trying to be the biggest wave or making the biggest splash, when the important concern should be the quality of the water. We in essence are the water, not a wave. To continue the metaphor, we should primarily concern ourselves with ridding the water of the pollutants.

The cosmos has been in the process of evolution over the past fourteen billion years. In the beginning change came very slowly. It took over a billion years for the first stars and galaxies to form. The process of cosmic evolution has seemed to greatly accelerate in the past couple hundred years though, and I would suggest that much of the reason is the result of the Enlightenment. Pinker in his important book *Enlightenment Now* (2018) explains the importance of the enlightenment:

> *What is the enlightenment? In a 1784 essay with that question as its title, Immanuel Kant answered that it consists of "humankind's emergence from its self-incurred immaturity," its "lazy and cowardly" submission to the*

"dogmas and formulas" of religious or political authority. Enlightenment's motto, he proclaimed, is "Dare to understand!" and its foundational demand is freedom of thought and speech. "One age cannot conclude a pact that would prevent succeeding ages from extending their insights, increasing their knowledge, and purging their errors. That would be a crime against human nature, whose proper destiny lies precisely in such progress."

With the advent of the Enlightenment has come tremendous cultural and technological advancement. It has also brought evolution of morality. Pinker goes on to say:

> *The thinkers of the Age of Reason and the Enlightenment saw an urgent need for a secular foundation for morality, because they were haunted by a historical memory of centuries of religious carnage: the Crusades, the Inquisition, witch hunts, the European wars of religion. They laid that foundation in what we now call humanism, which privileges the well-being of individual men, women, and children over the glory of the tribe, race, nation, or religion...*
>
> *A humanistic sensibility impelled the Enlightenment thinkers to condemn not just religious violence but also the secular cruelties of their age, including slavery, despotism, executions for frivolous offenses such as shoplifting and poaching, and sadistic punishments such as flogging, amputation, impalement, disembowelment, breaking on the wheel, and burning at the stake. The Enlightenment is sometimes called the Humanitarian Revolution, because it led to the abolition of barbaric practices that had been commonplace across civilizations for millennia.*

Humanity has evolved as the result of learning how to reason, how to critically think, and to grow out of mindless allegiance to religious and secular authorities. With the evolution of thinking came new values such as individual freedoms, liberty, justice, fairness, democracy, and repulsion to cruelty. This conception of morality has led to decreased misery and increased happiness for greater and greater numbers of people. It also has led to the acceleration of evolution of the cosmos. It has led to progress in the goal of attaining the kingdom of God which Jesus talked about. This, in my opinion, is the purpose of life- to evolve as a person and to contribute to the evolution of the cosmos- to contribute in bringing about the "kingdom of God."

Let me return to Jesus' declaration that the two great commandments are to love God and to love one's neighbors. Love of neighbors means a love for all humans, and many (including myself) would say all of life. What does it mean to love God? Jesus makes clear in Matthew 25 that by showing love to our neighbors we are showing love to God. Are there other ways to love God? I believe we show love to God by consciously promoting the evolution of the cosmos.

As a Christian, this means that there is much more required of me than to just subscribe to and profess a certain belief. It requires that I consciously strive to learn, to think, to introspect, to share, to become in touch with my feelings, to show compassion, and to love. It requires that I be open to new ideas. It requires that I not live in fear. It requires the hard work of being loving to those that are so easy to hate. It requires that I consciously work toward the evolution of the cosmos. The cosmos evolves by compassion and caring for others. Put simply, the cosmos evolves because of love.

I have described what I think morality is. Let me now spend a little time talking about what I think morality is not. It is not about sex, per se, although our society has often intertwined morality with sexuality. This is perhaps to a large extent due to the Catholic Church which teaches that procreation is the only appropriate reason for sex, and that sexual expression should only occur within a monogamous marriage. The position of the Catholic Church is that any sexual behavior outside of this is immoral, and that would include premarital sex, masturbation, promiscuity, homosexuality, prostitution, and the use of contraception.

This point of view is heavily influenced by anthropocentrism- the belief that humans are qualitatively different from all other life forms. Of course, this is not true. Various scientific disciplines including genetic research has shown conclusively that all of life has evolved from a single source and that all of life is related.

For the last two billion years when sexual reproduction first evolved, biology has made necessary a sex drive. The drive for sex is as natural as breathing, eating, urinating, and defecating. It is biology. It is natural for children to be curious about sex and other's bodies. It is natural for post-pubescent teenagers to explore sexuality. It is natural and normal for humans to express themselves sexually, not just for procreation but to be physically close to a cathected loved one. It is normal for some people to be homosexual, just as it is in the rest of the animal kingdom.

Although sexuality per se is not immoral, sexual *behaviors* can be immoral though. In my opinion morality is a continuum between self-centeredness and selfishness versus caring about others as much as we care for ourselves. And so sexual behaviors are immoral if done out of selfish desires with disregard for others' wellbeing. This can range from treating another human being as merely a sexual object with no regard or respect for them as a person all the way up the continuum to violent rapes. The key to moral sexual behavior is treating others with love and respect. A related issue to sexual morality is sexual *responsibility* such as behaviors that do not cause unwanted pregnancies, disease, and physical or emotional harm.

There are other things that I do not consider to be immoral such as eating shellfish or pigs, working on Saturdays, divorce, cursing one's parents, and having sex with your wife if she is menstruating. These are all things forbidden in the Old Testament of the Bible. These are the types of rules and regulations commonly found in the legal codes that existed prior to the Axial Age in which we find more familiar expressions of morality.

Philosophy often makes the distinction between "natural" evils and "moral" evils. Natural evils are things that harm people that are not the result of bad intentions, such as hurricanes, earthquakes, and disease. I am not sure why they are considered *evil* except for the fact that we humans do not like when they happen. Natural disasters certainly can cause tremendous human misery. However, I would suggest that the misery caused by natural disasters pales in comparison to the misery caused by moral evil.

The So-called Natural Evils

The rate of deaths from natural disasters, happily, has gone steadily down. It is not that we have less earthquakes, hurricanes, meteors, and pandemics though. It is because of the Enlightenment; the reliance on reason, technology, and scientific methodology that we have been better able to mitigate the negative effects. As Steven Pinker (2018) explains:

> *It's that a richer and more technologically advanced society can prevent natural hazards from becoming human catastrophes. When an earthquake strikes, fewer people are crushed by collapsing masonry or burned in conflagrations. When the rains stop, they can use water impounded in reservoirs. When the temperature soars or plummets, they stay in climate-controlled interiors. When a river floods its banks, their drinking water is safeguarded from human and industrial waste. The dams and levees that impound water for drinking and irrigation, when properly designed and built, make floods less likely in the first place. Early warning systems allow people to evacuate or take shelter before a cyclone makes landfall. Though geologists can't yet predict earthquakes, they can often predict volcanic eruptions, and can prepare the people who live along the Rim of Fire and other fault systems to take lifesaving precautions. And of course a richer world can rescue and treat its injured and quickly rebuild.*

Pinker (2018) shares many interesting statistics about how our lives are improved as the result of the principles of the Enlightenment. In the mid-18th century life expectancy was around

29 years where likely it had been for thousands of years. For Europeans and the Americas, it was slightly higher at 35 years. "But starting in the 19th century, the world embarked on the Great Escape, the economist Angus Deaton's term for humanity's release from its patrimony of poverty, disease, and early death. Life expectancy began to rise, picked up speed in the 20th century, and shows no signs of slowing down." Life expectancy in the world had risen to 71.4 in 2015.

What I will do now is discuss three world issues that I believe are among the greatest threats to humankind, and which are primarily the result of our human moral failings. Since these problems are the result of *moral* failings, I believe they should be a primary focus of concern for religions and churches.

War, Power and Autocracy

War is absurd. It is senseless death and destruction. Its cause is greed, selfishness, and hatred for others. Humans are only one of two species who engage in the practice, with the other being chimpanzees. A third species, bonobos, are genetically very similar to both chimpanzees and humans (we all share 96.6% of our DNA), but behaviorally they are very different. They do not engage in war. They are quite nonviolent. They seem to be like the hippies of the 1960s subscribing to the slogan "make love, not war". When confronted with strangers rather than getting aggressive, they engage in sexual contact. While some might consider such casual sexual activity negatively, I would suggest it is much preferable to killing one another!

War is as old as mankind. Rulers have initiated wars to obtain territory, economic resources, and power. Rulers over the ages have not cared about the fate of defeated peoples, and even have not cared about the fate of their own peoples. Wars were initiated primarily for the glory and power of the ruler. Pinker (2011) opines:

> *Conquest was what governments did. Empires rose, empires fell, entire populations were annihilated or enslaved, and no one seemed to think there was anything wrong with it. The*

historical figures who earned the honorific "So-and-So the Great" were not great artists, scholars, doctors, or inventors, people who enhanced human happiness or wisdom. They were dictators who conquered large swaths of territory and the people in them. If Hitler's luck had held out a bit longer, he probably would have gone down in history as Adolf the Great. Even today the standard histories of war teach the reader a great deal about horses and armor and gunpowder but give only the vaguest sense that immense numbers of people were killed and maimed in these extravaganzas.

One can get a good sense of the rise and fall of empires in reading the Old Testament Scriptures of the Hebrew people. One of the first empire builders was the Akkadian king, Sargon the Great (2334-2279), who had perhaps the first standing army in which to conquer various Mesopotamian city states.

After that there was a succession of various empires: the "Old Babylonian" empire of King Hammurabi, the Egyptian empire, the Assyrian empire, the "New Babylonian" empire, the Persian empire, the Greek empire, and the Roman empire. The only people who really mattered were the rulers- the kings, the pharaohs, the emperors. Other people existed to serve the needs of the tyrants who sought power, wealth, and "glory." Enemies and subjects alike were subjected to horrendous and unbelievable atrocities including genocide, slavery, terrorism, and torture.

Empires rose and fell in Asia as well. One of the most infamous world conquerors was Genghis Khan, who was quoted to have said "The greatest joy a man can know is to conquer his enemies and drive them before him. To ride their horses and take away their possessions. To see the faces of those who were dear to them bedewed with tears, and to clasp their wives and daughters in his arms." The Mongol conquests of the 13th and 14th centuries were responsible for widespread devastation and the death perhaps of eleven percent of the world's population.

"The backdrop of European history during most of the past millennium is ever present warring. Carried over from the knightly raiding and feuding in medieval times, the wars embroiled every kind of political unit that emerged in the ensuing centuries" (Pinker, 2011). Pinker notes that the political scientist Peter Brecke compiled a list of European conflicts since 900 CE. There were 1,148 conflicts between 900 CE and 1400 CE, and 1,166 conflicts from 1400 CE to 2011 CE. These conflicts produced tremendous destruction and deaths. Matthew White (2012) reports that between 500 BCE and 2010 CE there has been three hundred and fifteen million deaths that have resulted from war and one hundred forty-one deaths from peacetime oppression.

The war that produced the most deaths was World War II with a death toll of 55 million (which include not only deaths from the battlefield but also indirect deaths of civilians from starvation and disease). However, when considering the world population at the time of the event, it ranks as only number nine on White's list of worldwide atrocities. In other words, if the world population at the time of WWII was 300 million, and 55 million died, that would amount to roughly eighteen percent.

There have been other atrocities which have accounted for more than an eighteen percent death toll. Number one would be the An Lushan Revolt of the 8th century, which I would dare guess few of us have ever heard of. As a result of the eight-year civil war during the Tang Dynasty of China, two-thirds of the empire's population (and a sixth of the world population) died.

Here are the rest of the top ten world atrocities (when adjusted to percentage of world population):

#2 Mongol Conquests 13th century: 40 million deaths
#3 Mideast Slave Trade 7th to 19th centuries: 19 million deaths
#4 Fall of Ming Dynasty 17th century: 25 million deaths
#5 Fall of Rome 3rd to 5th centuries: 8 million deaths
#6 Timur Lenk 14th-15th centuries: 17 million deaths
#7 Annihilation of American Indians 15th-19th centuries: 20 million deaths

#8 Atlantic slave trade 15th-19th centuries: 18 million deaths
#9 World War II 20th century: 55 million deaths
#10 Taiping Rebellion 19th century: 20 million deaths

As I am writing this yet another invasion and more atrocities are happening due to Vladimir Putin's invasion of Ukraine. This is yet another example of a ruthless dictator in search of empire and glory at the expense of untold lives- both Russian and Ukrainian and at a cost of trillions of dollars. For what? As with most wars, nobody will be the winner here. Millions of people's lives will be forever ravaged because of one ruthless, evil ruler.

If you think it is a no-brainer that war is evil and to be avoided, consider that the leader of the Russian Orthodox Church, Patriarch Kirill, has blessed Moscow's invasion of Ukraine. This is not an aberration. Religious leaders likely have been complicit in waging war ever since wars have been waged. History writer John Carr in his book *The Pope's Army: The Papacy in Diplomacy and War* (2019) notes "For much of its 2,000-year history, the Roman Catholic Church was a formidable political and military power, in contrast to its pacifist origins". He said that between 410 and 1870 CE "the popes employed every means at their disposal, including direct military action, to maintain their domains centered on Rome."
Pope Urban II initiated the first Crusades to the Holy Land. In a speech in Clermont, France in 1095 he implored the French crowd, whom Carr reports he called "beloved and chosen by God" to go to war against "an accursed race, wholly alienated from God" that had "invaded the lands of the Christians." The pope went on to say

> *For this land which you now inhabit, shut in on all sides by the sea and the mountain peaks, is too narrow for your large population; it scarcely furnishes food enough for its cultivator. Hence it is that you murder and devour one another, that you wage wars, and that many among you perish in civil strife...Jerusalem is a land fruitful above all others, a paradise of delights...Undertake this journey*

eagerly for the remission of your sins, and be assured of the reward of imperishable glory in the Kingdom of Heaven.

The religion of Islam has also has engaged in war. Muhammad was not only a spiritual leader but also a political and military leader. Islam spread in large part due to military conquests. "By the time of Muhammad's death in 632, a substantial part of Arabia was under Muslim control" (Christian et al, 2014). Following the death of Muhammad during the Rashidun Caliphate there was a twenty-five-year period of military conquests into the Byzantine and Sasanian empires. Eventually the Islamic empire became the largest empire in the world.

Historian of war, Evan Luard, in his tome *War in International Society* (1986) called the period from 1559-1648 the age of religious wars because religion was the dominant reason during this time period for war. "In Europe alone there were 112 wars in 89 years; an average of 1.25 a year. Of these 53 were international (0.59 a year) and 59 domestic (0.66 a year). In every year of the period there was at least one substantial war going on somewhere in the continent: in most years two; and in many three." War broke out between Catholics and Protestants, Christians and Muslims, Sunnis, and Shias.

Wars have been primarily waged by male rulers intent on the acquisition of wealth and especially power. Wealth and power go hand in hand. Wealth gives one power, and power gives one the ability to create wealth. Many authoritarian rulers have been psychopaths- a mental illness I described earlier in this book.

War has been one of the greatest impediments to the evolution of humanity. In the 20th century just three individuals have been responsible for tens of millions of deaths: Adolf Hitler, Joseph Stalin, and Mao Zedong. In addition to the human toll, destruction of infrastructure (buildings, roads, utilities, and so on) has cost societies billions or trillions of dollars. War not only impedes human evolution; it causes brief periods of devolution.

The characteristics of authoritarian rulers or "strongmen" have been delineated by Ben-Ghiat (2020) and many others. Authoritarians gain power by stoking fear and hatred toward out-groups. Research in social psychology suggest one of the most effective ways of creating cohesion in a group is to have an enemy to fight against. Disinformation has always been one of the greatest tools for creating hatred toward out-groups, and unfortunately the advent of social media and the internet in the past decades has greatly facilitated the ability to spread false information. Authoritarians are masters of using propaganda to shape public opinions including the use of the now famous "big lie." This term was coined by Adolf Hitler in *Mein Kampf* and refers to a lie so incredible that people believe it must be true as no one would have the audacity to just invent such a lie.

Authoritarians also gain power by gaining the support of the social elites- the rich and powerful in a society. They do this by promising them continuing power and money in exchange for their loyalty and financial support. The elites capitulate to the Faustian bargain. This includes not only billionaires but also politicians. At the time of this writing an entire political party (Republicans) have capitulated to an anti-democratic psychopath (Trump) to maintain power or because of fear for themselves or their families.

Authoritarians also gain power with their charisma, confidence, and virility. Many people are attracted to especially strong and *macho* men. Genghis Khan was infamous for his production of progeny during his military invasions. "Today eight percent of the men who live within the former territory of the Mongol Empire share a Y chromosome that dates to around the time of Genghis, most likely because they descended from him and his sons and the vast number of women they clasped in their arms." (Pinker, 2011). Mussolini "had extramarital sex with up to four different women daily during his twenty-three years in power. His sex life is best visualized as a pyramid. Rachele, his wife, was on top, then his major lovers Sarfatti and Petacci, and then a dozen or so regular partners who he saw once or twice a month. If he had children with the women, the relationships could go on for decades." (Ben-Ghiat, 2020). Ben-Ghiat also described other strongmen who had boasted about their virile powers including Putin, Gaddafi, Berlusconi, Duterte, and Trump.

Ben-Ghiat also reports that other key features of authoritarian strongmen are rampant corruption and violence. "However they use it, strongmen give violence an instrumental as well as absolute value. They believe that not everyone is born equal, and most also feel that not everyone has the right to life. Some people must be sacrificed for the good of the nation, and others simply get in the way."

Wars continue to occur because of the ongoing self-centeredness of humans and lack of care and compassion for others. I want to make clear here, however, that I am not against standing up for or defending oneself whether on a personal level or a national level. I also am not against military or police actions to protect people who are under attack (either individuals or large communities of people or nations). Our country's current involvement in helping the people of Ukraine to defend themselves from Russia's invasion is an example. The important qualifier is whether we are acting in love and for justice, or are we acting out of greed and self-aggrandizement. As Thomas Aquinas has written, for a war to be just it must be done with righteous intent and for a just cause, i.e., to stop evil.

Pinker makes a strong argument that human beings are making progress with becoming less violent and less self-centered. In part this is the result of three important developments: humanism, democracy, and commerce. With humanism came the belief that *all* people have value and rights. This was a revolutionary idea. Since our earliest human civilizations, most human beings were considered to be nothing more than chattel, with no more value than other animals. Ultimate value was given to pharaohs, emperors, and monarchs or to the tribe or nation. Again, Putin's invasion of Ukraine is a good example of this. Certainly, his actions do not benefit the common people of Russia.

Humanistic ideas have given rise to democracies- a form of government in which all the people can participate and are considered equal. Conflicts are resolved in democracies by consensual rules of law, and this ethic has then externalized to nations in their treatment of each other. Might no longer makes right. All people are believed to have value, even those in other countries. Pinker notes that data shows that democracies are the form of government "that inflicts the minimum of violence on its own citizens" and that democracies are "less likely to get into militarized disputes."

The rise in commerce between nations has also contributed to increased peace and decreased war. Wars are expensive. It is less expensive to just buy things from other countries and then to also make money by selling things to them. It is a win-win situation. Countries that trade with each other are less likely to war with each other.

Humanism, democracy, and the desire to cooperate instead of fight have evolved due to our increasing capacity for empathy, compassion, caring, and love. Humanity has been evolving although as is typical with progress, there are regressions. We seem to be in one of those periods of time right now. Autocracy has been gaining popularity throughout the world including, to the surprise of many including myself, in the United States with the election of Donald Trump. Perhaps we are not as "exceptional" as we thought we were. This is not normal politics- disagreement over the size of government or the amount of taxes. It is no less than the rise of evil. Truth (facts) are being confused with or replaced with "alternative facts" (i.e., lies). Hatred of people felt to be different than us is on the rise (e.g., immigrants, Muslims, Jews, people of color, gays, transexuals). I just read a recent survey that indicated that most Republicans do not find it disqualifying for a political candidate to express homophobic, racist, or anti-Semitic statements. From national leaders violence is being encouraged, American institutions are being weakened, corruption is rampant, laws are broken, and democratic norms are defiled.

Why is this happening. Greed and self-centeredness. Political pundits often remind us that the populace is mostly concerned about "kitchen table issues" such as the price of gasoline and groceries. In other words, people are mostly concerned about themselves. People also are motivated by fear and hatred of people they do not understand. Politicians can take advantage of this, and do- due to their own cravings for power. And Christians and other religious people are complicit in all these Faustian bargains.

I believe people can evolve. I believe this is the primary message of Jesus and the other great prophets. We are to love others as we love ourselves. *This* leads to the "kingdom of God" that Jesus talked so much about. I do not believe it matters that you "accepted Jesus as your Lord and Savior." That is like thinking marriage is nothing more than saying "I do" at a wedding. What matters is emulating the life of Jesus and putting into action his teaching to love others, just as in a marriage what matters is being a faithful and loving spouse and parent. As the love and care of others (including our enemies) increases, the world will change. The cosmos will further evolve. We need to learn that we are all part of the whole, and that harm to others is really, in the long run, harm to ourselves.

Poverty and Income Disparity

Our human ancestors were hunter-gatherers and lived in a generally egalitarian world; all people shared equally in the hunting and gathering of food and were considered equals. It was only with the formation of more complex societies that human populations began to stratify. Larger societies required leadership. Early tribes had chiefs. Even larger societies created social classes. These societies were "based on notions of social inequality. Such societies are ruled by a tiny group of elites, who hold monopolies over strategic resources and use coercion to enforce their authority. State-organized societies of the past were first ruled by priest-bureaucrats, then gradually came under the rule of secular kings, who sometimes became despotic monarchs, often with alleged divine powers." (Fagan & Durrani, 2014).

Societies existed with this type of stratification for thousands of years. Only a small group of people had power and mattered. Vast majorities of populations existed only to serve the needs of the few. This paradigm began to change with the development of a new form of government: democracy. In this new form of government everyone mattered and had some degree of power. The general population were able to choose their leaders. The beginnings of democracy can be traced to ancient Greece. "Athens established the most democratic government known to have existed within agrarian civilizations, and during the subsequent Golden Age, particularly under the rule of Pericles (469-421 BCE), even the poorest citizen in Athens had some say in government." (Christian et al, 2014). Since then, democracies have come and gone.

In modern times the United States has been known as a "beacon of democracy" and "exceptional" in its well-designed constitutional system of checks and balances. But like other democracies from the past, ours is under attack and is in danger of collapsing due to the greed of moneyed elites.

Not only am I a strong advocate of democracy, I am also an advocate of capitalism. I think it is the best economic system yet devised in that it rewards hard work and innovations and does not "enable" people. But for capitalism to effectively work, it must have "guardrails." Because human beings continue to be a morally challenged species (willing to forego honesty and fairness in the pursuit of power and money), there must be rules and regulations to keep people and companies in line. Many of capitalism's guardrails currently are being chipped away as are democracy's.

While I believe in capitalism and systems that reward positive behaviors and give consequences to mistakes or failure, I believe in fairness and a level playing field. The current American economic system is not fair. One of the few declarations that Trump made that I agree with is "The system is rigged." It is. Of course, Trump did nothing to rectify this and in fact made it worse. There is ever increasing income inequality. A headline from an October 8, 2020 Forbes magazine article said that the top one percent of U.S. households hold fifteen times more wealth than the bottom fifty percent combined.

A year later another Forbes article reported that the twenty richest Americans had a combined net worth of 1.8 trillion dollars, which they pointed out is greater than the GDP of Canada and almost equal to the wealth of the bottom fifty percent of the U.S. population. Yet a 2021 OMB-CEA report in 2021 indicate that billionaires pay an average federal individual income tax rate of only 8.2% which is often a lower tax rate than for average Americans. Some billionaires get away with paying no taxes at all.

Another way of presenting the huge discrepancies of income and wealth in the United States was presented by Kurt Andersen (2020). If we were to create a perfectly equal society in which every American had the same income and the same amount of wealth, each household would have a net worth of $800,000 and an annual income of $140,000. Now I am not suggesting that this should happen; I am a capitalist as I have said before, and I believe that hard work and innovative ideas should be rewarded. But what this does demonstrate is that currently we have an economic system that does not promote "the general welfare" which the preamble to the U.S. constitution cites as a primary reason for our government. Instead, we have a system that favors the rich and powerful at the expensive of the poor and middle class. Wealth brings power, and power brings wealth. The term to describe this is *crony capitalism*. This refers to an economic system in which business especially thrives not due to free enterprise but rather due to collusion between business and politics. As Trump said, "the system is rigged."

The system is even worse for people of color. I think that most people are probably aware that there is a gap between black people and white people in terms of income and wealth, but I would guess it would be a surprise to most just how huge that gap is. A Pew Research Center analysis from 2016 concluded that the median wealth of white households was $171,000 compared with $17,100 for black households and $20,600 for Latinx households. White households have on average ten times the wealth than black households have! Why is this? What has caused such a discrepancy?

For over two hundred years black slaves as they toiled year after year and decade after decade in the United States, accumulated no wealth whatsoever. Indeed, they were nothing more than an asset in someone else's wealth portfolio. Although slavery ended with the 13th amendment in 1865, the so-called "Jim Crow" laws soon went in effect, which mandated racial segregation in many states. Although these laws mandated racial segregation, there was supposed to be "separate but equal" treatment of the races. As you might imagine there was nothing equal about it in terms of educational opportunities, housing opportunities, job opportunities, and the criminal justice system.

Separate education was provided to white children and black children until the Brown v. Board of Education decision by the Supreme Court in 1954 which outlawed school segregation. Although school children are no longer separated by race *per se* in schools, they are informally segregated by socioeconomic status. Poor people receive inferior education, and children of color are disproportionately poor.

After the civil war, freed slaves in the south needed to find jobs, and cotton still needed to be picked. The freed slaves had no money to buy land to farm or even enough money to buys tools, fertilizer, and seeds and so they had to work for the landowners/former slave owners. "The arrangement was known as 'sharecropping,' but in truth, it was about taking, not sharing. Even in good years, a white plantation owner chiseled away at a sharecropper's earnings with his pen: some here for rent, more there for groceries purchased at the plantation store, still more for fertilizer, seeds, and tools, all bought on credit. The planter kept the ledger book, and it always added up in his favor." (Dyson & Favreau, 2022). People were not significantly better off under sharecropping than they were under slavery- still no opportunity to grow wealth.

An even worse predicament occurred for freed slaves who found themselves forced onto "chain gangs." "Black people toiled for no pay in mines, on plantations, and in factories. They were caught in this new system of 'convict labor' by a web of new laws, racist sheriffs, and corrupt judges, whose only goal was to force as many Black people as possible to work for nothing." "In all, Southern states forced hundreds of thousands of African Americans onto chain gangs as late as the 1950s- almost a century after emancipation was supposed to have wiped involuntary servitude off the map." (Dyson & Favreau, 2022)

Many Blacks left the south for the northern states to find jobs in factories. From the 1910s until the 1970s an estimated six million Black people migrated from the south to northern, midwestern, and western states in order to escape Jim Crow oppression and to find economic and educational opportunities. Yet even in the north there was significant discrimination. Many labor unions did not allow membership for Blacks. Discrimination in employment was perfectly legal until the 1964 civil rights act. Discrimination in places of accommodation (e.g., restaurants, hotels, stores, parks, etc.) also was legal prior to this act.

The fifteenth amendment to the constitution was passed by the U.S. congress in 1870; the amendment prohibits voting discrimination based on race or color. Despite this, states and local governments continued to find ways of getting around the law to keep people of color from voting. Government officials created poll taxes, literacy requirements and employed other roadblocks to keep Blacks from voting, not to mention frequently utilizing outright intimidation and terrorist tactics. State and local governments were able to legally create these barriers to keep people of color from voting until the Voting Rights Act of 1965. Now in the twenty-first century we once again have numerous attempts by state governments to create obstacles for people of color to exercise their constitutional right.

One of the most important tools for saving money for the future and for the accumulation of wealth has been home ownership, particularly because of the federal tax code. People of color have always been at a disadvantage here too, however. It was perfectly legal to prevent the sale of homes to non-whites in certain neighborhoods until the passing of the Fair Housing Act in 1968. I highly recommend the recent book by Michael Eric Dyson and Marc Favreau titled *Unequal: A Story of America*. The authors do a great job in presenting very clearly the history of systemic racism and discrimination in this country. They write:

> *In this country, having wealth is part of what it means to be free. It's what we have left when we subtract all our debts- the money and resources that let us pay for our homes, our bills, and other essentials. If there is money left over after we cover the bases, maybe we can pursue a dream, start a business, take a risk on a new career: it's not about having too much, but rather about having enough-*

enough to live a stable and happy life. Today, very few Black families have enough.

However you slice it, the math is straightforward: America has a racial wealth gap. It gets wider each year. And the heavy truth is that even when two people have the same level of academic achievement, the same degrees, and the same job prospects, if one of these people is Black, he or she is likely to have less money in the bank. There's a simple reason for this: most of the wealth people have comes in the form of an inheritance. An inheritance could be money given to you by a parent or grandparent; it could be a home or other property left to you in a will; or bills paid on your behalf. Whatever its source, an inheritance is something you didn't earn yourself; our family histories powerfully influence our lives, and our wealth, in the present.

As a community, Black people had their inheritance stolen. Why this is true begins with slavery, but the story does not end there.

Even after the passage of the 1968 Fair Housing Act, Black people remained at a significant disadvantage in terms of home ownership. When I was growing up in the 1970s "white flight" was a significant concern in the neighborhood in which I lived. The term refers to fears about loss of property value when people of color move into a neighborhood. When Black people would move in, home owners would rush to sell their homes and move before the property values drop. This was not an unfounded fear; property values would drop. What many white people are not conscious of is that property values would drop for the black home owners as well. Just think about it; a black family purchases a home in a nice neighborhood with the expectation that most of us have that over the years and decades that home's value will appreciate. But by buying the house they are contributing to the value of the home depreciating. Their investment is secure only if not many other people of color buy homes there.

Robert Reich, former secretary of labor and professor of economics and public policy, has written extensively about the problems of our current economic system.   Following WWII America had developed a thriving middle class which began to reverse in the late 1970s due in part to deregulation, decline of unions, decreased taxes for the wealthy, and decreased investments in education, infrastructure, and social safety nets.   The nation's wealth began to be accumulated only by the country's most wealthy.

> *Political power has shifted to the top along with the money.   Money has translated into large campaign donations to politicians who do the bidding of their wealthy patrons- reducing their tax rates, widening tax loopholes, gaining government subsidies and bailouts for their businesses, and slashing regulations that impinge on them but would otherwise protect the public...*
>
> *Let me be clear. Some inequality is inevitable; we are not born with equal talents and inherited abilities. Some inequality is also necessary if people are to have adequate incentive to work hard, invent, and innovate to the benefit of everyone...*
>
> *But at some point inequality becomes so wide it undermines democracy. It also hobbles an economy by reducing overall demand. The vast middle class no longer has the purchasing power to keep the economy going, while the small group at the top that's raking in the money spends only a fraction of it, speculates with much of it, and parks the rest around the world wherever it collects the highest return at the lowest tax. (Reich, 2010)*

Writing in 2010 Reich was also prescient in adding:

> *And at some point inequality becomes so wide it causes a society to fracture. Average people become so frustrated and fearful they become easy prey for demagogues hurling blame at anyone or any group that's a convenient scapegoat.*

The increase in power to the uberwealthy significantly worsened as the result of the 2010 Supreme Court decision of "Citizens United" which resulted in massive amounts of dark money flooding into politics. "Dark" refers to the fact that the contributors, who can contribute unlimited amounts of money, are able to remain anonymous. These contributors expect that their money will be an investment in their interests.

Earlier in this book I mentioned Democratic Senator Sheldon Whitehouse's book *The Scheme* (2022). He describes a well-organized scheme by big business and the uberwealthy to not only influence legislative objectives, but also to take control of the court system, particularly the Supreme Court (which has now been accomplished). "A hundred years ago, the 'influencers' seeking to manipulate the political process represented mills and railroads. A thousand years ago, they were feudal barons and greedy courtiers. Today they are major players in the financial, pharmaceutical, insurance, technology, and fossil fuel industries."

Power creates wealth, and wealth creates power. Money goes from big business and rich donors to politicians, and politicians create policy which benefits big business and the rich. Let me give you just one example. I am a medical provider. While I am free to charge whatever for my services, most people have some type of medical insurance (either a commercial insurance, Medicare, or Medicaid). Patients obviously would like their health insurance to pay for appointments with me rather than paying out of pocket. Most of the health insurances though set their own rates for services. In order to be accepted as an approved provider for them, I must accept the reimbursement rate that they set. Some insurances (particularly some Medicaid plans) are exceptionally low, and so I and others decline to participate with their plans. Some insurers are so large and cover such a large number of participants that it is necessary for me and others to participate with them (for my practice that would certainly be Medicare). The size of these insurers gives them clout.

This is not the case with pharmaceuticals, however. Despite the size and clout of Medicare, federal law prohibits Medicare from negotiating drug prices with the pharmaceutical companies. As the result, Americans pay more for their medications than do people in other countries. This makes no sense at all. It is contrary to free market philosophy. It would be like Walmart deciding to pay full wholesale prices. Because Walmart is so large and purchases wholesale goods in such bulk, they can negotiate much lower prices than smaller retailers. Medicare should be able to utilize their clout in this same way. Why in the world would our federal government prohibit Medicare from doing this? The pharmaceutical industry has spent over five billion dollars since 1998 on lobbying congress, more than any other industry. They have 1,600 lobbyists in the United States, and over 59% are former government employees. Vast sums of money are being spent to fight against government-run healthcare and to fight House bill H.R. 3 which would give the government the ability to negotiate and cap drug prices.

Climate Change

In chapter two of this book, I briefly talked about five great extinction events in the history of our planet. The first occurred 440 million years ago and was known as the Ordovician-Silurian extinction. The second was 365 million years ago and was known as the Devonian extinction. With both extinctions there was a 70 to 80 percent reduction in species. The next great extinction (Permian-Triassic extinction) was 252 million years ago and was the greatest of all extinctions: it resulted in the death of 95 percent of marine species and 75 percent of land animals. Out of this vacuum came the beginning of the reign of dinosaurs. The fourth major extinction occurred 201 million years ago (Triassic-Jurassic extinction) due to widespread volcanic eruptions which caused an increase in atmospheric CO2, acidification of the oceans and global warming. The result was the death of 76 percent of marine and terrestrial life on earth.

Then our planet's most famous extinction event occurred 65 million years ago; the Cretaceous-Tertiary extinction. The extinction was caused by a six-mile-wide asteroid that hit the earth in the Yucatan Peninsula. This was the event which caused the extinction of the dinosaurs. "As a consequence of the impact 65 million years ago, an estimated 90 percent of land-based species were wiped out, and 50 percent of all plant species. Every dinosaur disappeared; birds are their only descendants still alive. Animals larger than 50 pounds died. Only mini-mammals and cockroaches were left to dine on frozen dinosaur carcasses." (Christian et al, 2014). The good news for us is that it created a vacuum for mammals to evolve.

We have had five major extinction events in the history of our planet and numerous other minor extinctions. There certainly is no reason to believe it cannot ever happen again, particularly considering the effects on the planet from our own species, homo sapiens. Never in the history of our planet has a species had the ability to destroy life as we know it. Not only can this happen with nuclear weapons, but it is currently happening with greenhouse gases, i.e., carbon dioxide, methane, and nitrous oxide. Eighty percent of greenhouse gases come from carbon dioxide (CO_2) which get released into our fragile and thin atmosphere from the burning of fossil fuels (oil, natural gas, and coal). Plants and trees live off CO_2; unfortunately, deforestation has contributed to the crisis.

If one pays attention to popular press or the internet one might get the idea that global warming and in particular human's contribution to it is controversial. Among scientists it is not. There is nearly unanimous consensus among climate experts that the earth is warming and it is due mainly to human activities.

The general public often is confused about the validity of climate change due to a concerted disinformation campaign by industries that have a vested interest in maintaining the status quo. As Al Gore's bestselling book (and film) correctly opines, global warming is an "inconvenient truth." Nobody wants it to be true. This truth threatens business. It threatens our current way of life. We humans generally focus on the present, the immediate- not potential problems way out in the future. We are more concerned about how much it costs to fill up our car's gas tank than we are about damage to the planet in the future. However, the future is coming upon us a lot faster than we originally thought.

Whitehouse (2022) reminds us that concern about global warming used to be a bipartisan concern.

> *I came to the Senate in 2007. In those first years, climate change was a bipartisan concern. At least three strong bipartisan climate bills were kicking around in the Senate, and John McCain...had a strong climate platform in his 2008 Republican presidential campaign. Then in January 2010 all that bipartisanship stopped, as if a switch had been turned off. Climate progress died. The sudden shift came immediately after a bare majority of Republican-appointed justices set loose unlimited political spending in the Supreme Court's disastrous Citizens United decision.*

The glaciers of the world are currently melting at an alarming rate. "If Greenland's ice dome or the West Antarctic ice shelf melted or broke up into the sea, it would raise water levels worldwide between 18 and 20 feet" (Gore, 2006). If this were to happen Miami, Amsterdam, Calcutta, southern Manhattan, and much of Bangladesh would be underwater. "In Bangladesh and the city of Calcutta, 60 million people would be uprooted. That is roughly the entire population of France or the U.K. or Italy."

An April 2022 article in *Science* magazine (Penn & Deutsch, 2022) predicts the likelihood of mass extinctions in our oceans if global warming is not significantly decreased. "Climate change brings with it the increasing risk of extinction across species and systems. Marine species face particular risks related to water warming and oxygen depletion." The authors "found that under business-as-usual global temperature increases, marine systems are likely to experience mass extinctions on par with past great extinctions based on ecophysiological limits alone."

Global warming, income disparity, war, the proliferation of weapons of mass destruction in American society, racism, and white supremacy are all primarily the result of selfishness, greed, and lust for power and wealth. These are the human deficiencies that Jesus and the other great religious prophets primarily preached against.

The Common Good

In 2018 Robert Reich wrote a book called *The Common Good*.

The idea of "the common good" was once widely understood and accepted in America. After all, the U.S. Constitution was designed for "We the people" seeking to "promote the general welfare"- not for "me the selfish jerk seeking as much wealth and power as possible." During the Great Depression of the 1930s and World War II, Americans faced common perils that required us to work together for the common good, and that good was echoed in Franklin D. Roosevelt's "Four Freedoms"- freedom of speech, of worship, from want, and from fear.

During the years that I have been working on this book it seems that the United States has greatly devolved in terms of selfishness and lack of concern for the "common good." Even though I never had any children, I pay hefty taxes every year to pay for other people's children to attend school. I do this for the common good. I pay taxes for a host of other things that do not directly benefit me. I do this for the common good. I wear masks in public places and get vaccinated during a pandemic, not only to protect myself, but for the common good. I support basic health care for all Americans as a right because it benefits the common good. I support common sense gun laws (such as universal background checks which ninety percent of the US population supports and the banning of weapons of war which most Americans support) because it is for the common good.

If we are to call ourselves Christians our purpose in life should not be for the accumulation of power and wealth. The primary message of Jesus was an emphatic exhortation against power and wealth. Jesus *commanded* us to love God and our neighbors. Jesus in the Sermon on the Mount, probably the best summation of the teachings of Jesus, specifically blessed the poor, the gentle, the hurting, the merciful, those who seek justice, the pure in heart, and the peacemakers. Whereas Caesar Augustus was declared "Lord" because through power and might he created peace in the Roman Empire, Jesus was declared "Lord" because of an alternative view to peace- through love. Peace through conquest never lasts long. Peace through evolution of the human spirit brings us closer to what Jesus called "the kingdom of God." I believe the main teaching of Jesus was to promote the common good- to love our neighbor- all human beings.

Christianity became corrupted when the Roman emperor Constantine converted to Christianity and then Christianity became the official religion of the Roman empire. The small, persecuted Christian community that was known for brotherly love then became corrupted. Power does indeed corrupt, as the adage says. The powerless became the powerful, and the persecuted became the persecutors. The early Christians were known for providing for the poor, taking care of the widows, aiding the imprisoned, and helping the strangers (immigrants). Upon gaining political power they devolved into an organization (the Catholic Church) that continued to seek power through the initiation of wars and putting to death (and torturing) people who simply had differing opinions. It really is questionable upon looking at the history of Christianity and all religions whether they have been a force more for good or for evil.

A similar corruption has occurred within the American Christian church. "In the twentieth century, White Christian America developed along two main branches: a more liberal mainline Protestant America headquartered in New England and the upper Midwest/Great Lakes region and a more conservative evangelical Protestant America anchored in the South and lower Midwest/Ozark Mountains region." (Jones, 2016). There arose a schism in the Christian church between the "modernists" and "fundamentalists." The former has embraced the ideals of the Enlightenment and science and interpreted sacred scripture by considering historical context. The "fundamentalists" are characterized perhaps primarily by their insistence that scripture is the literal, inerrant word of God. So, when there is a perceived conflict between scripture and science, fundamentalists believe it is scripture that is to be believed rather than science.

Evangelicals began to seek political power with the creation of the "Moral Majority" in 1979. Founder Rev. Jerry Falwell's agenda was to oppose abortion, homosexuality, pornography, and the ban on prayer in public schools. Interestingly, abortion had not been an issue for evangelicals until the 1970s.

> Throughout the 1960s and into the early 1970s, abortion remained almost exclusively a Catholic issue. While Catholics watched in panic, eighteen states liberalized their antiabortion statutes between 1967 and 1973. Then in 1973, the Supreme Court legalized the procedure nationwide. In this same period, the Southern Baptist Convention adopted a 1971 resolution calling for legal abortion in a broad range of circumstances that included not just rape and incest, but "damage to the emotional, mental, and physical health of the mother."
>
> In 1979, the Southern Baptist Convention reversed its earlier conditional support for abortion, throwing its institutional weight behind a proposed constitutional prohibition on abortion. (Jones, 2016).

According to Jones, the Moral Majority ran more than $10 million in ads in support of Ronald Reagan for president in 1980. This was the beginning of the establishment of the religious right in American politics and the beginnings of the marriage of evangelical Christians with the Republican party. "When the Moral Majority officially disbanded in 1989, declaring its mission accomplished, other leaders and organizations moved to consolidate its gains and propel the White Christian Strategy forward into the 1990s. Pat Robertson and Ralph Reed of the Christian Coalition of America, James Dobson of Focus on the Family, and Gary Bauer and Tony Perkins of the Family Research Council spoke for White Christian American through a proliferation of statewide and local chapters of their organizations." (Jones, 2016).

In 2009 the Tea Party movement began. Ostensibly a movement to protest government overspending, many also believe the movement had racial overtones and was a reaction to the election of the nation's first black president. "Despite the official assertions that the Tea Party represented a new libertarian surge, nearly half (47 percent) of Tea Party supporters reported that they also considered themselves a part of the Religious Right or Christian conservative movement. Moreover, they were mostly social conservatives, with views on issues like abortion and same-sex marriage that would have dismayed libertarian purists." (Jones, 2016).

And now we have the marriage of white evangelicals with Trumpism, a movement that eschews traditional conservatism (commitment to democracy, free trade, legal immigration, balanced budgets, law and order, and small government) and which embraces views that are completely antithetical to the teachings of Jesus Christ. White Christian evangelicals were an integral part of Donald Trump's "base;" 77 percent of white evangelicals voted for Trump in 2016, and this ticked up to 84 percent in 2020 (June 30, 2021 Pew report).

I am going to be blunt here. We now must face the fact that white evangelical Christianity, professed followers of Jesus Christ, the "prince of peace" who advocated primarily for the love of all humanity and who preached against the love of power and money, has now devolved into an absurdity. The line from the old Christian hymn that says "they will know we are Christians by our love" might now be replaced by "they will know we are white evangelical Christians by our white nationalism, our desire for the proliferation of guns, our propensity to violence, our fear and hatred of immigrants (both legal and illegal) and homosexuals, and our primary desire for power and money.

There now are several evangelicals who are speaking out against the moral decline of white evangelical Christianity. A June 2022 article in *The Atlantic* by Tim Alberta highlighted this conflict: "The evangelical movement spent 40 years at war with secular America. Now it's at war with itself... To many evangelicals today, the enemy is no longer secular America, but their fellow Christians, people who hold the same faith but different beliefs."

There now are several prominent evangelicals who are critical of evangelical Christianity for two primary reasons: moral decline in subservience to power, and lack of intellectualism.

Evangelical Mark Noll who was a professor of history at Wheaton College, a preeminent evangelical institution, and now is professor emeritus at Notre Dame, wrote *The Scandal of the Evangelical Mind* in 1994. He said "the scandal of the evangelical mind is that there is not much of an evangelical mind." In an updated preface written in 2022 he wrote "the evangelical mind' sounds increasingly to me like an oxymoron." He goes on to say:

> As documented for many years by many scholars, journalists, pundits, reporters, and bloggers, when the American population is divided into constituencies defined by religion, "white evangelicals" invariably show up on the extreme end of whatever question is being asked.
>
> These evangelicals have been least likely to seek vaccination against the coronavirus, least likely to believe that evolutionary science actually describes the development of species, and least likely to believe that the planet is really warming up because of human activity. White evangelicals are also most likely to repudiate the conclusion of impartial observers and claim that the 2020 presidential election was "stolen." They are most likely to regard their political opponents as hell-bent on destroying America. They are least likely to think that racial discrimination continues as a systemic American problem. And in response to a question that is usually formulated poorly, they are most likely to believe that Scripture should be interpreted "literally."
>
> In each of these spheres, white evangelicals appear as the group most easily captive to conspiratorial nonsense, in greatest panic about their political opponents, or as most aggressively anti-intellectual.

Evangelical Rev. Jim Wallis and other church leaders wrote the "Reclaiming Jesus" declaration in 2018. It was signed by twenty-three Christian leaders. A summary of the declaration is on the website of Sojourners, the evangelical organization that Wallace heads. The complete declaration is available in Wallace's book

Christ in Crisis: Why We Need to Reclaim Jesus (2019). Their statement includes the following:

> *The current administration is at war with the values of Jesus Christ so clearly enumerated in the Bible. People who say they are Christians but support the Trump Administration (the TRUMP EVANGELICALS) are creating a religious dissonance that is fracturing the integrity of our faith.*

Writer Ben Howe, an evangelical and political conservative, wrote *The Immoral Majority: Why Evangelicals Chose Political Power over Christian Values* (2019). In this book Howe quotes evangelical leader Michael Farris (who was chairman of the Home School Legal Defense Association). Farris attended the first meeting of Falwell's Moral Majority in 1980. "The premise of the meeting in 1980 was that only candidates that reflected a biblical worldview and good character would gain our support." Evangelicals were livid about Bill Clinton's sexual indiscretions over a decade later but were forgiving about Trump who had at least nineteen accusations of sexual assault and/or harassment leveled at him and who bragged about his ability to sexually assault women with impunity. Why the double standard? Because with Trump the white evangelicals were gaining political power. Farris lamented "In 1980 I believed that Christians could dramatically influence politics. Today, we see politics fully influencing a thousand Christian leaders. This is a day of mourning."

White evangelical Christians have been obsessed with abortion and homosexuality as their preeminent moral issues (despite these being common practices during the time of Jesus, and that Jesus never has been known to comment on). Evangelical leaders have often rationalized their support for Donald Trump by claiming that their moral objectives were being achieved, and that God has always employed extremely flawed people to do His well, e.g., Cyrus of Persia.

Although abortion is often cited as the number one moral issues for evangelicals, Howe points out that two polls (one by LifeWay Research and the other by Pew Research) completed after the 2016 election of Trump suggest that abortion was not foremost on evangelicals' minds. In both polls the issues that mattered most to evangelical respondents were terrorism and the economy. Abortion ranked at the very bottom of the LifeWay research poll and fourth from the bottom in the Pew poll. What mattered most was individual physical and financial well-being. Howe (2019) summarizes his concerns about the evangelical church that he grew up in:

> *Evangelicals purported, for decades, to position the urgent need for the reestablishment of Christian values as the central doctrine of their political motivations. Above all else, we were tasked with growing God's kingdom, preserving His creation, helping the poor, and loving the downtrodden. Despite evangelical leaders' talk of character, their followers have the inverse priorities. That these leaders can't recognize that it's their hypocritical actions which have led to this gap between abstract ideals and real-life priorities is precisely reflective of how they've chosen to misuse the mantle of leadership.*

> *By directly defying their stated desire, ignoring the character of Donald Trump, and creating a "Christian" culture that has become divisively self-interested and bitterly self-righteous, these leaders have taught their flocks to value the things of the world, rather than the things of Christ.*

> *Brutality is the new outreach. Subjugation is the new persuasion. Pragmatism is the new morality. Winning is the new religion.*

> *But all of this failed to answer that final and important question. Why?*

> *Such a simple answer: selfishness.*

A New Reformation

In 1517 Martin Luther published ninety-five theses in which he criticized the Catholic Church. Primarily his concern with the church was the practice of clergy selling *indulgences*. For a price, sinners allegedly could reduce their time in purgatory for their sins. The Protestant Reformation is usually considered to have started with Luther's theses. There were many other leaders in this movement to reform the church, including John Calvin and Huldrych Zwingli. Out of this reform movement came the ideas of *sola scriptura* (the idea that scripture is the sole source for proper doctrine) and *sola fide* (that the pardon of sin from God comes through faith and not by doing good works).

In my opinion it is time for a new reformation. Both the Protestants and the Catholics are missing the most important principles, including a return to the idea that to be a Christian one is to follow the teachings of Jesus and to emulate his life. Jesus preached against the pursuit of power and money. Jesus was against materialism. Jesus preached against tribalism, including tendencies to put loyalty to family above God. Jesus preached against self-centeredness; instead, we are to care for the downtrodden, the "least of these." Above all Jesus called us to love all- even our enemies!

I have no doubt that Jesus would have been against the sale of indulgences; after all, the purpose of the practice was for the Catholic Church to increase power and money. It was a practice in which powerful people took advantage of the ignorant and uneducated masses.

Jesus also did not tell us to consult our New Testaments for any questions about theology. No New Testament then existed. Scripture was written decades later in order to capture the life and teachings of Jesus that had been shared only orally over the decades.

Various scriptures were written in the first two centuries after the life of Christ. It was not until the fourth century that a New Testament canon came into being. There were many disagreements about what writings belonged in this canon. Many people now turn to their New Testament for definitive knowledge about what is "the word of God", but it must be realized that it was various councils (where politics were involved) that decisions were made about which of the many scriptures were deemed "orthodox" or correct and which scriptures were then deemed "heresy" or incorrect. After studying the history of the formulation of scripture, I do not believe it is inerrant and the one and only "word of God." I do believe that scripture has value though when it is considered in its historical context.

Why did Jesus dedicate his life to communion with God and the preaching of love and justice? These values go along with another major theme of Jesus' teachings: the *Kingdom of God.* Biblical scholar Marcus Borg (2006) wrote "Ask any hundred New Testament scholars around the world, Protestant, Catholic or non-Christian, what the central message of Jesus was, and the vast majority of them- perhaps every single expert- would agree that his message centered in the kingdom of God." "It is about a transformed world, a world of justice and plenty and peace, where everybody has enough and where, in the striking phrase from the prophet Micah, 'No one shall make them afraid.'"

I believe it is time for a second Christian Reformation- one that returns the focus to the teachings of Jesus. I believe it is time to return to the religion of Jesus and away from the religion that others created later about Jesus. Biblical scholar John Shelby Spong (2018) also calls for a new Christian reformation.

> *Christianity is called to be a community of self-conscious people who have transcended all of the boundaries that divide one human being from another...Christianity is charged with the task of creating a place in which all can hear about and contemplate the meaning of life and thus be introduced to that which is ultimately real...Christianity must be a place in which human oneness is practiced and where human engagement with that which is eternal can be probed. This is finally what Christianity must come to mean.*

What I envision is a reformation of not just Christianity but of all religion- to go *beyond* religion (to go beyond a system of beliefs which I might define as the conviction of ideas that are without significant evidence).

The idea of going "beyond religion" was also discussed by the Dalai Lama in his book Beyond Religion: *Ethics for a Whole World* (2012). "The fundamental problem, I believe, is that at every level we are giving too much attention to the external, material aspects of life while neglecting moral ethics and inner values." "If people lack moral values and integrity, no system of laws and regulations will be adequate. So long as people give priority to material values, then injustice, corruption, inequity, intolerance, and greed- all the outward manifestations of neglect of inner values- will persist."

The Dalai Lama's solution is the cultivation of a new secular ethics (that goes beyond religion) that centers on *compassion*. "The essence of compassion is a desire to alleviate the suffering of others and to promote their well-being."

The central principle for a new ethics that I would advocate is *conscious evolution* toward the goal of what Jesus called the Kingdom of God. When we look at the big history of the cosmos- seeing the cosmos' history in its entirety- the one quality that most characterizes it is evolution. The history of the cosmos is incredibly long from our perspective, and during that history there have been remarkable changes which includes several emergent events and ever-increasing complexity. In my view the information we now know suggests that the cosmos, which includes both physical matter/energy and non-physical entities such as ideas and consciousness, are all part of a whole, and this whole has been in constant evolution. God is the ground of being- of all beings. God is the ground of the entire cosmos- of our universe and perhaps multiple universes. The goal of God I believe is evolution. I believe it is our job to actively assist evolution, perhaps to the eventual end of an *omega point*, as envisioned by Pierre Teilhard de Chardin. It is our job to help bring to fruition what Jesus called the "Kingdom of God."

How do we assist evolution? First, we don't engage in activities which actively cause destruction and devolve the physical world and culture, activities such as war, greed, the pollution of the planet, anti-intellectualism, dishonesty, and the creation of absurd conspiracy theories. The universe evolves with acts of compassion (the Dalai Lama's preferred term), empathy, the desire for fairness and justice, and love (the preferred term of Jesus, the apostle Paul, and many others). We as individuals, we as a culture, we as a species, and we as a component of the cosmos evolve as the result of love. Love is the fertilizer that grows the cosmos.

Some people believe that the Kingdom of God will occur as the result of supernatural intervention by God. I do not believe this. I do not believe in the supernatural or in magic. I believe that since the Axial Age our species has developed morality, what religious historian Karen Armstrong has called the "great transformation" (who I quoted in the introduction of this book). It was the beginning of a transformation for *some* humans from a value system of self-interest only to a value system where there was ever increasing love and compassion for an ever-widening circle of people.

As human beings continue to evolve morally and culturally it is our responsibility, I believe, to effect the changes necessary to evolve. The Hebrew prophet Micah notes that God has told us what is good: "to do justice, and to love kindness, and to walk humbly with your God." (Micah 6:8)

The cartoon below says it well, I think.

Alcoholics Anonymous is an organization that is said to be a spiritual program. Chapter five of the A.A. "Big Book" describes how the A.A. program works; it is about a willingness "to grow along spiritual lines." "We claim spiritual progress rather than spiritual perfection." I believe that religion can learn a lot from A.A. and other twelve-step programs.

For one thing, A.A. is very clear about its mission (which is to help alcoholics establish a program of recovery for alcoholism) and requirements for membership (the desire to quit drinking). I agree with the Dalai Lama that while many people of various religious beliefs and backgrounds object to the rigid dogmas and rules that are part and parcel of most religions, many would be receptive to an organization that operates for one simple mission: to promote love and justice, or as the Dalai Lama puts it "to alleviate the suffering of others and to promote their well-being." This is what evolves the cosmos. This is what leads us to the *Kingdom of God,* as Jesus put it. This is what leads us to *Nirvana,* as the Buddha put it. This is what leads us to *moksha,* as the Hindus put it. This is what leads us to the *Tao,* as the Taoists put it.

There is much about A.A. as a spiritual program that aligns with this mission. A.A. stresses the need for "rigorous honesty." Their suggested program of recovery, which by the way is a suggested way of living for everybody, not just people with addictions, involves "twelve steps." Step three suggests that we "turn our will and our lives over to the care of God *as we understand Him.* It does not matter whether one is Christian, Jewish, Hindu, Muslim, agnostic, atheist or whatever. There are no tests of faith, no creeds to subscribe to. What they do suggest is finding a "Power greater than ourselves." That greater power is for everyone to determine for themselves. The goal according to the Big Book is for spiritual progress.

The Big Book also diagnoses the root of the problem for alcoholics as being selfishness and self-centeredness. "That, we think, is the root of our troubles." I believe that is the primary pathology of humanity in general.

Religion can also learn from A.A.'s inclusivity. Religions are often very exclusive; not everyone is welcome, and free thinking is frowned upon if not out-rightly forbidden. Many churches, for example, do not welcome people who are divorced or homosexual. My own religious tradition, Christianity, has a history of putting to death individuals who did not hold "orthodox" beliefs.

In the churches in which I grew up the congregations were often asked to stand to recite the Apostles Creed or the Nicene Creed; it was assumed that these were beliefs that we all subscribed to and were really a requirement for membership. A.A., on the other hand, is welcoming of all, no matter who they are or what they believe.

I am proud of the statement of inclusion that my own church (Park Congregational Church UCC of Grand Rapids) formalized in 2011:

As Jesus demonstrated by his life and teachings we fully welcome into the life of Park Church and value all people regardless of beliefs or doubts, age, color, gender identity, sexual orientation, physical, mental, or emotional ability, or economic status. We value and celebrate the rich diversity of all God's creation.

No one is excluded from the life or leadership of Park Church: nothing about who God made you to be could exclude you from full participation at Park Church.

No matter who you are or where you are on life's journey you are welcome here!

At Park, you can be who God made you to be: Yourself

Whereas religions might be characterized as doctrinaire, rigid, restrictive, and exclusive, I can envision something "beyond this" where the one unifying ideology is love for all of life and the promotion of justice and fairness in order to consciously evolve ourselves and the cosmos. I can envision a movement whose entire purpose is the promotion of morality- to encourage increased selflessness and compassion and to discourage self-centeredness, greed, and the lust for power and money.

In contrast to religion which generally bases its precepts on ancient traditions and authorities, I envision a philosophy that is based on empirical evidence, reason, and commitment to truth. I envision a philosophy that values education- not just education to make more money or to advance in a career, but education that helps us evolve as individuals morally and spiritually. As individuals evolve, culture evolves, and as cultures evolve, the cosmos evolves. I envision a philosophy that values humanism and enlightenment thinking. I envision a philosophy that actively works against racism, sexism, homophobia, tribalism, xenophobia, and all other *isms*. I envision a philosophy in which every individual is encouraged to think and to question authorities.

I believe we need a new religion that is extravagantly inclusive- whose only requirement is the promotion of conscious evolution which is achieved through the promotion of extravagant love for all of God's creation and the promotion of justice and fairness for all people. It would be a philosophy that eschews the lust for power and money. This was the religion of Jesus and the early Christians before Christianity became corrupted. It would be a reversal of present-day Christianity which has to a large extent has been co-opted by our culture's preoccupation with power and money. Our world needs people of good will to come together to change the world for good.

I realize that I am not likely to find a receptive audience for these ideas with fundamentalists or most evangelicals; those who are coming from a tribal, warrior, or traditional consciousness. I do hope to find some receptivity among those who are at least moving toward a modernist or higher level of consciousness. This would include those who consider themselves atheist, agnostic, or "spiritual but not religious." Most current atheists and agnostics were not raised to be atheists or agnostics. These are individuals who likely came to their beliefs by a willingness to think and reason and to be open-minded.

Progressive Christian writer, pastor and blogger John Pavlovitz in his book *If God Is Love Don't Be a Jerk: Finding a*

Faith That Makes Us Better Humans (2021) recalls that during a Q&A a man asked him if he was considering starting a church. Pavlovitz said that he was not because he appreciates being "authentic" and speaking his mind on issues. He thought that might not be appreciated as the pastor of a congregation. "The man shared with me that he and other atheist friends have been following my blog; it resonates with them, and he believes many people not currently at home in organized religion would be interested in being involved in something living out the values he sees in the writing. It gave me great pause. This has become a refrain I've heard echoed thousands of times over the past three years: people are hungry for redemptive community that makes the world more loving, more compassionate, and more decent- no matter what it's called."

A Church for the 21st Century: Growing Up, Waking Up, Cleaning Up, and Showing Up

The word "church," like the word "religion," might be irredeemable for many people. I have spoken to numerous people who continue to have significant "baggage" as the result of rejection by churches, particularly gay people. How ironic that an institution that is supposed to reflect the love of God should cause so much harm to so many people. It reminds me of a bumper sticker I saw years ago: "Dear Jesus, please protect me from your followers." As I am writing this in the year 2023, many of our American institutions are failing, and perhaps the institution in decline the most is the American church.

Yet the desire for community continues to be strong, as does interest in spirituality. Abraham Maslow's Hierarchy of Needs points out that the need for community and belonging is one of mankind's most basic needs. A definition of community is "a feeling of fellowship with others, as a result of sharing common attitudes, interests, and goals." The data that I shared in the introduction of this book suggests that many people, particularly younger people, reject the attitudes, interests, and goals of the traditional church, i.e., being anti-gay, judgmental, hypocritical, old-fashioned, anti-science and rejecting of enlightenment principles.

I believe it is time to create a new kind of church- one that is inclusive, open-minded, loving, and committed to justice and reason. What I believe we need are communities that encourage spiritual growth, that encourage us to be who we are and to grow to our fullest potential. I believe Ken Wilber summarizes well what I think the goals for church should be: helping people to "grow up," "wake up", "clean up", and "show up".

An essential element for spiritual growth is education. "Growing up" is the result of cognitive, emotional, moral, and spiritual development. We grow up by learning, and we learn by education, introspection, and experiencing life. For children and young adults, we have developed programs of study in school and problems to struggle with in order to encourage the development to mature adults. Unfortunately, growth stops for many people after reaching adulthood and the completion of formal education. It is my belief that education could and should be a lifelong process, and that individual human growth should be an ongoing process right up until death.

Research has suggested that with education, contemplation and self-examination people can progress through stages of spiritual development. I believe the institution that *could* provide such education for ongoing spiritual growth is the modern church.

What should the curriculum be for adult spiritual development? Human development and especially spiritual development have been a prevailing interest of mine throughout my life and is the reason that I studied psychology and became a psychologist. It is the reason for writing the books that I have written. All my writing is about information that I feel is important for spiritual development.

As has been done traditionally in Christian churches, I believe that Bible study should be part of a curriculum for a modern church, although the curriculum should include not only what the Bible says but how the Bible came to be, including learning who wrote the books, what was the historical context of the writings, and who decided what should be in a Biblical canon and the reasons for choosing these writings and rejecting others. Christians generally have no idea about the diverse writings that were considered scripture that did not make it into the Biblical canon, and who it was that made the decisions about a canon and the beliefs that were determined to be "orthodox." Most Christians have no idea about the politics and the disputes about what are "correct" Christian beliefs that occurred centuries after Jesus lived and died and which are still propagated today. This is the information I wrote about in *Evolution of the Bible*.

I think the curriculum should also include education about other religions and their scriptures. I think it is important to learn how various religions developed and particularly to learn about the similarities in religions as they evolved and how the various religions influenced each other (syncretism). There is much to be learned from other spiritual traditions, and in fact in essence most of the great spiritual traditions have a great deal in common. This is the information I wrote about in *Evolution and Syncretism of Religion*.

The curriculum of a modern church should also include education about morality and ethics. Morality has become the central principle in religions since the advent of the Axial Age. It brought forth a paradigm shift from self-centeredness to ever increasing circles of care- from concern for only oneself and one's family to care for the tribe, to care for the nation, to care for all humanity, to care for all life. What does it mean to be moral? Why is something right or wrong? Why should we be moral? This is what I wrote about in *Evolution of Morality and Psychopathology of Evil*.

An associated issue to morality is the issue of values. Whether conscious or unconscious, we all have a "values hierarchy." What are the things that you value the most in life? When people observe your life, do they see that your actions reflect those values? I had previously mentioned the leader of the Arizona senate who felt the U.S. constitution was divinely inspired. He expressed that a major value for him was to follow the constitution. Despite reporting under oath that former president Trump put tremendous pressure on him to go against the constitution and acknowledging that Trump was intent on lying and cheating, he confessed a day later that if Trump was the Republican candidate for president again, he would vote for him. This makes one wonder what his most important values are. Being Republican? Tax cuts? Not being voted out of office? Jesus made clear what his top values were: loving God and loving one's neighbors. What are your most important values? Do you live by them? What are your moral principles?

An even more important issue to spiritual growth than education is critical thinking. Education on critical thinking would involve a complete paradigm shift for churches which primarily teach people *what* to think rather than *how* to think. This is the topic of chapter one of this present book. There is a quotation that is attributed to Gautama Buddha, although there is dispute about whether the quote is an accurate translation of what he said or thought. Nevertheless, regardless of the authorship I completely agree with the sentiments of the quote:

> *Do not believe in anything simply because you have heard it. Do not believe in anything simply because it is spoken and rumored by many. Do not believe in anything simply because it is found written in your religious books. Do not believe in anything merely on the authority of your teachers and elders. Do not believe in traditions because they have been handed down for many generations. But after observation and analysis, when you find that anything agrees with reason and is conducive to the good and benefit of one and all, then accept it and live up to it.*

I also would advocate education in "big history," the focus of chapter two of this book. Spirituality, I believe, is about seeing the "big picture," the so-called view from "30 thousand feet". It is about the development of an accurate "worldview" and the development of an accurate "life map." This is greatly enhanced by a study of "big history" which attempts to give us answers about who we are, where we came from, and what our destiny might be. These are questions that people have sought throughout history.

The ancients devised myths to attempt to answer such questions. Many churches continue to propagate such myths. Since the enlightenment we now have various academic disciplines such as archaeology, astronomy, physics, biology, chemistry, psychology, and history that have given us new knowledge to answer these fundamental questions of existence. A church suitable for relevancy in the 21st century should relegate ancient myths to history and embrace modern knowledge in our ongoing quest to develop accurate world views.

When looking at the universe in its entirety the word that best characterizes its history to me is *evolution*. There is a single theme that runs throughout the entire story of the universe's history: ever increasing complexity and the emergence of qualitatively new and novel phenomena. Why is this? How might this affect our world view? What might this have to say about God? What might this have to say about us?

Science has given us new knowledge about the immensity of the universe, and now with the new James Webb space telescope we will be learning even more. How does modern knowledge about the immensity of time and space affect our perception of God? I believe a modern church needs to stress the notion that God is the *ground* of being rather than being a *being*. Paul R. Smith (2011) beautifully explains the theology of panentheism:

> *Panentheism is very different from theism and pantheism. With theism, God is always separate from the universe. With pantheism, God is the universe and nothing else. With panentheism, God is in the universe, and the universe is in God. Theism sees God as a separate being, separated from everything. Pantheism sees God as everything, and God is limited to the everything of creation. Panentheism sees God both beyond everything and, at the same time, as part of everything. God is in everything, and everything is in God. God is more than us and yet also very close to us. God is within us and we are within God.*

Whereas growing up primarily comes as the result of intellectual processes, *waking up* is usually the result of direct experiences. The focus is not just on learning about God, but about experiencing God. Many experience God through nature- by observing a spectacular sunset, by pondering the stars, by seeing natural wonders such as the Grand Canyon, or the solitude of being in the woods or on the beach. The great cathedrals of the world also have been built to reflect the presence of God- awe inspiring architecture, stained glass windows, the reverberation of great pipe organs, or the beauty of choral music. As discussed previously in this book individuals have also developed skills in meditation to experience God. By silencing the mind's chatter (which is not easy to do) one can find God in the emptiness. I believe it is the task of the modern church to help individuals *experience* God.

One of the things I think traditional church worship services do well is give parishioners an hour each week to contemplate the "big picture" - a time to get away from our normal routines and harried lives to think about the things that are important. It can be a time to clarify values and principles and to consider whether one is living a life consistent with these values. Church sanctuaries often seek to provide an environment that encourages contemplation about God and ultimate truths by providing architecture, art and music that transports us from our normal ordinary lives. I think it is unfortunate though that most Christian churches take a very theistic view of God, i.e., as a humanoid being out there somewhere as opposed to being the spirit that imbues all including ourselves.

Rather than teaching a separateness of humanity and God, I believe a modern church should help us to gain an awareness of the interconnectedness of life and God. I have written a great deal in this book about the oneness of the cosmos and the interconnectedness of all life. This is a belief suggested not only by physics but by spiritual prophets throughout the world and over the ages. Albert Einstein in a letter written in 1950 wrote:

> *A human being in part of the whole, called by us "Universe," a part limited in time and space. He experiences himself, his thoughts and feelings as something separated from the rest- a king of optical delusion of his consciousness. The striving to free oneself from this delusion is the one issue of true religion. Not to nourish the*

delusion but to try to overcome it is the way to reach the attainable measure of peace of mind.

I would hope that the church of the 21st century would become a resource for a host of spiritual practices to become closer to God and to experiences greater emotional, mental, physical, and spiritual health. The realization that the entire cosmos is one would hopefully contribute to more cooperation, compassion, care, and desire for justice.

Cleaning up refers to taking care of all the things that interfere with me being my "higher self." It means dealing with unresolved traumas from the past, learning skills to manage anger, recognizing and developing tools to deal with addictive behaviors, recognizing and correcting unhealthy and unhelpful habits, and resolving grudges and resentments. It is about recognizing things that are suppressed (i.e., things I consciously push from awareness) and things that are repressed (things that bother me that I have no conscious awareness of). It is about dealing with behaviors that I am guilty about, and it is about dealing with aspects of myself that I am ashamed of. Often it is helpful to seek assistance from a counselor or psychotherapist to resolve such issues.

I think the modern church might be a place where work on *cleaning up* also might happen. Group therapy is a powerful modality of treatment for dealing with all the above concerns. Therapy groups are powerful when participants are encouraged to be authentic and are shown acceptance for being so. One learns that one is not alone in having problems and doubts. As a group develops cohesion, there is a sense of "we-ness" that develops. The emotional support of others is crucial for emotional and spiritual growth. Groups are helpful for reality testing, e.g., "Am I crazy for thinking this way?" They are helpful for ventilating about things that have been suppressed. As trust in the group develops one becomes willing to share about things one has always been afraid to share, particularly when other group members open up about similar issues. It is the things that are most difficult to talk about that are most important to talk about, but it is crucial to find a safe place to do this.

I know from personal experience that many people would be interested in a group experience to explore spirituality, and currently there is a dearth of settings to do this. Religions and churches traditionally have been institutions that tell people what to believe and think, not places where people can explore their own thoughts and feelings. A key ingredient in professional counseling or psychotherapy is that the therapist is not a guru who gives answers but rather a facilitator that encourages clients to discover their own answers (although education may well be part of the process in terms of giving clients facts and knowledge gained from research).

I discussed previously in chapter three "Christian counseling" and "nouthetic counseling" in which people seek Christian counselors who tell them what to think and how to act based on a certain Biblical viewpoint. Nouthetic counselors want to make psychotherapy more like the traditional church, in which an "authority" tells people what they should do and think. I would advocate for just the opposite, i.e., that the church should be more like professional psychotherapy in that congregants are supported, listened to, respected, and encouraged to come to their own decisions about beliefs and how to live their lives.

Showing up is about putting love and compassion into action. In what ways are we making the world a better place? In what ways are we serving humanity (as opposed to trying to take as much as we can)? Jesus said in the 25th chapter of Matthew that those who inherit the kingdom of God are those that feed the hungry, give drink to those who are thirsty, are welcoming to the strangers, who clothe the naked, who tend to the sick, and who visit the imprisoned. We care for the downtrodden and poor not because we will be personally rewarded by God in some way, but because it is the right thing to do. We are called to not only care for individuals but to confront systems of oppression.

I can envision a day when the bulk of humanity realizes that all of life, and indeed all the cosmos, are one. We need to think of the cosmos as a single entity that is constantly evolving, and at times during this evolution various emergent events occur, as I have discussed in this book. Who knows what future emergent events might occur that we have no ability to anticipate?! When we truly realize that all of existence is a single entity, we begin to realize how foolish it is to promote the health and growth of *parts* at the expense of the *whole*. When we come to discover that much of life is not zero-sum, we will become less greedy and self-centered and will work toward the growth and happiness of all.

The establishment of the "Kingdom of God" is not likely to happen in our lifetimes and may not occur even in the next centuries. Perhaps it will take many thousands of years to come to pass or more. However, I do believe that there will come a time when we outgrow our violence, pettiness, greed, and selfishness. We eventually will succeed, I believe, just because it makes sense to do so. I can envision a spiritual philosophy that advocates for the conscious evolution of the cosmos. There will be long-term benefits for sure, but there also will be short-term benefit because the qualities that grow the cosmos are love and justice (love put into action). As I previously said, love is the fertilizer that grows the cosmos.

I believe that the spiritual development of humans will be an ongoing process as talked about in chapter three of this book. I envision a time when in our ongoing pursuit of truth, we will no longer rely on unquestioning subservience to authority figures or writings. Tradition will be replaced by reason, empiricism, reflection, and introspection. Allegiance to partisan tribes and to charismatic personalities will evolve to allegiance to values and principles that extol love and compassion for all of life.

I continue to pray along with Jesus "Thy kingdom come." May the cosmos evolve to perhaps an omega point- where God's love evolves to its complete and final manifestation.

Questions for Contemplation or Discussion
Chapter Six. Conscious Evolution

1. What is the basis for morality?   What makes something "good" or "bad"?

2. Do you agree with the author that morality is a construct that is on a continuum?

3. Do you agree with the author that the world's problems are primarily the result of immorality?

4. Do you believe the universe is evolving? Do you think you are able to assist in its evolution?

5. What is your purpose in life?

6. What do you most value? Is there any principle or value that you would be willing to die for?

Bibliography

Abrams, Nancy Ellen (2015). *A God That Could Be Real: Spirituality, Science, and the Future of our Planet*. Boston: Beacon Press.

Alberta, Tim (2022), *How politics poisoned the church*. The Atlantic (June, 2022).

Albom, Mitch (1977). *Tuesdays with Morrie: An Old Man, a Young Man, and Life's Greatest Lesson*. New York: Doubleday,

Andersen, Kurt (2017). *Fantasyland: How America Went Haywire*. New York: Random House.

Andersen, Kurt (2020). *Evil Geniuses: The Unmaking of America*. New York: Random House.

Armstrong, Karen (2006). *The Great Transformation: The Beginning of Our Religious Traditions*. New York: Anchor Books.

Bekoff, M. (2008). *The Emotional Lives of Animals: A Leading Scientist Explores Animal Joy, Sorrow, and Empathy- and Why They Matter*. Novato, CA: New World Library.

Bekoff, M. and Pierce, J. (2009). *Wild Justice: The Moral Lives of Animals*. Chicago: The University of Chicago Press.

Ben-Ghiat, Ruth (2020). *Strongmen: Mussolini to the Present*. New York: W.W. Norton & Co.

Blackmore, Susan (2017). *Consciousness: A Very Short Introduction*. Oxford, UK: Oxford University Press.

Borg, Marcus (1997). *Jesus and Buddha: The Parallel Sayings*. Berkeley, CA: Ulysses Press.

Borg, Marcus (2006). *Jesus: Uncovering the Life, Teachings, and Relevance of a Religious Revolutionary*. New York: Harper One.

Boyce, Mary (1979). *Zoroastrians: Their Religious Beliefs and Practices*. New York: Routledge.

Canda, E.R. (1997). *Spirituality. Encyclopedia of social work: 1997 supplement (19th ed.)*. Washington, DC: NASW Press.

Capra, Fritjof (1975). *The Tao of Physics: An Exploration of the Parallels between Modern Physics and Eastern Mysticism*. Boulder: Shambhala.

Carr, John (2019). *The Pope's Army: The Papacy in Diplomacy and War*. Yorkshire, UK: Pen and Sword.

Chaisson, Eric (2001). *Cosmic Evolution: The Rise of Complexity in Nature*. Cambridge, Mass: Harvard University Press.

Chaisson, Eric (2006). *Epic of Evolution: Seven Ages of the Cosmos*. New York: Columbia University Press.

Chalmers, David J. (1996). *The Conscious Mind: In Search of a Fundamental Theory*. New York: Oxford University Press.

Christian, David (2005) *Maps of Time: An Introduction to Big History*. Berkley: University of California Press.

Christian, D.; Brown, C. & Benjamin, C. (2014) *Big History: Between Nothing and Everything*. New York: McGraw-Hill.

Coogan, Michael D. (2011). *The Old Testament: A Historical and Literary Introduction to the Hebrew Scriptures, 2nd Ed*. New York: Oxford University Press.

Coontz, Stephanie (2005). *Marriage, a History*. New York: Viking.

Dalai Lama (2012). *Beyond Religion: Ethics for a Whole World*. New York: First Mariner Books.

Daniels, M. (2013). *Traditional roots, history, and evolution of the transpersonal perspective*. In Friedman, H. and Hartelius, G. (Eds.), The Wiley Blackwell handbook of transpersonal psychology. West Sussex, UK: John Wiley & Sons Ltd.

Dawkins, Richard (1989). The Selfish Gene. Oxford, UK: Oxford University Press.

Dennett, Daniel (1991). *Consciousness Explained*. New York: Back Bay Books.

Dennett, Daniel (2018) DENNETT ON WIESELTIER V. PINKER IN THE NEW REPUBLIC

De Waal, F. (1996). *Good Natured: The Origins of Right and Wrong in Humans and Other Animals*. Cambridge, MA: Harvard University Press.

De Waal, F. (2013). *The Bonobo and the Atheist*. New York: W.W. Norton & Co.

Dowd, Michael (2007). *Thank God for Evolution: How the Marriage of Science and Religion Will Transform Your Life and Our World*. New York: Viking Penguin.

Dyson, Michael Eric & Favreau, Marc (2022). *Unequal: A Story of America*. New York: Little, Brown and Company.

Easwaran, E. (2007). *The Upanishads*. Tomales, CA: Nilgiri Press.

Ehrman, Bart (2012). *The New Testament: A Historical Introduction to the Early Christian Writings, 5th Ed.* New York: Oxford University Press.

Einstein, Albert (2014). *The World As I See It.* Snowball Publishing.

Fagan, B. and Durrani, N. (2014). *People of the Earth: An Introduction to World Prehistory, 14th edition.* New York: Pearson.

Fowler, James W. (1981). *Stages of Faith: The Psychology of Human Development and the Quest for Meaning.* New York: HarperCollins.

Fowler, James W. (2000). *Faithful Change: The Personal and Public Challenges of Postmodern Life.* Nashville: Abingdon Press.

Funk, Robert, Hoover, Roy and the Jesus Seminar (1993). *The Search for the Authentic Words of Jesus: The Five Gospels.* New York: Macmillan Publishing.

Gore, Al (2006). *An Inconvenient Truth: The Crisis of Global Warming.* New York: Viking.

Haidt, Jonathan (2012). *The Righteous Mind: Why Good People Are Divided by Politics and Religion.* New York: Vintage Books.

Harari, Yuval Noah (2015). *Sapiens: A Brief History of Humankind.* New York: HarperCollins.

Hartelius, G., Rothe, G. & Roy, P. (2013). *A brand from the burning; defining transpersonal psychology.* In Friedman, H. and Hartelius, G. (Eds.), The Wiley Blackwell handbook of transpersonal psychology. West Sussex, UK: John Wiley & Sons Ltd.

Howe, Ben (2019). *The Immoral Majority: Why Evangelicals Chose Political Power over Christian Values.* New York: Harper Collins.

Huxley, Aldous (1944). The Perennial Philosophy. New York: Harper Perennial Modern Classics.

Isaacson, Walter (2007). Einstein: His Life and Universe. New York: Simon and Shuster.

Ivanhoe, Philip (2003). *The Daodejing of Laozi.* Indianapolis, IN: Hackett Publishing.

Jaspers, Karl (2010). *The Origin and Goal of History.* New York: Routledge.

Jaynes, Julian (1976). *The Origin of Consciousness in the Breakdown of the Bicameral Mind.* New York: Houghton Mifflin Harcourt Publishing.

Jones, Robert P. (2016). *The End of White Christian America.* New York: Simon and Shuster.

Kahneman, Daniel (2011). *Thinking, Fast and Slow.* New York: Farrar, Straus and Giroux.

King, Ursula (2001). *Christian Mystics: Their Lives and Legacies throughout the Ages.* Mahwah, New Jersey: Hidden Spring.

Kinnaman, David (2007). *Unchristian: What a New Generation Really Thinks About Christianity...and Why It Matters.* Grand Rapids, MI: Baker Books.

Kinnaman, David (2011). *You Lost Me: Why Young Christians Are Leaving Church.* Grand Rapids, MI: Baker Books.

Klein, Ezra (2020). *Why We're Polarized.* New York: Avid Reader Press.

Kobes Du Mez, Kristin (2020). *Jesus and John Wayne: How White Evangelicals Corrupted a Faith and Fractured a Nation.* New York: Liveright Publishing.

Kohlberg, Lawrence (1971). *Stages of moral development as a basis for moral education.* In Beck, C.M., Crittenden, B.S. & Sullivan, E.V. (Eds), Moral Education: Interdisciplinary Approaches. New York: Newman Press.

Kohlberg, L. & Power, C. (1981). *Moral development, religious thinking, and the question of a seventh stage.* In Kohlberg, Lawrence, Essays on Moral Development Vol. 1: Philosophy of Moral Development. San Francisco, CA: Harper & Row.

Kohlberg, L. & Ryncarz, R.A. (1990). *Beyond justice reasoning: moral development and consideration of a seventh stage.* In C.N. Alexander & E.J. Langer (Eds.), Higher stages of human development: perspectives on adult growth. New York: Oxford University Press.

Kuhn, Thomas (1962). *The Structure of Scientific Revolutions.* Chicago: University of Chicago Press.

Laughlin, Robert B. (2005). *A Different Universe: Reinventing Physics from the Bottom Down.* New York: Basic Books.

Lewis, C.S. (1952). *Mere Christianity.* New York: HarperCollins.

Luard, Evan (1987). *War in International Society.* New Haven: Yale University Press.

Macalister, Todd (2008). *Einstein's God: A Way of Being Spiritual Without the Supernatural.* Berkeley, CA: Apocryphile Press.

Maslow, A. (1971). *The Farther Reaches of Human Nature.* New York: Viking Pess.

Maslow, A. (2014). *Toward a Psychology of Being*. Floyd VA: Sublime Books.

McIntosh, Steve (2007). *Integral Consciousness and the Future of Evolution: How the Integral Worldview is Transforming Politics, Culture and Spirituality*. St. Paul, Minnesota: Paragon House.

McIntosh, Steve (2012). *Evolution's Purpose: An Integral Interpretation of the Scientific Story of Our Origins*. New York: SelectBooks.

Nagel, T. (1974). *What is it like to be a bat?* Philosophical Review 4:435-50.

New Revised Standard Version Bible (1989). Division of Christian Education of the National Council of the Churches of Christ in the United States of America.

Nicholi, Armand (2002). *The Question of God: C.S. Lewis and Sigmund Freud Debate God, Love, Sex, and the Meaning of Life*. New York: The Free Press.

Noll, Mark (2022). *The Scandal of the Evangelical Mind*. Grand Rapids: Eerdmans.

Pavlovitz, John (2021). *If God is Love Don't Be a Jerk: Finding a Faith That Makes Us Better Humans*. Louisville: John Knox Press.

Peck, M. Scott (1978). *The Road Less Traveled: A New Psychology of Love, Traditional Values, and Spiritual Growth*. New York: Touchstone.

Penn, J. and Deutsch, C. (2022). *Avoiding ocean mass extinction from climate warming*. Science, Vol. 376, 524-526.

Phipps, Carter (2012). *Evolutionaries: Unlocking the Spiritual and Cultural Potential of Science's Greatest Idea.* New York: Harper Collins

Pinker, Steven (2011). *The Better Angels of Our Nature: Why Violence Has Declined.* New York: Penguin.

Pinker, Steven (2018). *Enlightenment Now: The Case for Reason, Science, Humanism and Progress.* New York: Penguin.

Pinker, Steven (2021). *Rationality: What It Is, Why It Seems Scare, Why It Matters.* New York: Viking.

Reich, Robert (2010). *Aftershock: The Next Economy and America's Future.* New York: Vintage Books.

Reich, Robert (2018). *The Common Good.* New York: Knopf

Ring, Kenneth (2006). *Lessons from the Light: What We Can Learn from the Near-death Experience.* Needham, Massachusetts: Moment Point Press.

Roberts, Alice (2011). *Evolution: The Human Story.* New York: DK Publishing.

Sagan, Carl. (1977). *The Dragons of Eden: Speculations on the Evolution of Human Intelligence.* New York: Random House.

Smith, Paul R. (2011). *Integral Christianity: The Spirit's Call to Evolve.* St. Paul, MN: Paragon House.

Spong, John Shelby (2018). *Unbelievable: Why Neither Ancient Creeds Nor the Reformation Can Produce a Living Faith Today.* New York: HarperCollins.

Stengel, Richard (2019). *Information Wars: How We Lost the Global Battle Against Disinformation & What We Can Do About It.* New York: Grove Atlantic.

Vander Maas, Craig (2016). *Evolution of the Bible.* Grand Rapids, MI: Integral Growth Publishing.

Vander Maas, Craig (2017). *Evolution and Syncretism of Religion.* Grand Rapids, MI: Integral Growth Publishing.

Vander Maas, Craig (2019). *Evolution of Morality and Psychopathology of Evil.* Grand Rapids, MI: Integral Growth Publishing.

Wallis, Jim (2019). *Christ in Crisis: Why We Need to Reclaim Jesus.* New York: Harper One.

White, Matthew (2012). *The Great Big Book of Horrible Things: The Definitive Chronicle of History's 100 Worst Atrocities.* New York: W.W. Norton.

Whitehouse, Sheldon (2022). *The Scheme.* New York: The New Press.

Wilber, Ken (1995). *Sex, Ecology, Spirituality: The Spirit of Evolution.* Boston: Shambhala.

Wilber, Ken (1998). *The Essential Ken Wilber: an Introductory Reader.* Boston: Shambhala.

Wilber, Ken (2000). *Integral Psychology: Consciousness, Spirit, Psychology, Therapy.* Boston: Shambhala.

Wilber, Ken (2001). *Quantum Questions: Mystical Writings of the World's Great Physicists.* Boston: Shambhala.

Wilber, Ken (2007). *The Integral Vision.* Boston: Shambhala.

Wilber, Ken (2017). *The Religion of Tomorrow*. Boston: Shambhala.

Wootton, David (2015). *The Invention of Science: A New History of the Scientific Revolution*. New York: Harper Collins.

Wright, Robert (2009). *The Evolution of God*. New York: Little, Brown and Company.

Index

Laughlin, Robert, 183, 303

Leibniz, Gottfried, 220

leptons, 173, 183

Leviticus, 31, 66, 133

li, 8

liberal arts education, 143-144

limbic system, 107–108, 161, 195, 203, 206, 210, 243

Locke, John, 72

Loevinger, Jane, 115

Loftus, Elizabeth, 41

Logos, 8, 161–162, 214

Luard, Evan, 259, 303

LUCA (last universal common ancestor), 89

Lucy (fossil), 83

Luther, 12, 38, 247, 280–281

M

Macalister, Todd, 172, 303

Maccabees, 67

MacLean, Paul, 106–107

malignant narcissist, 140

Malthus, Thomas, 72

Malthusian cycles, 72

Mao Zedong, 45, 259

Marcionites, 34

Maslow, Abraham, 114, 149–150, 247, 288, 303

Maxwell, James Clerk, 165–167, 178, 191

McIntosh, Steve, 116, 131, 305

Mead, Margaret, 78

meme, 226

Mencius, 12, 221

Mencken, H.L., 59

Merton, Thomas, 215

Mesopotamia, 36, 64, 66, 68, 133, 206

meuons, 173

Micah, 134, 282, 284

Middle Ages, 9

mirror test, 204

Montesquieu, 72

Moses, 18, 31–32, 36, 133, 249

motivated reasoning, 29-30

Moynihan, Daniel Patrick, 60

multiverse, 190–191

Musk, Elon, 63

Muslims, 35, 50, 121, 259, 262

www.ingramcontent.com/pod-product-compliance
Lightning Source LLC
Chambersburg PA
CBHW072032020426
42338CB00033B/1908/J